The merchants of Moscow, 1580–1650

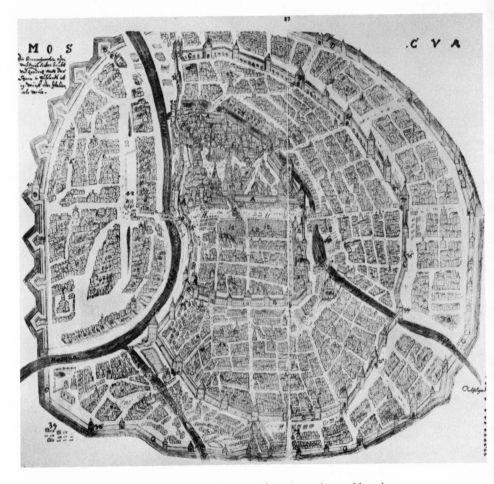

Frontispiece: Moscow in the 1660s (from Augustin von Meyerberg,
Al'bom Meierberga [Saint Petersburg, 1903], p. 45)

The merchants of Moscow

1580–1650

PAUL BUSHKOVITCH

Department of History, Yale University

CAMBRIDGE UNIVERSITY PRESS

CAMBRIDGE

LONDON   NEW YORK   NEW ROCHELLE

MELBOURNE   SYDNEY

For A. V. B.

Published by the Press Syndicate of the University of Cambridge
The Pitt Building, Trumpington Street, Cambridge CB2 1RP
32 East 57th Street, New York, NY 10022, USA
296 Beaconsfield Parade, Middle Park, Melbourne 3206, Australia

First published 1980

Printed in the United States of America
Typeset by The Composing Room of Michigan, Inc., Grand Rapids, Michigan
Printed and bound by the Murray Printing Company, Westford, Massachusetts

Library of Congress Cataloging in Publication Data
Bushkovitch, Paul.
The merchants of Moscow, 1580–1650.
Bibliography: p.
1. Merchants – Russian Republic – Moscow – History.
2. Moscow – Commerce – History.
3. Russia – Commerce – History. I. Title.
HF3630.M6B83 381'.0947'31 79-14491
ISBN 0 521 22589 2

CONTENTS

PREFACE

The purpose of this book is to present a detailed account of the merchants of Moscow in their formative period, and on this basis to reevaluate some widely held assumptions about the nature of trade and industry in seventeenth-century Russia. It has been clear for decades that the Moscow merchants were the richest and most significant group in the Russian merchant class, but there has never been an attempt to present the history of the group as a whole. We have only a few studies of individuals or subgroups within the Moscow merchants. There have been several studies of specific aspects of Russian trade, and of provincial towns such as Ustiug Velikii and Tikhvin, but very little attention has been paid to the city of Moscow and its merchants. Furthermore, no attempt has been made to describe in detail, and where possible, quantitatively, the history of the trade at the main port of Archangel and the relationship of the Moscow merchants to that trade. Historians of Russia have continued to reflect on the fate of the Russian economy over centuries and to characterize in detail the supposed relationship of the merchants to the state, even though the history of the most important contingent of Russian merchants and their activities in the main branches of trade and industry remains largely unknown.

It is necessary to introduce some basic factual information into the discussion of these larger problems. I have undertaken here to describe in detail the economic history of the Moscow merchants, restricting myself to the period 1580–1650, with some remarks on the second half of the seventeenth century. There are two reasons for this restriction. First and most important is the fact that these years were decisive in the formation of the Moscow merchants, the period during which they became part of the international trade network that was centered on the new maritime powers of Holland and England. The second reason is methodological: Because the sources of Russian commercial history are alternatively scarce and too numerous to use, historians have usually advanced their opinions on trade and the merchants on the basis of random illustrations taken from the eve of Peter's reign and then proceeded to assert that they were describing the whole of the century. I have attempted to analyze the earlier part of the century and to show that the basic pattern of life of the Moscow merchants at the end of the century was clearly established by 1650.

Because no extensive literature exists on the history of Russian trade, the historian cannot confine himself to the role of the Moscow merchants. He must provide his own background. The Russian trade at Archangel and the trade of the Russians with Persia have been almost completely neglected; the trade with Poland can be reconstructed only in fragments. Accordingly Chapters 3 through 6 of this book offer what is essentially a history of Russian foreign trade in the period under discussion, with special attention paid to the role of the Moscow merchants. This emphasis on foreign trade does not result from a conviction that it was somehow "primary" in Russian commerce: There is not enough data to warrant such a conclusion (or the opposite). Rather, it results from the relative neglect of foreign trade by historians of Russia. Only the Russian trade via the Baltic Sea has been thoroughly studied, and then less from the Russian than from the Swedish-Livonian point of view: The data must be reinterpreted to be of value to the historian of Russia. The history of the domestic market in Russia is more difficult to deal with because the sources are abundant (after 1650) only for markets in towns of secondary or tertiary importance. In particular, there is no record of the trade in Moscow itself before the 1690s. As a result, our discussion of the internal market in Chapter 7 concentrates more on Siberia and the Russian North than on Central Russia, although it is possible to make some conclusions about the Russian domestic market and its relationship to foreign trade and the salt industry. Chapters 8 and 9 describe the unique role of the Moscow merchant in seventeenth-century Russia's main industry, salt production, and the relationship of the merchants to the state. Seventeenth-century Russia was more or less an absolute monarchy, and the state could have played a major role in hindering or helping the merchants. Russian historians have almost invariably asserted that the role of the state was purely negative because it robbed the merchant of his time and wealth through onerous demands of service and gave him nothing in return. As we shall see, the reality was not so one-sided and considerable doubt may be cast on this traditional view.

This evaluation of the role of the state is an integral part of the widely held assumption that the Russian merchant of this period was poor and backward, and that there is not much to be said about him. This view is not wholly wrong but it is inadequate. From the broadest historical perspective, the Russian merchant was clearly "backward," that is, was neither as rich nor as powerful as his counterpart in Amsterdam or London. But is this a valid standard of judgment? We do not learn very much from this comparison because the most general consideration of Russia's social and economic position in the 1600s would lead to this conclusion. We learn nothing about the internal dynamics of the merchant class or of the Russian economy as a whole. One aim of this book is to demonstrate that more is to be learned by setting the Russian merchant in the context of the merchants of Eastern Europe, a region whose economic complexities and contradictions in this period were shared by the Russian state.

The tradition of Russian historiography is largely responsible for the exclusive emphasis on backwardness in the literature. The first important work on trade and the merchants in this period was that of N. Kostomarov, the Ukrainian regionalist and populist of the 1850s and 1860s.[1] Kostomarov established the basic conception of the seventeenth-century Russian merchants, describing them as poor, ignorant, and crushed by the arbitrariness and competition of the government. The populist line was continued in reference to the Moscow merchants by M. V. Dovnar-Zapol'skii, whose 1912 study is in one of the few prerevolutionary works devoted to the trade and crafts of Moscow. Both men were liberal populists and regionalists (Dovnar-Zapol'skii a Belorussian) who saw the history of Russia as the march of an ever more powerful autocracy that easily crushed all manifestations of regional and popular life.[2] They also subscribed to the populist economic theories that maintained that capitalism, being an artificial product of state policy, had never played any role in Russian history. Clearly there was no room for the Russian merchant in such a view of history. Dovnar-Zapol'skii in particular saw seventeenth-century Moscow as the residence of a few enormously rich merchants, allied with the state to suck the lifeblood of the provinces. This populist view was then reinforced by more academic interpretations. The legal historians of the 1860s, such as A. D. Gradovskii, and the greatest of

Russian historians, V. O. Kliuchevskii, maintained that the basis of the ranks of the richest Moscow merchants was the requirement to serve the state in the collection of taxes, in their view purely an onerous burden.[3] These merchants received higher rank and status under compulsion from the state, which needed their service. The populists at least made an elementary attempt to uncover the history of the merchants' economic activities, but Kliuchevskii and the legalists were uninterested in this problem. The result was an interpretation of the history of the merchant class based on scanty economic data and an extremely narrow view of their legal status.

The advent of a Marxist historiography after 1917 changed the interpretation of the role of the merchant class far less than it affected other aspects of Russian history. The leading Marxist Soviet historian of the 1920s, M. N. Pokrovskii, held to a number of eccentric theories in this area (identifying Marx's "merchant capital" with the state in Russia) and probably hindered more than he helped the situation. Nevertheless, a number of serious, concrete studies appeared in the 1930s, mainly from the pens of K. V. Bazilevich and S. V. Bakhrushin, which radically altered the factual base of the discussion.[4] Both of these historians accepted a Marxist interpretation of Kostomarov's views, with the result that their conclusions were not very novel; but they provided the first detailed studies of merchant families, regional groups, and government commercial policy. Unfortunately, neither of them devoted much time to the merchants of Moscow or Central Russia, preferring to concentrate on the North and Siberia. After the Second World War, the main emphasis shifted to the formation of the "all-Russian market" and the history of early industrialization. It might be thought that this emphasis would be fruitful for the history of the merchant class, but such was not the case. The industries of the seventeenth century were written off as "feudal" or "semifeudal" because of the presence of unfree labor alongside free labor, without much consideration of the economic aspect of the question. The formation of the all-Russian market was reduced to the appearance of interregional ties, an important theme to be sure, but not the only subject of interest in the area of internal trade. None of these studies ever seriously challenged the idea that Russian merchants and trade were backward: Instead they merely reinterpreted the comparison with the West. In contrast with the situation in England, they showed, capitalism remained at the most rudimentary stage, indeed so rudimentary as to scarcely deserve the name. In the last twenty years the Russian merchant has been described as even more primitive, if possible. N. N. Pavlenko, for example, maintains that there were no signs of capitalism before the end of the eighteenth century, thus consigning the seventeenth-century merchant to the Middle Ages.[5] This attitude among Soviet historians has not been conducive to research on the history of the merchant class. Nevertheless, historians such as Ustiugov, Serbina, and Zaozerskaia, whose main attention has been devoted to industry, have provided much information on the merchants. An important study has been produced of the northern town of Ustiug Velikii, and the work of R. I. Kozintseva and N. N. Repin on the period 1680–1725 has provided important new data on trade in that period. Kozintseva has also clearly demonstrated the minor role of the treasury in the Russian trade of Peter's time, even though this was a period of heavy expenditure.[6]

In the West, the work of Erik Amburger has been devoted to the role of the foreigners in Russia, which he (following the lead of Russian historians) overemphasizes. Samuel H. Baron has studied the composition of the highest rank of Russian merchants, the *gosti*, coming to the conclusion, very much in the tradition of Russian historians, that the state was the main obstacle to economic development.[7] The West German historian Wolfgang Knackstedt has recently offered a new and challenging view of medieval Moscow, arguing that the residence of the Grand Prince (and later Tsar) of Moscow in the city was the basis of the relationship of the court and government to the population of the city, including the merchants.[8] Although Knackstedt has made a fundamental contribution to our understanding of the medieval city, no such attention has yet been granted by any historians to the city after 1550. The historians in Russia and the West have failed to analyze either the history of the Russian merchants as a whole or any important contingent of the Russian merchants. Moreover, the history of the trade at Archangel has not been sufficiently explored to provide the basis for conclusions. This history of the Moscow merchants is an attempt to fill that gap.

Acknowledgments

A great many people have helped me in the research and writing of this book. The late Michael Cherniavsky provided inspiration and guidance in the initial stages. Nina Borisovna Golikova of Moscow State University guided me through the archives of seventeenth-century Russia with intelligence and generosity. Marc Raeff took on the supervision of the dissertation when it was merely a mass of raw data and gave me invaluable assistance in making it into its present form, and he has never failed to give encouragement and advice when it was needed. The staffs of the Lenin Library, the Central State Archive of Ancient Acts (Moscow), the Leningrad Section of the Institute of History of the USSR Academy of Sciences, and the Gemeente Archief, Amsterdam, provided essential assistance. In particular, I would never have been able to exploit the holdings of the Gemeente Archief without the assistance of its director, Dr. Simon Hart, who generously shared the results of decades of classificatory work in seventeenth-century notarial records. My research in the USSR was made possible by the International Research and Exchanges Board (New York) and in Amsterdam by the A. Whitney Griswold fund of Yale University. At various stages I have benefited from the reactions and comments of Samuel Baron, Alexander Erlich, Arcadius Kahan, Andrzej Kaminski, Edward Keenan, Edgar Melton, and J. W. Smit.

P. B.

1

Moscow and its merchants, 1580-1650

The Russian merchant

The Russian merchant of the seventeenth century seemed a strange figure
by the side of his contemporary in Western Europe. Unlike the English or
Dutch merchant, he was not part of a vast network of overseas trade nor
was he the beneficiary of great empires in America and Asia. He rarely
left his own country, used no sophisticated bookkeeping or financial techniques, and by the standards of Amsterdam or London was not a man of
tremendous wealth. Compared to the merchants in the centers of European commerce he appeared backward indeed. Against the background of
Eastern Europe, however, the Russian merchant was not so unique because most of the distinctive features of his economic activity were shared
by the merchants of Prussia, Poland, and the Habsburg lands. They too
did not participate in the great currents of European overseas trade, and
although probably aware of the more sophisticated techniques of the English and the Dutch they, like the Russians, lacked the capital to form
great trading companies and financial institutions like those of the West.

The political and legal status of the Russian merchant also set him apart
from his counterparts near and far. The English merchant was not only a
subject of the King, but was usually one of the propertied minority of
townsmen who elected a member of Parliament from their borough. The
Dutch merchant, as a citizen of Amsterdam or some other town, had an
important voice in the affairs of state at every level. Even in Eastern
Europe, the merchant had some political importance legally established, if
not always honored. The town in Eastern Europe emerged from the end
of the Middle Ages with some autonomous rights: mainly those of self-

government and representation in the local diet. In the absolutist states these rights were severely curtailed – in the Habsburg lands in the sixteenth century and in Prussia in the seventeenth. In Poland, the peculiar constitution of the Commonwealth allowed the towns to retain their legal position, but the decline of the towns' economic base after 1650 undermined their actual position in the state: Only Danzig continued to play a role in Polish politics. The legal and political position of the East European merchant was very weak by the end of the seventeenth century. The Russian town, in contrast, had never been a legal corporation and possessed no rights as such; it was not even theoretically a legal entity. Nevertheless, some forms of self-government existed: The townsmen were required to elect from among themselves a number of judicial-administrative officers. This legal structure was an essential element in the life of the Russian merchants, an element without which much of their purely economic history must remain incomprehensible. Unfortunately, most historians of the administration of the towns in this period write from a strongly legalistic viewpoint that makes it difficult to give an account of the real political and administrative life of the towns and to avoid the error of describing what the law intended instead of what actually happened.

This state of affairs has less to do with the Russian towns of the seventeenth century than with the world of the Russian historians of the nineteenth: From the writings of the liberal legal historian B. N. Chicherin (1856) onward, a dominant theme was the absence in Russia of the traditions of local autonomy supposedly present in the Germanic world since the Middle Ages. An extremely abstract view of the legal history of Northwestern Europe was used as the basis for understanding the institutions of pre-Petrine Russia. The historians of the nineteenth century found no legally enshrined safeguard of the autonomy of Russian towns and concluded that these towns must have been powerless. At no point did they consider the actual workings of the town administration in connection with its social and economic reality; at every point they substituted law for life. This outlook has had a tremendous impact on the Russians' view of their own past and continues to be influential among Western historians of Russia. Furthermore, one cannot escape the impression that Soviet historians have implicitly accepted the doctrine of the powerlessness of the town: The Marxist critique of the legalistic view led them, understandably, to concentrate on the economic side of urban history, but this led also to the neglect of the history of urban administration. Thus the nineteenth-century understanding of the political-administrative role of the city in Russia remains substantially unchallenged, in spite of the fact that it is based on evidence and a type of argument that would not be accepted by most historians in the West or in the USSR. The result of this situation is that even a determined attempt to uncover the reality of urban administration in pre-Petrine Russia will tend to fall back on the description of a legal theory.[1]

The fundamental legal distinction applied to the population of seventeenth-century Russia was the distinction between those who were "burdened" (*tiaglye*, that is, those who paid the direct taxes) and those who were not. Almost all peasants and townsmen were burdened; the church (in most cases) and the nobility were not. Thus, in law the townsmen seemed to merge into the peasant mass. However, economic and social reality divided the townsmen from the peasant. Since the end of the sixteenth century, almost all Russian peasants outside the North were serfs: under the power of a noble or ecclesiastical lord and forbidden to move without his permission. Only the crown peasants (11 percent of all serfs) were somewhat better off, being closer in status to the virtually free peasants of the North and Siberia. This basic difference in Russian society was barely reflected in the law, but it was none the less fundamental. In contrast to the peasant serf, the townsman had no lord but the Tsar and had much greater freedom of movement. The merchant of Moscow, like the merchant of most other towns in Central Russia, possessed this over-whelming privilege of not being a serf in the midst of millions of peasants who were serfs.

Within the towns, however, a small minority of townsmen (mostly artisans) were, in effect, serfs. These men were the property of the great ecclesiastical lords, and possessed the dubious advantage of living in "white places," that is, they were freed from the burden (*tiaglo*). The rest of the townsmen, living in "black places" paid the burden and formed the legal community of the town. This community elected an elder (*starosta*) from among the "best" (i.e., richest) townsmen and a number of assistants (*tseloval'niki*) to assist him in his duties – the collecting of the burden from the town and the exercise of judicial authority at the lowest level. It also elected the "toll and tavern chief" (*tamozhennyi i kabatskii golova*) and a group of assistants (also called *tseloval'niki*) to carry out the administration of the toll collection and state tavern monopoly in each town. All these offices were held by the richest merchants, and all the prominent merchants of a given town held all the offices at one time or another in their lifetime. In the two or three largest market towns (Archangel, Moscow,

Astrakhan) the toll and tavern chief was appointed by the financial office in Moscow responsible for the town, rather than elected by the townsmen. He was not, however, a bureaucrat but a great merchant of Moscow or some other commercial city. In one way or another the merchants stood at the head of the basic financial apparatus in the towns.

Looking at this system of elected financial officers, it would seem that the merchants had a great deal of power over the financial affairs of the state. However, this is not the conclusion drawn by the historians of Russia who have written about the merchants of the financial administration: The traditional view is that these offices were merely burdensome service obligations. The performance of such duties was supposed to signify the "binding" of the merchant to the town, and the binding of the urban population to the state, a view based mainly on the analysis of the theoretical legal significance of these obligations. The emphasis has been placed on the duty of the chief and his assistants to make up the deficit if the amount of money collected in a given year fell below the amount collected the previous year, and on the supposedly ruinous effect of this requirement. No attempt has been made to assess the likelihood of such an event, although it is obvious that either prolonged inflation or prosperity would reduce it to a minimum. It will be shown later that there is evidence that the merchants had some power in the financial sphere.

The city of Moscow

At the beginning of the seventeenth century, Moscow was a city built wholly in the tradition of the medieval Russian town. It possessed few large, open spaces and the center, pierced here and there by narrow streets, was a crowded jumble of mostly wooden houses and fences. For its time it was a large city, with almost a hundred thousand inhabitants. Spreading out in a circle from the Kremlin for several miles, the city was divided into five parts: the Kremlin, the Kitaigorod across Red Square from the Kremlin, the White City surrounding both, and the Earthen City in a concentric ring around the White City. Across the Moscow River to the south of the Kremlin was the Zamoskvorech'e. In the Middle Ages virtually the entire population had lived in the Kremlin and Kitaigorod, both protected by massive walls that still stood complete in 1700. After the unification of the Russian state at the end of the fifteenth century, the new capital burgeoned, and the White and Earthen cities became important and densely populated parts of the city for the first time.

The growth of Moscow resulted in a change in the social complexion of the population in the different parts of the city. Formerly, not only the court and the church but much of the boyar aristocracy, and even minor nobles and craftsmen, had lived in the Kremlin. By 1600 the requirements of court and administration had pushed most of the boyars out, and by 1700 the boyar palaces within the Kremlin walls were almost extinct. Many boyars moved their residences across Red Square to the Kitaigorod, but this could not be a long-lasting solution. The Kitaigorod was becoming the commercial and ecclesiastical center of Moscow, and as such, more and more crowded. The reason for this expansion was the proximity to Red Square, the main marketplace of Moscow. The square, which was only called the "Market" until about 1650, was not then the large, open space created by the architects and city planners of the eighteenth and nineteenth centuries, but rather a small area enclosed on one side by the Kremlin and on the other side by the "trading rows" – the shops and stalls of the Moscow merchants. The only broad, open space was in front of the cathedral of the Intercession of the Virgin (St. Basil the Blessed), the memorial to the victories of Ivan the Terrible. Here was the *lobnoe mesto* (place of execution), the scene of most of the riots and revolts of the Muscovites, and the place where the Tsar spoke to the people when the occasion arose. But it was the marketplace that was the center of attention at most times, and it was the marketplace that drew the merchants to the Kitaigorod. Here the great merchants competed for space with the church and the boyars who still lived there. The Kitaigorod formed a rectangle with three main streets running east away from the Kremlin. To ease traffic and keep down fires the government required the main streets to be paved with logs and to be some twelve meters wide, but this rule was usually violated so that the streets were actually much narrower. The lesser streets were little more than alleys between the houses. Most of the population lived in the other three districts of Moscow, which contained people of every rank from beggars to boyars. The boyars already preferred certain streets to the west of the Kremlin (such as the Prechistenka) which in succeeding centuries became the great aristocratic streets of Moscow. The inhabitants of the White and Earthen cities and the Zamoskvorech'e, however, were mostly artisans, traders, or soldiers, joined by some of the great merchants.[2]

The houses of the great boyars, which dominated the streets and clearly provided models for the merchant houses, had a number of distinctive features, quite different from the norm further west. By the end of the

Map 1. Moscow in the
seventeenth century
Key:
 1. Red Square
 2. "Trading Row"

Monasteries:
 3. Chudov
 4. Zaikonospasskii
 5. Bogoiavlenskii
 6. Androniev
 7. Novospasski

Palace Settlements
 8. Kadashevo
 9. Khamovniki
10. Old and New Koniushen-
    nyi

"Black" settlements and hundreds:
11. Arbatskaia
12. Vorontsovskaia
13. Golutvinskaia
14. Dmitrovskaia
15. New Dmitrovskaia
16. Ekaterininskaia
17. Kozhevnitskaia
18. Kuznetskaia
19. Miasnitskaia
20. Nikitskaia
21. Novgorodskaia
22. Ordynskaia
23. Pankratievskaia
24. Pokrovaskaia
25. Rzhevskaia
26. Semenovskaia
27. Sretenskaia
28. Troitskaia
29. Ustiuzhskaia
30. Chertolskaia
31. Aleskeevskaia
32. Old Foreigners' settlement
    (to 1652)
33. New Foreigners' Settle-
    ment (after 1652)

State and church:
34. Tsar's palace
35. Patriarch's palace
36. Land Office
37. Foreign Office

sixteenth century, the nobility of Northern Europe was already beginning
to construct the Renaissance and neoclassical palaces that have been the
typical aristocratic dwellings until the present century. In Russia this
fashion did not appear until the 1680s, and most aristocratic and merchant
houses were still built in the traditional Russian style. Few secular buildings of the pre-Petrine era remain, and almost none of the wooden buildings that constituted the vast majority of boyar houses. Hence their appearance must be reconstructed from drawings and the remaining stone
houses. The most distinctive feature of the Russian urban house, either
that of a noble or that of a great merchant, was the fact that it did not have
its facade on the street, but rather, that it stood in the center of a yard
surrounded by a fence. The passerby in the street saw only a row of fences
with barns and stables behind them, broken by elaborate gateways
through which he might catch a glimpse of the house. Behind the house
was usually a garden, both to supply the kitchen and to provide some
color: We hear of flower gardens at least by 1650. The house itself was
utterly unlike the structures that prevailed in Western Europe, either
among nobles or among the burghers. Usually it had a partly sunken
ground floor (called *podklet'*) that served as a storeroom and servants' quarters, and above it was the first floor with the dining rooms and receiving
rooms of the householder. These two floors were of stone if the owner was
extremely wealthy, but even if they were stone, the third floor was usually
wooden: Wooden walls were warmer in winter and preferred even by the
wealthiest boyars until the eighteenth century. The internal arrangement
did not follow any conscious aesthetic plan, and usually the rooms were
simply built in a long row with short halls between the rooms, causing the
house to be long and narrow. As the houses grew larger, and as the boyars
had to provide for the practice of dividing the house into a women's and a
men's part in accordance with the Russian aristocratic custom of seclusion
of the women, some of the houses were built in an L-shape. Only at the
end of the century did the enfilade arrangement of the rooms give way to a
boxlike ground plan of a square broken up into four quadrants. In the
house of a great boyar the rooms were low and ill-lit, the gloom relieved
by painting the walls and ceiling in bright colors and complex floral patterns. Imported cloths, silver utensils, richly decorated ikons, and elabo-
rately carved furniture filled the rooms, the atmosphere of heavy luxury
conveying an oppressive sense of rank and dignity. The exterior of the
house was not as elaborate as the interior, but the assymetrical facade, the
carved window frames, and the elaborate decoration of the front staircase

and the roof would have made the house picturesque to modern eyes, if not to the classical taste of Peter's time.[3]

This was the kind of house that the great merchants of Moscow admired and tried to imitate when they could. Certain features were present even in the dwellings of merchants of moderate wealth: the fenced-in yard with the barns and stables around the edge, the position of the house in the center, the garden in the back. Other features were absent: the richness of decoration, the separate women's half of the house, the great size, and often elaborate plan. Indeed the merchant's house resembled more the house of the prosperous northern peasant than that of the great boyar. Above the *podklet'* most merchants kept the ancient three-part plan of the peasant house, that of an entrance hall in the center (with the stove) and on each side a room of about equal size – one where guests were received and entertained and one where the family lived. A richer merchant usually built a third floor, especially if the first two were stone, and this was the family's usual place in daily life. The very richest merchants imitated the boyars' technique, building houses on the L-shaped plan and later (after 1700) imitating the neoclassical creations of the imported architects. Until the end of the century, however, most merchants continued the traditions of Russian domestic architecture. Lesser merchants and artisans stayed even closer to this tradition, building only small wooden houses of one room and an entrance-hall-cum-storeroom (the *seni*) with no *podklet'* and often without any yard or only a very small one. Few such houses survive even in drawings, but they may be imagined from the small number of examples of stone houses of the lesser townsmen dating from the very last years of the seventeenth century. Many a great merchant began his life in just such a house, and of course most of the population of Moscow lived in such houses for the whole of their lives.

Moscow in the seventeenth century was the largest city in the Russian state. A good estimate of the size of the population is very hard to come by because the censuses of the seventeenth century are all incomplete and were made at different times. The population of the city was quite complex: According to the Soviet historian S. K. Bogoiavlenskii there were in Moscow around 20,000 households of musketeers (*strel'tsy*) and other soldiers and 17,470 households of civilians. (A large portion of the army was stationed in Moscow, and the soldiers were expected to partially support themselves by trading and crafts.) Of the civilians, some 50 percent were townsmen of varying legal status, who made up the "urban" society of Moscow. The rest included some 20 percent gentry and boyars with their servants, 8 percent government officials, 10 percent clergy, and smaller groups as well.[4] These figures should be thought of simply as estimates, especially because the townsmen were the largest but least accurately counted group, and it may be presumed that their numbers were larger than the censuses report. It is impossible to evaluate the exact extent of participation of the soldiers in commercial activities, although it is well known that they did participate in large numbers. Furthermore, there were a number of so-called palace settlements, originally founded to serve the needs of the Tsar's palace, but that by this period were also largely commercial in character. The commercial and artisan population of Moscow was thus much larger than the quarter of the whole that a literal reading of the figures implies.

The legal and administrative structure of Moscow was much more complicated than that of other towns. In most provincial towns, tbe urban population formed a single unit that elected its elder and toll chief as described above. The nonmilitary population of Moscow, however, was divided into four large groups. These four were (1) the ordinary townsmen; (2) the palace and treasury settlements; (3) the monastery and ecclesiastical settlements; and (4) the foreigners.[5]

The ordinary townsmen, those who lived in black places and paid the burden, formed the largest group and were in turn divided into a number of "hundreds" (*sotni*) and "demihundreds" (*polusotni*), whose origin is obscure, but whose functions in the seventeenth century are fairly clear. Each hundred was a self-contained administrative unit on the model of a provincial town, with its own elder and his assistants responsible for the collection of the burden from that hundred. The hundred and demi-hundred elders did not, however, collect the toll, which in Moscow was collected by a single central office, the Great Toll Office (*Bol'shaia Tamozhnia*), normally headed by a great merchant appointed by the government. The elders of the Moscow hundreds were also subject to the courts of the Land Office (*Zemskii prikaz*), an office of the central administration entrusted with the general administration of the city of Moscow. In Moscow there were some twenty-five hundreds, demihundreds, and other settlements (*slobody*) to which ordinary townsmen belonged.

The second large group comprised the palace and treasury settlements, whose members had originally supplied the court with its needs in cloth, food, and services of many kinds. Some of these settlements were still mainly occupied with the service of the court, such as the Tsar's stables (*koniushennaia sloboda*), but even in these groups some men were traders or artisans. More important were the groups who were, in fact, no longer primarily servants of the court, but rather merchants and artisans whose economic role differed in no respect from that of other townsmen. Such were the *kadashevtsy*, members of the most numerous of the palace settlements (372 households in 1653) who were concentrated in Kadashevo, a district of the Zamoskvorech'e (whence their name). Apparently founded in the sixteenth century, the Kadashevo settlement was originally intended to weave cloth (mainly linen) for the Tsar's court, but by 1613 this obligation was reduced to an annual supply of cloth paid for by the *kadashevtsy*, who spent their time on trade. The richest merchants among the *kadashevtsy* were the most important merchants of the palace settlements and were wealthier than all but a few merchants in Moscow as a whole. All the palace settlements retained some feature of their original status as court servants. They were free of the burden (and thus not part of the legal community of Moscow), they often performed some symbolic task as a vestige of their original position, and they paid an *obrok*, a money rent paid by each household in part as a sign of its subject status to the Tsar. When they were judged, they had to go to the courts of the palace offices or the treasury court rather than to the Land Office.

The third group, not nearly as large as the first two, comprised the monastery and other ecclesiastical settlements, numbering about twenty-six but usually small in population. The members of this group were subject to their owners, and were essentially serfs of the monastery or Patriarch, although by occupation they were small traders or artisans rather than peasants. Some may have been artisans working to supply the household of the Patriarch or other great churchmen, but they also turn up as traders working on their own. They were, in a sense, the predecessors of the serf-craftsmen of the eighteenth- and nineteenth-century cities. Both the palace settlements and the ecclesiastical settlements aroused a certain hostility in the ordinary townsmen because they were both excluded from the payment of the burden, and thus increased the taxes for the rest of the population: These settlements provided an escape for townsmen trying to evade the taxation imposed on the black hundreds and demihundreds.

Finally, the fourth group of the urban population comprised the foreigners, who were mainly Dutch and German. They were organized on the Russian system with an elder, but were judged not by the Land Office but by the Foreign Office (*Posol'skii prikaz*). The palace, ecclesiastical, and foreign settlements were fairly distinct and lived in clusters of adjoining streets, so that the legal status coincided with a definite district of the town. The hundreds and demihundreds, in contrast, were less concentrated and to some extent intermingled with each other and with the other three major groups, usually, however, with some street as a focus.

It is clear that the city of Moscow, with its variegated pattern of settlements and statuses, did not have a unified administration. A large segment of the city's population were soldiers and thus under the authority of the *Streletskii prikaz*, the Musketeer Office, whereas the palace and treasury settlements were subject to the palace and treasury. The majority of the nonmilitary population, the ordinary townsmen who lived in black places, were subject to the Land Office. Located on Red Square where the Historical Museum now stands, this office was the nearest approximation to a city administration of Moscow. It was headed by a great nobleman and served by a staff of *d'iaks* (officials), and was the main police office and criminal court for the majority of the townsmen. It had the duty of regulating and recording any transfer of real estate within the city, and served as commercial court, judging cases of debt and other litigation arising from commercial transactions. It was charged with the maintenance of public order, the suppression of immoral games, the fighting of fires, the repair of the streets, and the general upkeep of the city. To support these operations it collected a number of direct "local" taxes from the townsmen (distinct from the burden, which went to the central state treasury). Some insight into this aspect of its activity can be gleaned from the account of its tax collection compiled at the request of the *Razriad*, the Military Office, soon after the accession of Tsar Alexei Mikhailovich in 1645. The Land Office reported three main sources of revenue, beginning with the "paving money" (*mostovye den'gi*). This tax was collected every six years (because the wooden paving was renewed at this interval) from each shop and house and amounted to about 5,100 rubles in 1642–3. Second, every year the some 3,000 white places of the city provided the "gate money" (*reshotochnye den'gi*), about 207 rubles or three kopecks per house. This tax maintained the grillwork gates that were placed on all major intersections at night to prevent crime. Third, the millers and draymen (*izvozchiki*) of Moscow provided a further 834 rubles. It is not surprising to find that the shops on Red Square, the main market, which paid 1,127 rubles toward the paving money in 1625–6 and 1634–5, had been granted a complete exemption from 1642–3. Because all the richest merchants had shops here, it is not hard to guess who benefited the most from this measure. These taxes provided the Land Office with its own income, but it was sometimes required to collect taxes for the treasury: Perhaps the burden passed through its hands, and it is certain that in 1638 and 1639 it collected from 1,221 houses of the black settlements an extraordinary tax called *povorot-nye den'gi* amounting to 2,442 rubles that went to support the army. The Land Office had at its own disposal only some thousand rubles annually besides the 5,000–6,000 rubles to last six years.[6] It also collected judicial fees from its courts, but the size of these is impossible to determine. It is difficult to escape the impression that the upkeep of Moscow was not high on the government's list of priorities.

None of the regular taxes collected by the Land Office were very large. The burden also (cf. Chapter 9) was not a great sum for the town to provide, because the bulk of the taxes paid by any town community was the enormous sums that came from the tolls and tavern monopoly. However, these taxes were inevitably distributed unequally among the urban population: The burden was supposed to be distributed by the town community, but the highest payments per household were only a few rubles, trivial sums for a great merchant. The same was true for the local assessments made by the Land Office. The extraordinary taxes such as the *piatinnaia denga* (fifth) or *povorotnye den'gi* were a more serious matter, but even here the records of the sums collected do not show large sums paid by the merchants. More serious for the merchant were the tolls, which he had to pay on all goods bought and sold. For the small man, merchant or artisan, however, these direct taxes were onerous, because even a tax of half a ruble on a household whose income was measured in rubles, not thousands of rubles, could be a great hardship.

The Moscow merchant

Above the mass of the townsmen in wealth and legal position stood three groups of merchants who had a rank and organization of their own. The most important of these were the *gosti*, followed by the *gost'* hundred and the woolen drapers' hundred (*sukonnaia sotnia*). The *gosti* were the richest and most privileged merchants, in most cases owning a house and warehouse in the Kitaigorod, across Red Square from the Kremlin, where they rubbed shoulders with the most prominent boyars, clerics, and officials. Although they often acted as a group, there seems to have been no formal organization like the hundreds: The *gosti* were merely a group of merchants given a certain rank by the Tsar. Mutual interests and family ties drew the *gosti* together, but they did not constitute a corporation in any sense. The *gost'* hundred, however, was organized like the hundreds of ordinary townsmen, possessing an elder and perhaps some other rudimentary organization. The members of the *gost'* hundred stood one rank lower than the *gosti* and many of its members became *gosti*; it was not uncommon for the son or nephew of a *gost'* to spend some years in the *gost'* hundred. Both *gosti* and the *gost'* hundred were free of the burden and were not judged like ordinary Muscovites in the Land Office. Below the *gost'* hundred stood the woolen drapers' hundred. Other than the fact that it seems to have been subject to the Land Office, little is known about this group. It is clear that it had no particular connection with woolen cloth by 1600 because that commodity was traded by merchants of all ranks and stations. The group was often included in public documents after the *gosti* and *gost'* hundred, implying that it was in some way a privileged group. Virtually no members of it are known to have been men of great wealth (in contrast to the *gost'* hundred), and in the second half of the seventeenth century it gradually fades from view.

In the history of the Moscow merchants the most important sector of the population was the *gosti*. Most of the richest and most active merchants in the city held the rank of *gost'*, although a few *kadashevtsy* and members of the *gost'* hundred equaled them.[7] The *gosti* thus accounted for all but a few of the merchant elite of Moscow. The title was granted to only about thirty men at any one time in the seventeenth century, and carried with it sufficient privileges to raise the holder above the mass of the Russian merchants in legal status. Legally the *gost'* was no longer a member of the town community: He did not contribute to the burden, and his house was considered a white place like an ecclesiastical or boyar property. He could own land and serfs in the countryside and was free of the state tavern monopoly (he could make his own beer and vodka).[8] Most of the *gosti* were Muscovites, although in the larger towns other than Moscow there were often one or two merchants of this rank and five or six merchants in the *gost'* hundred: This work will deal mainly with the Moscow *gosti*, however, because the provincial *gosti* were a distinct group. The rank of *gost'*, as well as membership in the *gost'* hundred, was awarded by the Tsar but the criteria are unknown.

Generally, the wealthier merchants of Moscow and the main provincial towns were given the rank of *gost'* or *gost'* hundred. It has been assumed without proof that the purpose of such an award was to require the richest merchants to serve the Tsar, and that the *gosti* were therefore an artificial creation. The existence of stable *gost'* families in Novgorod (the

Emel'ianovs), the fact that most Moscow *gosti* were the children of Muscovites, and consideration of the economic forces in Russian trade effectively refute this view. In any case, the service performed by the *gosti* did not tie them to Moscow. In the sixteenth century, the main form of *gost'* service seems to have been diplomatic, with *gosti* being sent to England, the Low Countries, and the Emperor, possibly because in their dealings with foreign merchants they had learned German or Dutch or at least knew a little about Western Europe. In the seventeenth century, *gost'* service was perhaps less honorific but equally important. *Gosti* were usually appointed to head the toll and tavern administration in the great centers of Russian trade – Archangel, Moscow, and Astrakhan – from at least 1613, if not from the 1590s.[9] The *gosti* were also prominent in the collection of extraordinary direct taxes such as the fifth (*piatinnaia den'ga*), and in the commercial operations of the treasury. (The members of the *gost'* hundred and even the woolen drapers' hundred were often assigned less important tasks of the same type.[10]) It has been assumed that this service was purely an onerous burden, but too little is known of the internal operations to confirm or deny this assertion. As we shall see, there is some evidence to the contrary.

A history of the merchants of Moscow is thus mainly a history of the Moscow *gosti*. Before the commercial activities of the *gosti* can be investigated, it is necessary to solve an important preliminary question: Were the *gosti* a stable group, or was the rank of *gost'* merely granted to a man who had just become rich and who had no successors in that position? The traditional view of Russian historians has been that there was no continuity among the *gosti* and that therefore the capital they accumulated was dispersed at their death. The problem of the stability of merchant capital cannot be approached directly, and the method has been to search for stable merchant families and assume that the capital will roughly follow the fortunes of the family. Only recently has any attempt been made to go beyond the illustrative method and to look at the merchant class as a whole in order to find out who the *gosti* were.[11] As will be shown, there was a certain amount of stability among the Moscow merchants, at least over two or three generations. The real problem here lies not so much in establishing the historical facts of Moscow merchant families as it does in working out a meaningful definition of "stability": What does the stability of a merchant group mean in seventeenth-century Europe, particularly Eastern Europe? Russian historians tend to assume that, whereas Russian merchant fortunes rarely lasted very long, the West was characterized by stable merchant dynasties lasting over generations, if not centuries. This was not, however, the case. As long ago as the 1890s, Richard Ehrenberg, one of the pioneers in the economic history of European commerce and merchants, said in speaking of Antwerp in the period 1480–1550: "Only the greatest trading houses flourished for several generations, and as a rule the development [of a commercial house] came to an end in the third generation." In that period the same was true of English provincial towns.[12]

In Eastern Europe the same chances of continuance faced the merchant family. The purely demographic chances of family survival were very low. In Buda and Pest in the period 1490–1526 only 10 percent of the great merchants and patricians had living grandsons at their death, and only half had one or more male children. Thus the chance of simple continuity of the family surname was only one in two. It has been suggested that the demographic factor was the most important in the rapid turnover of the urban elite. This explanation need not be accepted, but the fact of rapid turnover is clear. In Krakow, still an important commercial center until the last years of the seventeenth century, it was exceptional for the grandson of a seventeenth-century merchant to retain the social position of his grandfather. Only in the most commercially advanced centers of Europe, such as Amsterdam, was there great continuity among merchant families. This continuity may be partly the result of better records because it is easier in Amsterdam than in most Eastern European cities to follow the fortunes of a specific family and its capital. In addition, the superiority of commercial technique and organization gave the Dutch an advantage over virtually every merchant class in Europe, not only the Russians. Finally, the Dutch of the Golden Age were not just merchants: Investment in land, in financial operations, and in the great trading companies like the East India Company gave them additional security in the face of the fluctuations of commerce. Whereas a Russian or even a German merchant could be wiped out by a single loss, the Dutch merchant had other investments to carry him through a bad period. Outside of London and Amsterdam only a few cities like Hamburg could boast such continuity among merchants. Certainly in many Central European cities that had stagnated since the end of the Middle Ages, a stable elite continued to control the city, but this is a wholly different type of continuity from that of the Dutch merchant families. In Eastern Europe and the less advanced cities of the West, the merchants' lot was very uncertain.[13]

The history of the *gosti* begins in the middle years of the sixteenth century, the earliest reference being the signatures of twelve *gosti* to the resolution of the Assembly of the Land of 1566. For the first time the term *gosti* signified a specific rank, rather than simply a general term for a merchant. By the time of the Assembly of the Land in 1598 the *gost'* hundred and the woolen drapers' hundred had also appeared.[14] All these men were certainly residents of the city of Moscow, but at the same time *gosti* appeared who were not Muscovites. This fact is not insignificant because the tendency has been to treat all *gosti* as Muscovites, with the result that the concentration of the merchant class in Moscow has been somewhat exaggerated. In Novgorod there was a *gostinnaia sokha* among the taxation units that clearly included merchants titled *gosti* by the 1570s if not earlier. In Yaroslavl one Nikita Nikitnikov was already called *gost'* and was rich enough to own a house in Kazan in the 1560s.[15] Nikitnikov was certainly the ancestor of the Nikitnikov family, still important and titled Yaroslavl *gosti* in the seventeenth century, before it moved to Moscow. In Novgorod and Pskov the Emel'ianov and Stoianov families persisted until the time of Peter as local *gosti*. In the important northern town of Ustiug Velikii the Usov-Grudtsyn, Reviakin, and Bosoi families kept their main seat of operations in the town and only maintained a subsidiary office in Moscow.[16] All these Ustiug families were members of the *gost'* hundred by at least 1613, and they lasted through most of the seventeenth century. Some members of the family called themselves Muscovites and lived at least part of the time in the capital, but the commercial operations of the family required them to keep Ustiug as their center. This sort of double base in one merchant family was not unusual in the case of towns closely connected to Moscow. Ustiug was an important station in the fur trade between Siberia and Moscow, and the merchants had to take account of this. Yaroslavl was closely tied to Moscow for almost all branches of trade, a fact reflected in the fate of the Gur'ev-Nazar'ev-Chistoi family, part of which stayed in Yaroslavl while part founded a new branch in Moscow that rose to great wealth and position.[17] Cities more loosely tied to Moscow, such as Novgorod, did not have such split merchant families, and indeed most Moscow merchants from provincial towns lost their family connections in their native town, although often they maintained close commercial ties. The relations between *gosti* of Moscow and the provincial towns were determined primarily by the shape of Russia's economic network.

In spite of the relative paucity of sources, it is possible to follow the history of the *gost'* families from the middle of the sixteenth century to the end of the seventeenth. Because the main problem is the economic stability of merchant families, it is important to consider not only the continuance of a family at *gost'* rank, but also its commercial history as a whole, insofar as it can be traced. The major shifts in the trade of Russia, and of Moscow in particular, are also clearly relevant and demand consideration.

The history of the *gost'* families begins with the twelve men who appear among the signatories of the resolution of the Assembly of the Land of 1566.[18] Six of these men had ancestors who had traded with the Near East through the Crimea or Poland in the previous century: Afanas'ev, Khoznikov, Suzin, Tarakanov, Podushkin, and Kotkov. Some of the Tarakanovs were moved from Moscow to Novgorod after its capture by Grand Prince Ivan III Vasilevich at the end of the fifteenth century, and this Tarakanov may have become a *gost'* in Novgorod. One more *gost'*, Glazev, also came from a family of Novgorod merchants.[19] Thus, in the first list of *gosti* extant, six or seven are known to have come from families important in trade for some hundred years; five of these families were from Moscow, two from Novgorod.

The *gosti* mentioned in 1598 present more problems and are harder to trace. Of the twenty-one names, only ten can be identified. Two were the sons or grandsons of Bulgak Savanin, a *gost'* in 1566 (Bogdan Semenov Bulgakov and Men'shoi Semenov Bulgakov), and one (Ivan Iur'ev) was his nephew. One *gost'* in 1598, Ivan Mikhailov Churkin, was a simple merchant (*kupets*) in 1566.[20] Three of the *gosti* in 1598 were descendants of the so-called *smol'niane* of 1566. There is some debate over the precise meaning of this term, which literally means only "men of Smolensk": Were they merchants living in Smolensk in 1566 or Muscovites whose ancestors were moved to Moscow after the Russian capture of Smolensk in 1514? In a document of 1549 they are referred to as *svedentsy Smol'niane, pany moskovskie*. The term *svedentsy* implies that they were already moved, but from where to where? They could have been Muscovites moved to Smolensk, as happened in the case of Novgorod. Their presence at the Assembly of the Land in 1566 suggests that, whatever their earlier fate, they were living in Moscow at the time of the Assembly.[21] In any case, they were involved in trade via Smolensk, which means the trade with Poland, and two of these 1566 *smol'niane*, Afanasii Ivanov Iudin and Stepan Ivanov Kotov, were *gosti* in 1598. Furthermore both had descendants who were important seventeenth-century merchants and *gosti*. A third *gost'* of 1598, Grigorii Ivanov Tverdikov, was certainly a relative of the *smol'nianin* Ignatii Tverdikov of 1566. The Tverdikov family also survived well into the next century. Not so successful were the descendants of three other 1598 *gosti*. Iurii Bolotnikov remained a *gost'* himself until the 1620s, and his son Stepan Iur'ev Bolotnikov was in the *gost'* hundred by 1613; but the father died in 1628 and the son in 1633.[22] The *gost'* Bogdan Trofimov Poryvkin seems to be represented in the next generation by a Nikifor Poryvkin, active about 1620, who had a house in the Kitaigorod with his brothers Anikei and Ivan. The house suggests that the family had once been wealthy, but Nikifor occupied himself not so much with trade as with denouncing bribery and graft among the merchants in the state service after 1613.[23] One *gost'* in 1598, Timofei Vykhodets, was a Novgorod merchant in the 1580s, but had no descendants known to be wealthy merchants.[24]

Most of the *gosti* of 1598, however, cannot be traced back, and most of the *gosti* of 1566 did not have commercially active descendants. The reason for this change is not to be sought merely in a general "instability" of the Moscow merchant class. The fact was that Russian trade experienced a major shift in the course of the sixteenth century. In 1500 the most important branch of Russian foreign trade was the trade in Near Eastern goods, mainly fine cloth, at Kaffa in the Crimea. Most of the *gosti* of 1566 whose activities and families can be identified were associated with that trade. By 1598, the direction of Russian trade had shifted to Archangel and the trade with the Dutch and the Muscovy Company. Thus, the particular skills, the knowledge of roads and languages, and even of the goods traded in Kaffa were no longer important. The men who were wealthy in 1566 could reorient their fortunes only with difficulty, and it is not surprising that the Smolensk merchants superseded them. The trade with Poland in the sixteenth century was a trade in the same goods as the Baltic trade and the Archangel trade: Anglo-Flemish woolen cloth for furs, wax, flax, and hemp. The knowledge and skills of the Smolensk merchants made them the natural heirs of the old Kaffa traders in the new commercial situation that emerged at the end of the sixteenth century.

Between the Assembly of the Land of 1598 and the next group of sources on the *gosti* in the 1620s came the political and social upheaval known as the Time of Troubles. Because much of the action and warfare took place around Moscow itself from the summer of 1608 to 1613, it is to be expected that the Moscow merchants found themselves in a dangerous position, and many must have perished or suffered irreparable losses in trade. A large number simply fled the city, and had to be ordered back by the new government in 1613. It is therefore not surprising that sixteen out of twenty-one *gosti* of 1598 had no descendants who remained *gosti* or wealthy merchants for long. The discontinuity, however, was not as great as might be supposed from these figures because five of the 1598 *gosti*, together with lesser Moscow merchants, produced half of the *gosti* after the restoration of internal order in 1613–15.

From about 1620 to the end of the century fairly complete lists of the *gosti* can be compiled from a variety of sources. In the 1620s, about a half of the *gosti* of Moscow were the descendants of merchants active and wealthy, if not themselves *gosti*, in the sixteenth century. Bakhteiar and Kirilo Bulgakov, who were clearly not young men in 1620, were probably the sons of the Bulgakovs of 1598. The *gost'* Vasilii Ivanov Iur'ev was certainly the son of the *gost'* of 1598 Ivan Iur'ev and was thus a cousin of the Bulgakovs. He owned land in the Kolomna district and had three merchant sons, Vasilii, Ivan, and Il'ia, who were landowners in the Moscow district. Vasilii and Il'ia Iur'ev also had a house in Moscow in 1626. The three sons were active merchants in the 1640s; a Vasilii Fedorov Iur'ev was a *gost'* from 1646 to 1675, and his son in turn in the 1680s. Thus three and possibly five generations of Iurievs were active merchants from 1598 or even 1566 to 1710.[25] The *gost'* S. I. Kotov of 1598 undoubtedly was the father of the three Kotovs who were *gosti* in the 1620s, and the *gost'* Tomilo Tarakanov was certainly related to the Grigorii Tarakanov of 1566.[26] Besides the Kotovs, who had sprung from the *smol'niane*, the two Tverdikovs and three Iudins were from the same group, making about one-quarter whose ancestors had been connected with the Smolensk trade. Half of the *gosti* in the 1620s were members of families connected with Moscow by at least 1598, and, if the *smol'niane* are accounted Muscovites in 1566, half of the *gost'* families were connected with Moscow back to the middle of the sixteenth century. Furthermore, the Tarakanov and Kotov (Kotkov) families were active in the Crimean trade before 1500, so that some of these families may have gone back three generations or more.

The half of the *gosti* of the 1620s who were not of old Moscow families came from a variety of provincial towns, but the most important of these new merchant immigrants to Moscow were those who came from Yaroslavl – Nazar Chistoi, Nadeia and Naum Sveteshknikov, Grigorii Nikitnikov, and Vasilii Lytkin. Nazar Christoi later became a *dumnyi d'iak*, or high official, and was killed in the Moscow revolt of 1648 at the peak of his political career. The Nazar'ev and Gur'ev branches of the family remained in Yaroslavl and were still important merchants there in

the second half of the century. Little is known of Lytkin, but Nadeia
Sveteshnikov and Grigorii Nikitnikov were the two richest merchants in
Moscow, and except for the Stroganovs, the two richest merchants in the
whole Russian state. Nikitnikov was a descendant of the Yaroslavl *gost'*
of the 1560s who owned a house in Kazan, and he was an important local
leader in Yaroslavl in the Time of Troubles. He was involved in both the
first and second militias, and therefore was one of the men who helped
bring the Romanovs to the throne.[27] Sveteshnikov was an important
supplier to the court in 1613–14, when he was still called *iaroslavskii gost'*.
Both of these families died out in the plague of 1654.[28] Thus, five *gosti*
came from Yaroslavl, about 15 percent of the total. Grigorii Shorin came
from Viaz'ma, apparently from a prominent merchant family there.
Semen Shorin was active already in 1584, and in 1596 headed the toll
collection in Smolensk.[29] Smirnoi Sudovshchikov must have been from
Kaluga, as his brother Tret'iak Sudovshchikov was called *kaluzhskii gost'* in
1615, and Smirnoi paid taxes on a house in Kaluga in 1614. Smirnoi
Sudovshchikov was one of the signatories to the election document of
Mikhail Romanov as representative of Kaluga.[30] The other *gosti* in the
1620s cannot be traced earlier than that decade, although most had descendants active in the later part of the century.

In the 1630s there were only nineteen *gosti*. Some of the men who left
the ranks of the *gosti* were replaced by relatives, such as Nazar Chistoi,
who was replaced by his brother Anikei (Almaz) Chistoi. The Shorin
family reappeared in the 1640s, and Oblezovs continued as merchants in
the *gost'* hundred. Those who disappeared completely were the ones about
whom least is known, like Bolotnikov or Eroksalimov: They were probably not wealthy to begin with and perhaps without male descendants.
More than half of the *gosti* active in the 1630s were still the Muscovites of
old families that were active in the previous decade or their sons. Only one
new man from the provinces received the rank of *gost'* in Moscow, Bogdan
Tsvetnoi of Murom.[31]

In the 1640s the number of *gosti* increased slightly to twenty-one. Ten
of them had been *gosti* for twenty years or were the children of these *gosti*
and thus firmly settled in the capital. Two new *gosti*, Bogdan Shchepotkin
and Andrei Spiridonov, had been in the *gost'* hundred in Moscow in the
1630s.[32] One man is of unknown origin and eight were from the ranks of
provincial merchants. Two, Kiril Bosoi and Vasilii Fedorov (Fedotov)-
Gusiatnikov, known as Skoraia Zapis', came from Ustiug Velikii.[33] Peter
Volkov and Ivan Kolomiatin came from Kolomna.[34] Semen Cherkasov,

Fedor Venevitinov, and his son Afanasii came from Murom. Daniil Pankrat'ev came from Galich.[35] His father, Grigorii Grigor'ev Pankrat'ev, was
a merchant who moved to Moscow and eventually became an official in
the treasury. His son Daniil continued the commercial activities of the
family, and in the latter part of the century they were important salt
producers in the Russian North.

These findings make it apparent that the elite of the Moscow merchants
were as stable a group as could be expected in the seventeenth century.
Some families did last over several generations, although not always at the
same rank. There is a distinct rise and fall in the history of a family, but
this fact is neither unexpected nor unique to Moscow. Furthermore the
Moscow merchants possessed a distinct local base in the city. About half
were old inhabitants of Moscow from the middle of the sixteenth century
to the middle of the seventeenth century. That the proportion of new men
from the provinces should be relatively high, about a quarter of all merchants, is not surprising considering that the period was one of great
commercial expansion. The new men come from the towns closely connected with Moscow: Yaroslavl, Ustiug Velikii, Galich, and the towns of
the upper Oka River such as Kaluga, Kolomna, and Murom. They do not
(after the sixteenth century) come from Novgorod or Pskov, nor from
Nizhnii Novgorod or Kazan. In the commercial network of the Russian
state there were certain groupings within the national market, and the
formation of the Moscow merchant class reflected that fact: Most came
from the North or Central Russia. Indeed it will be shown that there was a
gradual expansion of mercantile activity from 1500 to 1700, and that the
provincial towns benefited from this process as much as Moscow. In 1500
Russian trade with the Near East and Western Europe was confined to a
few places – Moscow, Novgorod, Pskov, the Crimea – and virtually all Russian merchants involved in it came from the three main Russian towns. In
the first half of the seventeenth century, merchants from a great number
of minor towns came to Archangel to trade, and by 1710 virtually all
Russian cities, dozens of small towns, and even many trading villages were
represented at the Archangel fair. In a situation like this, it would be
difficult to keep certain of the richest provincials from joining the ranks of
the Muscovite merchant elite. It is more remarkable that the native Muscovites were not swamped by immigrants from the provinces with newly
founded fortunes coming to take the richer prizes of the capital.

The formation of the Moscow merchant elite so closely reflected the shifts and turns of trade in Russia that it is difficult to see what influence the government's policy could have had on it. Yet the tradition of Russian historical writing has been to assert that the *gosti* were an artificial group concentrated in Moscow by an overcentralized state that was solely interested in service and in draining the merchants of their wealth. This view has never been supported by much empirical evidence but has instead been based on general considerations. Only two pieces of evidence have been cited. First, the practice of drafting artisans from other towns for government works projects in Moscow – surely a situation so different as to merit no serious consideration. Second, the petitions that resulted from the revolt of 1648: In these petitions many recently arrived merchants requested leave to return to their native towns and complained of the great burden of service. But surely it is naive to take such petitions at face value. Submitted at the end of one of the most serious revolts in Moscow's history by the members of a merchant elite under attack from the mob, these petitions were hardly objective descriptions of the situation.[36] All Russian petitions of the time that request some privilege or relief open with the stereotyped assertion of the petitioners' complete ruin (*do kontsa razorilsia*) and reveal nothing but the petitioners' dissatisfaction. Moreover, the privileged status of the *gosti* and *gost'* hundred was one of the objects of the mob's fury. Thus the request of the great merchants to serve in the provinces from which they came and to return to the status of ordinary townsmen, either in Moscow or in a provincial town, meant their removal from the eyes of the rebellious Muscovites. When the Muscovites were not sacking their houses, the *gosti* showed no desire to return to a more humble status. The government's attempts to get merchants from the provinces to move to Moscow were simply failures when such moves did not coincide with the merchant's commercial interests. In 1637 and apparently again in 1646 the government ordered a number of members of the *gost'* hundred in Ustiug to move to Moscow: "zhit' na Moskve dlia nashikh [the Tsar's] sluzheb." However, when the revolt of 1648 broke out, Stepan Usov and Vasilii Bosoi were both still living in Ustiug, and indeed had to flee for their lives from the mob. The 1637 order had specifically ordered "the sons of Aleksei Bosoi" (i.e., Kirill, Vasilii, and Andrei) to move to the capital, but in fact the Bosoi family continued to operate from Ustiug, sending only the younger brother, Andrei, to Moscow where he acted as agent for the family. It is not known whether Andrei went to Moscow as a result of the government's orders, but certainly his functions there were necessary to the family business. The merchants may have found the government's orders annoying, but they often did not follow them when they did not choose to.[37]

By the end of the sixteenth century Moscow was a flourishing commercial city as well as the Tsar's residence and seat of government. This commercial prosperity continued, in spite of the Time of Troubles and lesser disasters, throughout the seventeenth century, and it carried the merchants of Moscow on to fortune. The Moscow merchants were the wealthiest and weightiest element among the merchants of the Russian state, and this not merely because of their connections with the court and their service to the Tsar, but because of their prominence in all branches of Russian trade, both the trade with the West and (as far as we can tell) inside Russia. But this prominence was not a monopoly. The Muscovites had rivals not only in London and Amsterdam but in Novgorod and Yaroslavl, Ustiug and Kazan, and even in the many villages of peasant-traders scattered along the roads and rivers of rural Russia. It is the commercial role of the Moscow merchants that formed the basis of their prosperity, and that therefore provides the basis for an evaluation of their ultimate role in Russian history.

2

The conditions of trade in seventeenth-century Russia

The most important fact in the commercial geography of Russia in the sixteenth and seventeenth centuries was the lack of direct and easy access to the markets of Western Europe. This obstacle has been stated and discussed innumerable times in the literature on Russian trade, and has even been considered a major element in the history of Russian culture. Nevertheless, it is not strictly true. Until the Time of Troubles, Russia possessed (and had possessed since the ninth century), a strip of coast between Narva and the mouth of the Neva known to the Russians as the *Izhorskaia zemlia*, from the name of the Finno-Ugric tribe *Izhora*, one of the original constituents of the Novgorodian state in the Middle Ages. Furthermore, the route from the mouth of the Neva up to Lake Ladoga, through the southern corner of the lake, and up the Volkhov River to Novgorod, was the historic route of Russian trade with the West. It was used at the time of earliest-recorded Russian history by the Varangians, as part of their route to Byzantium, and Russian merchants sailed to Denmark and Sweden by this route in the eleventh and twelfth centuries. After the establishment of the Hansa in the Baltic, the Hanseatic merchants used it until the closing of the Hansa "factory" in Novgorod (1494). Thus, Russia was not literally cut off until 1617. However, Russia did not use the coast in the sixteenth century, and most trade passed through Reval or Narva and was then carried into Russia by land or river. Ivangorod, in Russian territory across the river from Narva, failed to provide an effective rival to Narva. Why did this change take place? Perhaps the problem was that the Dutch replaced the Hansa as the primary shippers of the Baltic in the late fifteenth century, and at the same time larger ships came into use in the Baltic. The new ships could not sail up the Volkhov to Novgorod as the older Hansa ships had, and thus were compelled to stop in deep water ports like Reval and Narva. For the Dutch this was not a serious problem because the larger ships were one of the reasons for their success, but for the Russians it meant the end of direct trade with Western Europe merchants. Henceforth the Revalers firmly established themselves as middlemen between the Dutch and English and the Russians.[1]

For this reason the appearance of the English in the mouth of the Northern Dvina in 1553 was a major event, and the northern route became the chief highway of Russian commerce with the commercial centers of Europe at that time, England and the Netherlands. The sea route ran from the North Sea ports (London, Hull, Amsterdam, and the smaller ports of North Holland and Friesland) along the coast past Norway and Lapland to Archangel. The Dutch had been trading in Lapland before they moved on to the Northern Dvina mouth in the 1570s, and it was still common around 1600 for their ships to stop at Vardø, Pechenga, or Kola and trade in the products of the Arctic fisheries, before they sailed on to the mouth of the Northern Dvina. Archangel was not founded until 1585, and until then the main town was Kholmogory, several miles upstream, where the river was too shallow for ships with 50–100 lasts of cargo, or in the seventeenth century, ships with as much as 250 lasts. The English dropped anchor off the island of Iagry in the Dvina mouth, which they called Rose Island because of the wild roses that grew there. The English also called the port St. Nicholas, the name of the largest island in the bay. The Dutch anchored in the Pudozhemskii channel of the Northern Dvina until 1583 when the Danish fleet, jealous of the Dutch penetration into the Russian markets, attempted to raid the Dutch trading fleet. The Dutch merchants petitioned for a safer harbor opposite the Monastery of St. Michael the Archangel, and in 1583–5 the town of Archangel was constructed. The Tsar ordered that both the Dutch and English merchants transfer their dealings to Archangel, but the English held on to Rose Island until 1591. In contrast, Jan van de Valle had a warehouse in the new town by 1586.[2]

The voyage from Holland or England to Archangel was long, arduous, and dangerous. The journey from Texel, the island off North Holland that was Amsterdam's port, to Archangel took around four weeks if there was no trouble. Generally the captains tried to leave in late spring if possible, and arrive in Archangel by June because the fair lasted only until the end of August. The ship usually lay in port for about a month, and tried to start the return voyage in September, although it was still possible to come home safely in October. After October the storms off Norway's North Cape made the voyage very dangerous. The ships that made the journey from Holland were large, somewhat heavier than the usual Dutch ship going to the Baltic, and often armed. Armament was not only heavy, but required a larger crew and thus drove up the cost of the voyage. For the Amsterdam–Archangel–Amsterdam voyage the price per last fluctuated between twenty and thirty guilders for the end of the sixteenth and first half of the seventeenth centuries.[3] The requirement of armament naturally added to the cost, but it is probable that this affected only ships stopping in Lapland in addition to Archangel. The need for arms came from the Danish King's claim to require a pass from the Dutch for the Lapland trade, a requirement they tried to avoid. The presence of a Danish fleet cruising off the northern coast of Norway was undoubtedly the reason for the cannon; certainly Russia had no fleet to provide a reason for armaments. Sometimes the returning Dutch ships did not stop in Holland at all but sailed straight from Archangel to Livorno on the Tuscan coast, an enormously long voyage that was very expensive and made a large, heavy ship an absolute necessity.[4] The trade with Archangel was certainly not an easy task, and it is no wonder that the Dutch, with their superior ships and crews, were able to hold their control over it so long.

Archangel did not have a proper port with piers because the water was too shallow near shore, and the entire cargo had to be transferred to lighters and brought to the bank piecemeal. Indeed, the river was fairly shallow all the way up to Archangel. Of the three channels in the mouth, only two, the Pudozhemskii and Berezovskii channels, were usable. In the first half of the seventeenth century the government forbade the use of the Berezovskii channel, probably to prevent smuggling. By 1646 the Pudozhemskii channel had silted up too much, and as a result the government ordered the use only of the Berezovskii channel; however, it seems that both continued to be used to some extent until the end of the century. Once the ships had reached the river mouth they had to wait for a Russian *nosnik*, a pilot, to take them into the actual harbor.[5]

In the harbor, the ship master had to present a list of the goods to the toll chief (*tamozhennaia golova*), who was invariably a Moscow *gost'*. The purpose of this was to make sure that all the goods were sold with the payment of the toll because evasion of this payment was a serious problem for the Russian authorities, as everywhere. Dutch ships often anchored in unfrequented parts of the bay or in the smaller channels of the Northern Dvina and sold off the side of the ship to Russian smugglers. One of the

Map 2. Russia 1618–1654

devices to hinder smuggling was the requirement that all trade take place in the Merchants' House (*gostinnyi dvor*), a large complex of stalls and storage rooms built together into one large building. Such a building usually existed in any Russian town (for trade with foreign or out-of-town merchants), but the Merchants' House in Archangel was probably the largest of them all. It was wooden until the fire of 1667 caused it to be rebuilt in stone, and contained 170 storage rooms and probably roughly the same number of stalls.[6] On what legal basis a merchant acquired a stall or storage room in the Merchants'. House cannot be known with any certainty; apparently he paid a fee of some sort (*obrok*) and had to petition the toll administration for space. Once granted space, the merchant seems to have been able to keep it, but whether (for example) space in a Merchants' House could be inherited is unknown. Most prominent Moscow merchants had storage rooms or a stall in the Archangel Merchants' House. In April 1614 Grigorii Nikitnikov and Vasilii Iudin (both *gosti*) had storage rooms, and the *gost'* Mikhilo Smyvalov was granted one too. Vasilii Lytkin, a Yaroslavl merchant who soon became a Moscow *gost'*, was granted one in that year, near the storage room of Vtoroi Chistoi, of the important Chistoi merchant family of Yaroslavl.[7]

Trade at Archangel between Russians and foreigners was supposed to be only wholesale, and although this rule was evaded in practice, the foreign merchants were confined to selling at Archangel and going home. As we shall see later, they were not able to penetrate internal markets to an extent that would challenge the Russian merchants. The trading was only supposed to take place in the period of the fair, from June 1 to September 1. This restriction sometimes created difficulties if the fleet was late and only arrived in July, and in 1679 permission was given to extend the period of trading past September 1.[8]

Once the buying and selling had been completed, the task was to ship the wares to the south. This had to be done as swiftly as possible because it had to be completed before the rivers froze. From Archangel south along the Northern Dvina the route ran to the Sukhona River, and up the Sukhona past Ustiug Velikii and Tot'ma to Vologda, the end of the river route. Vologda was the most important way station on the route to Moscow because it was here that the merchants and their wares waited out the period of bad roads in the spring and fall. The Merchants' House here was a wooden, two-story building built after the Time of Troubles, ninety-two by ninety-three meters in area, with forty one storage rooms, a sort of hotel, and a church of Sts. Peter and Paul. In addition a number of

Moscow merchants, the *gosti* Vasilii and Ivan Iudin, Ivan Kolomnetin, and Mikhailo Glazovoi had their own houses, as did the Stroganovs, many important northern merchants, and the Dutch and English. The town had in 1627 about 1100 householders, and thus a population of perhaps 5500–6600. Many Muscovites also had shops in the market place: Grigorii Nikitnikov, *gost'*; Mikhail Neupokoev, *gost'* hundred; Mikhalko and Bogdashka Glazovskii, *gost'* hundred; the "Moscow German" Andrei Buk; Grigorii Iudin, *gost'* hundred; Ortiushka Fedorov, *kadashevets*; and Bogdashko Sadyvnov and Sidorka Maksimov of the Hunters' Settlement in Moscow.[9] There were also a number of houses belonging to the Dutch and to the Muscovy Company.

With all these facilities it was not difficult to wait the few weeks until the snow was deep and hard enough for the sleds to travel. Then the whole group began to move south along the Moscow road, leading out of Vologda. This route is described in numerous passes (*proezzhie gramoty*) of the seventeenth century. It ran to Yaroslavl, and then on to Pereiaslavl' Zalesskii, Rostov, and Moscow. Generally merchants traveled over it in the winter by sled, but if necessary it was possible to travel in summer with carts. Much less is known about this last part of the route, and it appears that no important stops were made except for Yaroslavl, where many merchants stopped and where some went on to towns along the Volga. Those who traded on the Volga must have been largely from Yaroslavl itself because there is little record throughout the century of merchants from Kazan or Nizhnii Novgorod trading at Archangel.

The second major trade route of Russia was the Volga. The great emporium on the Volga was Astrakhan, where the Persian ships came from the ports of Gilan and the Khanate of Shemakha (both Persian dependencies), the great centers of silk production. These were mainly small ships that sailed in convoy, hugging the western coast of the Caspian Sea in fear of the Turkmen pirates who flourished along the eastern coast. Most of these merchants were Armenian subjects of the Shah because except for those on diplomatic missions, only a few Russians went to Persia. Besides the Armenians and Azerbaijanis, Central Asians came to Astrakhan, both by sea and by the caravan route across the steppe. By the end of the seventeenth century Indian merchants had settled in Astrakhan, but it is not clear when they first came; it seems that the first Indians traded in Russia about 1640.[10] Astrakhan was a town of some significance with a permanent (and polyglot) population. Nevertheless, it was a town whose life was seasonal, and its permanent population was largely a garrison and a group of artisans and seasonal laborers who worked the salt marshes. These salt marshes, the fisheries, and the Oriental trade were the three attractions of Astrakhan, and the Muscovite merchants were heavily involved in all of them, along with the merchants of Nizhnii Novgorod and Kazan.

The river route of the Volga was just as important as the Northern Dvina and grew more important as the river valley was settled farther and farther down. Downstream travel was easy because the crew simply drifted and steered for the most part. Upstream the boat had to be rowed. The boats, chiefly the *doshchanoi strug*, were fairly large and required twenty-six rowers as well as a cook (normally a young boy) and a pilot. Such a boat belonged to Grigorii Nikitnikov in 1622–3. On the whole, these boats were the property of the merchants trading in Astrakhan, rather than of the merchants of any Volga town in particular. This was in contrast to the Northern Dvina, where most boats belonged to Vologda shippers and merchants.[11]

The first major stop upstream was Kazan, but it does not seem that Kazan merchants (at that time mainly Russians, not Tatars) played an important role.[12] Kazan was simply a stopping place whose importance was increased by the confluence of the Kama and thus the arrival of the salt from Solikamsk. From Kazan the route to Moscow led to Nizhnii Novgorod, the usual starting place for the Volga boats, and then overland to Moscow. Sometimes the Oka was used, but if the practices of Kalmykov in the second half of the century are typical of the previous generation, it was more common to carry the wares by carts (or sledges in winter) overland to Moscow. The carriers were generally peasants from the villages along the way, who did this as supplementary labor in the winter. This arrangement was possible because the Volga trade, like that at Archangel, was seasonal. The boats left Nizhnii Novgorod after the ice cleared and sailed down to Astrakhan, and returned in the late summer. The cargo then sat in warehouses in Nizhnii Novgorod until the snow was packed hard, and then was taken by the peasants to Moscow. On their return journey by sled the peasants brought the Russian and European goods to Nizhnii Novgorod to wait for the spring. Another variant of this route was to use Yaroslavl instead of Nizhnii Novgorod, but it is impossible to know how widespread this was, or whether only Yaroslavl merchants used it.

The other great road used by the Muscovite merchants was the road that led directly west to Wilno. This road was used for commerce until at least 1650, in spite of the frequent wars. The road ran from Moscow to Mozhaisk, then to Viaz'ma, Dorogobuzh, and Smolensk. Until the Time of Troubles Smolensk was an important entrepôt for Russian and Polish trade. But afterward there is little evidence of either its importance or decline. In any case, beyond Smolensk there were two possible routes. One went southwest to Mogilev, which became a major city only in the sixteenth century, as a result of the growing trade with Russia. The older route ran directly west to Wilno, which after 1550 was less important than Mogilev, although it continued to hold second place. Few Russian merchants went farther west than this, although there are occasional records of Russian merchants in Poznań, the great center of the overland trade in Russian and Polish furs.[13] The Russian merchants in Wilno had a separate *gostinnyi dom*, first granted them in 1495 but apparently not built until at least 1503.[14] All these routes overland required that the Russian merchants in Moscow hire their own carts and sledges that would take them at least as far as the border.

There was another route into the Polish-Lithuanian state, the route southwest to Briansk, and the Svinsk fair at the Uspenskii monastery on the edges of Briansk itself. This fair was one of the largest markets for furs, which were sold not only to Ukrainian merchants from Kiev and other towns, but also to the Nezhin Greeks and the Armenians of Kamenets-Podol'skii. Some Moscow merchants did go on as far as Nezhin and Kiev, but on the whole little is known of this route. The route to the Crimea, which formed an important part of Russian trade in the fourteenth and fifteenth centuries and continued for at least a generation or two after the Ottoman Turks captured Kaffa, seems to have fallen into disuse. Indeed, many of the furs sold at the Svinsk fair or Nezhin went on to Constantinople, but they were shipped by Ottoman subjects or by Greek and Armenian merchants who lived in Nezhin, Kamenets, or Lwow. If we hear little of Nezhin and Kiev from the Russian side, we hear nothing of Kaffa. Direct Russian trade with the Crimeans was strictly a border trade between Voronezh and the Don Cossacks on one side and Azak (Azov) on the other.[15]

In the seventeenth century, the Baltic route was no longer of first importance. The traditional route still ran from Western Europe (Lübeck, Hamburg, Amsterdam) through the Livonian cities, which were from the end of the Livonian War part of the Swedish Kingdom. (Riga, which was conquered by the Swedes from Poland only in 1621, did not play an important role in trade with Russia until late in the seve, teenth century.)

The route went by sea as far as Reval, then along the coast to Narva, and overland to Novgorod. Another possibility was from Reval by land to Dorpat, and then to Pskov. Russian merchants, mostly from Novgorod and Pskov, did travel to Reval; Muscovites were rare in Livonia. In Reval the Russians traded not with the Dutch or Hansa merchants, but with the Revalers who acted as intermediaries, according to Reval's guest-right. This guest-right prohibited merchants from other towns from trading with one another directly; they had to sell all their goods to a Reval merchant. In Narva, the English had the right of trading directly with the Russians from 1665, but only in the 1680s did this right bear fruit in increased English trade in the town. On the whole, the competition of the Archangel route meant the virtual stagnation of the Baltic route to Russia until the end of the century.[16]

A totally new branch of Russian foreign trade that appeared only after the Treaty of Stolbovo (1617) was the Russian trade with Stockholm and the Finnish towns along the route from Russia to the Swedish capital. This trade route was dominated by Novgorodians, merchants from Tikhvin and other small towns of the Northwest, and the Russian and Karelian peasants of the Lake Onega district. Some Muscovites did trade along this route however. The Russians collected at the old center of Russian Karelia, Korela, which the Swedes called Kexholm, arriving there by a number of roads. From Kexholm they generally crossed the Karelian Isthmus to Viborg and then took Swedish ships to Stockholm. Some preferred the land route via Helsingfors to Åbo, then the main city of Finland, and then by boat through the Åland Islands to Stockholm. In Stockholm there was a "Russian House" (*russkii dvor*) in accord with the provisions of the Treaty of Stolbovo, but little is known other than the fact of its existence. This route was naturally a summer route because it depended on harbors in Finland being ice-free. This new route was the result of the increasing productive capacity of the Swedish economy, and consisted of the exchange of copper and high-quality Swedish iron for the Russian exports normal at that time: hides, lard, hemp, flax. In contrast, the Reval route brought to Russia much the same assortment of commodities as the Archangel route, and thus was sensitive to competition from the latter.[17]

In general, two aspects of the trade routes between Russia and Europe should be noted. As has been pointed out in every work on the subject, they were long, dangerous, impossible in winter, and expensive. The Dutch ships to Archangel had to carry a larger crew than the ships to the

Baltic because the policy of the King of Denmark rendered armaments necessary. The arms also required (beside their own expense) larger, and hence more expensive, ships. The route via Reval was shorter, safer, and therefore less expensive than the northern route, but the Dutch could not trade directly with Russia because of the Reval guest-right. The Polish route was too expensive because it was entirely overland. Thus, Swedish policy and territorial acquisitions in 1617 were not the only obstacles to Russian trade with the West. The Neva route was in disuse after the 1480s for economic reasons, thirty years before Sweden began to shake itself free of the Danes. The economics of Dutch trade in the Baltic created the "barrier," which was only strengthened by Sweden's commercial policy. Russian foreign trade could not expand significantly until the larger English ships of the beginning of the eighteenth century began to come to Archangel in greater numbers. The capture of Riga and the founding of St. Petersburg completed the fundamental change in Russian trade that began at that time, by providing a shorter and cheaper sea route to Russia.

The status of the foreign merchants

An extensive literature already exists that touches on the legal status of the foreign merchants in Russia, but does little more than describe in detail the negotiations on this topic as part of the diplomatic history of Russia.[18] An exception to this treatment is found in the literature on the Muscovy Company,[19] and in I. P. Shaskol'skii's recent work on the treaty of Stolbovo.[20] However, only Shaskol'skii directed his attention to the problem of the legal status of foreign merchants and the presence or lack of privileges in trade. Thus, in spite of the considerable literature on the question, many of our conclusions must come from Shaskol'skii.

The group with the greatest privileges was the Muscovy Company. The history of its privileges and the fluctuations of those privileges until the expulsion of the English in 1649 is well known and need not be repeated here. Only the following rights need be considered: (1) Englishmen who were not members of the company could not legally trade in Russia; (2) the company had the right to have houses in Archangel, Kholmogory, Vologda, and Moscow; and, most important, (3) the merchants of the company did not pay the customs duties in Russia. Furthermore, the company merchants had the right to be tried only in the Foreign Office (*Posol'skii prikaz*), but it seems that virtually all foreign merchants had this right. These privileges seem to give the company a commanding position among the foreign merchants, and the historians of the beginning of this century drew that conclusion, citing the petitions of the Moscow merchants against the English as evidence.[21] These petitions, however, must be treated as vast exaggerations because the Dutch swiftly outstripped the English in commercial importance after 1590. Because the Dutch merchants had a much less favorable status in Russia, the privileges of the Muscovy Company must be regarded as far less significant than they appeared to earlier historians.

Shaskol'skii asserts that of all the foreign merchants, only the subjects of the King of Sweden had rights as a nation based on a state treaty. This statement is literally true, but is excessively legalistic. Indeed the English *company*, rather than merchants of the English *nation*, had privileges, but the distinction is only theoretical. Almost all English merchants were working for the company, although there were a few interlopers. The subjects of the Swedish King were in a less privileged position than the English, according to the Treaties of Tiavzino (1595) and Stolbovo (1617). The provisions of 1595 were largely intended to keep Russian trade with Western Europe through the Baltic Sea in the hands of the Revalers. Western European merchants could not land on the Russian coast and had to trade in Reval or Viborg. Only Swedish subjects could trade in Narva. In return, the Russians had the right to trade in all Swedish possessions. In 1595, this last provision was not very significant because the Russians only traded in Reval and Viborg at that time, and began to venture further afield only in the 1620s. After the Time of Troubles, when the Russian government wanted to keep the Swedes out of Novgorod, but also needed an alliance with Sweden against Poland, the position of the Swedes was somewhat improved. The towns that both sides could trade in were specified: Moscow, Novgorod, Pskov, and Ladoga for the Swedes; Stockholm Viborg, Reval, and Narva for the Russians. Russian merchants could only trade with Swedish subjects, and only with the men of the towns in which they were trading, not with peasants or merchants from other Swedish towns. (This merely affirmed Reval's guest-right.) The same was true for Swedish merchants in Russia. Both nations had the right to trading houses in the towns in which the right of trading was specified. A Charter of Grant (*Zhalovannaia gramota*) given at the same time to the Swedish merchants also granted them the right to be judged in the Foreign Office (*Posol'skii prikaz*).[22]

The group with the least privileges was the Dutch merchants. The merchants of the Netherlands were never granted a general charter of rights, nor was any treaty ever made with the States-General. Dutch merchants did receive individual Charters of Grant (*Zhalovannye gramoty*) from the Tsar, however, of which ten have survived and seven have been published.[23] There is no reason to believe that these were the only charters ever issued because Dutch merchants not named in them traded regularly in Russia, and there were houses and warehouses owned by the Dutch in Archangel, Kholmogory, Vologda, Yaroslavl, and Moscow. Furthermore, from 1625 on there was a Dutch church in Moscow, with a minister, one Johan Bulaeus. This church continued to exist into the eighteenth century (when it moved to St. Petersburg).[24] The only disadvantage the Dutch had was the lack of privileges in customs payments, which was also the case with the Swedes, and the need to obtain a statement of the right to trade, for which they undoubtedly had to pay. Obviously these disadvantages were not serious because the unprivileged Dutch virtually eliminated the Muscovy Company from the Russian trade well before 1649, when the execution of Charles I caused the Russians to expel the company. The English could not even eliminate the competition from Hamburg and Denmark, whose merchants were in the same unfavorable position as the Dutch.

Consequently the whole question of the privileges of the foreign merchants must be considered in a new light. In the sixteenth century it may be said that the main group of foreign merchants had considerable privileges, for the English at that time controlled the trade with Archangel. But the situation had begun to change as early as the 1580s, and by 1600 the Dutch had replaced the English as the main trading partners of the Russians at Archangel. In this context it is remarkable that Dutch attempts to secure greater privileges met with such an absolute lack of success. The refusal of the Russian government to grant any such privileges, given the scale of the Dutch trade, was probably the most significant act of Russian policy of that time, and marked the transition from the policy of Ivan IV in the 1550s, continued to his death, of favoring the foreign merchants. This policy was the first indication of the attitude that came to the fore in the *Novotorgovyi ustav* of 1667.[25]

Trade in Russian law and administration: the toll system of the Russian state

Russia did not possess at any time before Peter the Great a body of commercial law. There were laws that regulated aspects of commerce, but they were in large part laws relating to debt and reflected the traditional Christian prohibitions on usury and the complexities of the problem of debt-slavery. In general, commercial transactions came under the same body of law as other transactions and did not constitute a separate entity in Russian law. Unfortunately, very little work of substance has been done on this problem, and even the relatively obvious topic of usury has not been studied systematically. Consequently, a thorough account of the problem cannot be given here, and we will restrict ourselves to one basic problem that has attracted some interest, namely the history of the toll system (*tamga*) and the customs policy of the state. Russian (and foreign) merchants were, in theory, subject to a number of payments if they came to a town or market to trade. The most basic was the *rublevaia poshlina*, a percentage tax on the value of commodities bought and sold. Furthermore, there were separate taxes on certain commodities, such as horses, which were paid by item, not by value. Long lists of such itemized charges are found in the rates charters of the sixteenth century, but they had largely disappeared after 1613, being replaced by the percentage tax. There were also charges for using certain facilities provided by the state, such as warehouses (*ambarshchina*). The latter were varied, but amounted to very little of the total collection of the toll administration, and generally disappeared along with the per item charges after 1613. Certainly the disappearance of such charges was the result of the fall in the value of Russian currency at the end of the sixteenth century because the charges were fixed and consequently fell in value as the same rates continued to be the basis of the collection from the 1550s into the early years of the seventeenth century. Furthermore, a small charge (*proezzhaia poshlina*) was exacted from a merchant who merely passed the collection point. (This was similar to the old *myt*, which declined in importance after the mid-sixteenth century.) The term "toll collection" (*tamozhennyi sbor*) was also used to refer to the collections at the border towns and the internal customs duties exacted in Moscow or Ustiug Velikii.

The guest-right as such was unknown in Russia, but a system of differential taxation did exist, which served the same purpose. Until the reform of 1653 the principle of the taxation of sales was that in any given market the local merchant paid less than the merchant from another town or region. Generally the merchant in his home town paid nothing at all (at least of the *rublevaia poshlina*) or .5 percent, but rarely .75 percent. The out-of-town merchant paid 2 percent as a rule.[26] In the seventeenth century this differential narrowed somewhat.

This narrowing of the differential between merchants of the town and those from outside the town was the main change in the *tamga* system in the late sixteenth and early seventeenth centuries. Iu. A. Tikhonov argued that this change was clearly the result of a conscious policy that appeared several decades before the reform of 1653, and that this policy was the result of a response on the part of the government to the growth of a national market. As the regional markets grew into a single national market, the government adapted to the process by creating a unified toll system. This is undoubtedly true, but treats only one part of a complicated problem, as Tikhonov pointed out. Because this fundamental question in the history of Russian trade has not really been studied, it is necessary to try to fill in some of the gaps left by Tikhonov's preliminary work.

We know the rates in only some thirty five localities in Russia for the whole period from 1497 to 1653, so for the sake of clarity we shall present the data on the *rublevaia poshlina* for all of them, with some corrections and additions to Tikhonov. Table 2.1 shows separately the grants of the tolls to monasteries and boyars. Table 2.2 shows the rates in towns and other markets not privately owned.

It is clear from a comparison of Tables 2.1 and 2.2 that local merchants paid more at monastic markets. Clearly this was an attempt to get more revenue out of the monasteries' own peasants who were engaging in trade. It is also clear that Moscow paid proportionately much higher taxes than the other towns, and therefore its markets benefited the most from the equilization of the rates in 1653. Whether the merchants also benefited to the same extent depends on the pattern of their trade.

The trend toward unification of rates for local and out-of-town merchants is apparent even in this list. There are fewer towns after 1613 with no charge for local merchants. Furthermore, Tikhonov's examination of the toll books for Ustiug Velikii shows that these rates were not always observed, so that the actual rate exacted there was 1.5 percent for local merchants (in the rate charter nothing) and 2.5 percent for out-of-town merchants. In Sol' Vychegodsk, the actual rates were 1.25 percent and 2.5 percent.[27] In addition to a gradual unification of rates at each market, there was also a rise in the rates, especially after 1620, that was clearly the result of the financial needs of the state.

Generally there are a number of differential rates in the toll rates. In the second half of the sixteenth century, in some cases there were higher rates for merchants from different parts of the Russian state, as in the cases of

Dmitrov (1521), Ustiuzhna (1542–3), and Ves'egonsk (1563). In the seventeenth century only one town, Shuia (1614), preserved the higher rate for merchants from other regions of Russia. In the case of Shuia, Shuians paid nothing, out-of-town merchants paid 2 percent, and merchants from the lands of Novgorod, Pskov, Tver', Riazan', and Kazan paid 3.5 percent. Here we see clearly that those least favored were the merchants from Russian lands annexed by the prince of Moscow after the mid-fifteenth century. By 1614, this feature was clearly an anachronism, and it is not possible to know if it was enforced. If the trend of the collection at Ustiug Velikii was typical of the whole of Russia, it is likely that it was not.

Table 2.1. *Toll rates at monastic and boyar markets (in percent)*

Year	Market	Local	Nonlocal
1588	Eremeitsevo, Yaroslavl district (Yaroslavl-Spasskii)[a]	0.75	2.00
1591	Solovetskii Monastery	1.00	3.50
1592	Charonda and Korotkoe, Charonda and Beloozero districts (Dm. Godunov)[a]	1.50 (2.00)[b]	3.00
1595	Fedorovskoe, Yaroslavl district (Yaroslavl-Spasskii)[a]	0.75	2.00
1595	Klementevo, Moscow district (Troitse-Sergeev)[a]	0.75	2.00
1596	Rozhdestvenskoe, Meshchersk district (V. A. Shchelkalov)[a]	0.50	2.00
1602	Slovenskii Volochok, near Beloozero (Kirillo-Beloozerskii)[a]	1.00	2.00
1621	Rogachevo, Dmitrov district (Nikolo-Pesnoshkii)[a]	0.50	1.50
1621	Purdyshevskii Monastery in the town of Temnikov	0.50 (2.00)	2.00 (2.00)[b]
1641	Kholm, Bezhetskii district (Bezhetsko-Antonov)[a]	0.50	2.00
1652	Semendiaevo, near Uglich (Makariev-Kaliazin)[a]	0.75	2.00

[a]Names of owners.
[b]Rates for goods that had to be weighed (*veschie tovary*).
Source: Tikhonov, "Tamozhennaia," Table 1, p. 264.

Table 2.2. *Toll rates at towns (in percent)*

Year	Town	Local	Nonlocal
1497	Beloozero	none	3.00
1521	Dmitrov	—	1.50
1542-3	Ustiuzhna Zhelezopol'skaia	none	3.50
1551	Beloozero	none	3.00
1563	Ves'egonsk	0.75	2.00
156?	Oreshek	0.75	2.00
1571	Novgorod (Market Side)	none	2.00
1588	Dvinskii uezd	0.75	2.00
1590	Ustiug Velikii	none	2.00
1593-4	Tarusa	none	2.00
1595	Sol' Vychegodsk	none	2.50
			(3.50)
1596	Kargopol'	0.75	2.00
1606	Suzdal'	none	2.00
1613	Mozhaisk	$(1.25)^a$	$(2.50)^a$
1614	Shuia (and Galich)	none	2.00
1618-9	Sol' Vychegodsk	none	2.00
1619	Viaz'ma	0.50	2.50
1620-1	Perevitsk	1.00	3.00
1620-1	Moscow	2.00	3.00
		$(3.50)^a$	$(5.00)^a$
1620-3	Kaluga	0.50	2.00
1620-3	Yaroslavl	1.25	2.50
1622	Tot'ma	1.25	2.00
1633	Gorokhovets	0.75	3.00
		$(2.75)^a$	$(4.00)^a$
1653	National	2.50	2.50

^{a}Rates for goods that had to be weighed.
Source: Tikhonov, "Tamozhennaia," Tables 1 and 2, pp. 264–5; *DAI,* vol. 3, no. 27, pp. 104–6, for Moscow, Kaluga and Yaroslavl, which Tikhonov misdated; *Polnoe sobranie zakonov Rossiiskoi Imperii,* 45 vols. (Saint Petersburg, 1830), vol. 1, no. 107, pp. 302–5.

The most important stations in the toll system were the three main cities on the northern route: Moscow, Yaroslavl, and Archangel. Moscow had the highest rate in the country.[28] The rate at Yaroslavl was roughly the same as the actual rate at Sol' Vychegodsk and Ustiug, and as the rates of Tot'ma. This is also the same rate as in the main post-1620 station on the road to Poland, Mozhaisk. In contrast, Kaluga, Shuia, and Suzdal', all largely oriented to the internal market, had somewhat lower rates, especially for the local merchants. The great question, however, is Archangel. Before the construction of the town of Archangel (1583–5) it is probable that the tolls there were collected as part of the collection of the Dvina district. Two documents survive for the sixteenth century, a tax farm (*otkup*) of 1560 and a toll rate of 1588.[29] The tax of 1560 records the farming of the tolls for the area to fifty-one merchants of the Dvina district for the sum of 1,485 rubles, the farm to last one year. This set of rates does not include a *rublevaia poshlina*, but in the case of the payments on boats (which are roughly comparable), it seems that merchants from the Dvina district, Ustiug, Vologda, or the Central Russian towns, paid the lowest rate; merchants from the Vaga or other northern areas paid a higher rate; and merchants "*iz Korely i iz Novagoroda i iz Zamor'ia*" paid a still higher rate.[30] In 1588 most traces of the regional differentiation are gone, and all merchants from outside the Dvina as well as foreign merchants (except the Muscovy Company) paid the 2 percent rate. We do not know the evolution of this rate from then on except as it applied to the foriegn merchants (without privileges). The Dutch record that in 1646 the toll was raised from 1.5 percent and 2 percent to 4 percent and 5 percent.[31] This change is not recorded in any Russian source, and clearly was the result of the petition of the Russian merchants of that year against the foreigners. At the same time, the inland rate for foreign merchants was raised to 7 percent, whereas in most cases it had been previously 3.5 percent (2 percent in Tot'ma. In 1653, 1662, and the *Novotorgovyi ustav* (1667) there were further changes in the toll system. What changes there were for Russians in Archangel is not recorded. It is probable that Russians who were not from the Dvina continued to pay 2 percent after 1646 because the purpose of the change was to protect them from foreign competition.[32]

What conclusions can be drawn from this review of the evolution of the toll system? It is certainly clear that Tikhonov is right in finding a gradual unification of the toll system for Russian merchants. First, the regional differentials disappeared, and the territory of the old Novgorodian empire was brought into the Russian commercial system on equal terms by the end of the sixteenth century. Then, in the seventeenth century the differences in rates paid by local merchants and those from other towns decreased in size and disappeared in 1653. Also, the protectionist character of the system increased. There was a clear trend toward the protection of Russian merchants from foreign competitors, first within the country and then also at Archangel. In the 1550s and 1560s the chief foreign group trading at Archangel paid no tolls, but as the Dutch gradually edged the

English out, they were simply refused a general reduction in tolls and had to pay the high toll in Moscow. Finally, the rate revision of 1646 marked a definite move toward protectionism that culminated in 1667. However, not all rates were the result of the desire to favor or hinder one or the other group of merchants. The higher tolls in Moscow and the northern and Polish routes for Russian merchants were certainly not the result of a desire to discourage trade along those routes. Rather, they were simply based on the principle that the treasury could collect the largest revenues in those areas because they were the most prosperous. However, this fiscal principle ran counter to the growing wealth of the merchant class. Compared to the small sums assessed on the great merchants by the *tiaglo*, the tolls could be an enormous payment. Aleksei Zolotov, for example, sold goods at Archangel around 1630 for 5,000–10,000 rubles depending on the year (see Chapter 3). This means 100–200 rubles of *rublevaia poshlina* were paid in only one of his many transactions throughout Russia, whereas in the *extraordinary* tax of 1614 the highest sums paid were 200–250 rubles and more often the sums were lower. Clearly the *tiaglo* was much less than this extraordinary tax (and in any case *gosti* did not pay the *tiaglo*). Thus, even a rich merchant who did not have the good fortune to get into the privileged groups would find his toll payments much higher than his payments of the *tiaglo*. Certainly for the great merchants the critical part of the government's financial policy was the toll payment, not the direct tax. Consequently it is easy to understand the persistence of the petition campaign, even from great merchants like Nikitnikov and Sveteshnikov, for higher tolls on the foreigners and reform of the system in general. The problems of the town and the *tiaglo*, which have attracted so much attention from Russian historians, were largely the problems of the little man – the artisan and small trader of the local marketplace. For the wealthy merchants of every town it was the tolls, which formed the largest item in their own tax payments and which they had to administer, that formed the center of their own concerns.

3

The Archangel trade

Commerce at the end of the sixteenth century

The arrival of English ships in the mouth of the Northern Dvina in 1553 and the subsequent organization in England of the Muscovy Company in 1555 were two of the most important events in the history of Russian foreign trade. These English ships were not the first from the West to reach the Russian North – the Dutch had been fishing and trading off the Kola peninsula since the 1530s – nor did the event signify the beginning of Russian trade with Europe. Russia had been buying the products of Western Europe for centuries by 1553. The real significance of the English voyage was a reorientation of Russian foreign trade toward the new commercial centers of England and the Low Countries. In the century before 1553 Russia had traded (among European nations) mainly with the Livonian cities, which had taken up the mantle of the Hanseatic League as far as Russia was concerned, and with Poland-Lithuania. In both cases, Russia imported mainly the cloth of Flanders, England, and Central Europe (Silesia, Moravia, Saxony), and various other less important products such as Krakow metalwares. In return, the Russians sold furs, wax, and other products of the Russian forests that were in demand in Western Europe. After 1553, the selection of goods flowing in both directions remained roughly the same at first (with the exception of an increase in agricultural exports) but now the Russians dealt directly with the English and the Dutch, who were the main producers of most of their imported goods. In addition the English and Dutch merchants brought the same Central European cloth, as well as certain products of the Mediterranean and the East Indies, to which they had access through their colonial empires.

Of all the aspects of Russia's trade with the West in the period 1550–1700, the activities of the Muscovy Company have perhaps received the most attention from both Western and Russian historians. This degree of attention does not correspond to its actual importance. The Muscovy Company was indeed virtually the only group of merchants trading at the mouth of the Dvina between 1555 and 1580, and also one of the chief groups of merchants trading in the so-called Narva navigation (1558–81). However, already at Narva the Dutch were beginning to come in increasing numbers, and soon after the capture of Narva by the Swedes, the Dutch had replaced the English as the first among the Western European nations trading at the new port of Archangel. By 1600, in fact, the Dutch sent the majority of the ships going to Archangel, and by 1649, the Dutch were already far ahead of their English rivals. Even after the English were readmitted in the 1650s, they were never able to send even a fraction of the number of ships sent by the Dutch, until in 1701–10 the growing power of English shipping and the commercial policies of Peter the Great caused a radical change in favor of English ships and English merchants. However, for the entire period of the seventeenth century the story of commerce at Archangel is largely a story of Dutch-Russian trade.[1]

Ship traffic at Archangel, 1580–1650

There are a number of sources for the ship traffic at Archangel during our period. The figures in the works of Russian scholars all come from the records of the Novgorod Quarter, which administered Archangel. Apparently the Russians did not keep a regular account of the number of ships in the harbor before 1650, or if they did the records have not survived. Because the Russians collected taxes not from the ship as it entered the harbor (as in Western Europe), but from the merchant as he sold his goods, there may have been no need to keep such data. In any case, the available Russian figures come from requests for information from Moscow, generally in response to some unusual fluctuation in the tax receipts. Consequently, the figures in Table 3.1 may reflect unusual years. Incomplete as it is, Table 3.1 offers proof that the Dutch were the dominant group in Russian trade with the West after 1600. In the second half of the century, it seems that there was a slight increase in the number of ships from Hamburg and Bremen, but in view of the relations that existed between Holland and Hamburg in Baltic shipping, some of these ships may well have been freighted by Dutch merchants.

More complete information is provided by the recent research of the Dutch scholar Simon Hart on the Amsterdam notarial archives. These figures naturally only count those ships whose freighting contract passed through the hands of a notary, which did not include all ships. However, on a fairly dangerous run such as that around the North Cape, a notarial confirmation of the contract was more common than in shipping to the Baltic ports, and it is estimated that about 50 to 60 percent of the contracts were notarized.[2] The results are shown in Table 3.2. In other words, the average number of Dutch ships (traceable in notarial records) going to Archangel doubled twice between 1595 and 1640. This increase was followed by a sharp decline in the 1640s that reached its low point in 1646–7, but returned, starting in 1650, to the level of the 1630s. Because Table 3.1 suggests a slight decline in the number of English ships trading at Archangel after the late sixteenth century, it is clear that Russia's trade with the West at Archangel became largely a matter of trade with the Dutch.

Table 3.1. *Ship traffic at Archangel, 1582–1701*

Year	Total ships	English	Dutch	Other
1582	23	11	10	2
1589	14	6	4	4
1600	25	12	13	0
1604	29	9	17	3
1618	43	—	30	—
1621	67	—	—	—
1634[a]	51	(3)	(7)	(1)
1653[b]	30	0	13	17
1655	67	—	—	—
1658	80	4	60	16
1692	41	7	24	10
1698	54	—	49	—
1701	106	—	—	—

[a]In 1634 there were thirty-one grain ships, one ship bringing munitions to Russia and nineteen ships that came to trade. Apparently the grain ships contained only ballast and no tradable commodities. Of the nineteen ships that actually engaged in trade, only eleven came from known ports (given in parentheses). The year 1634 was a year of Russian grain subsidies to the anti-Habsburg powers in the Thirty Years' War.
[b]In 1653, besides the thirteen Dutch ships, there were six ships from Bremen, ten from Hamburg, and one Danish ship.
Source: Floria, "Torgovlia," pp. 132, 137, 140, 142; Ogorodnikov, *Ocherk*, p. 94; Repin, Dissertation, pp. 300–8, 402; TsGADA, f. 141, 1634, no. 31.

The Dutch practice of chartering ships in Hamburg, Bremen, and to some extent, the Danish ports, further strengthened the hegemony of the Dutch at Archangel because the few ships coming to the northern port that were not under Dutch or English flags were nearly all from those three places. These figures for Dutch shipping reveal not only the victory of Dutch over English merchants, but also the vast increase in the volume of trade at Archangel. One may estimate the actual number of ships to be about fifty to sixty from Holland and about ten from England, the Hanseatic towns,

Table 3.2. *Number of Dutch ships sailing to Archangel*

Years	Number	Average per year
1594–1600	60	8.6
1601–10	165	16.5
1611–20	160	16.0
1621–30	200	20.0
1631–40	292	29.2
1641	8	
1642	11	
1643	7	
1644	16	
1645	5	
1646	2	
1647	2	
1648	9	
1649	8	
1650	23	
1641–50	91	9.1
1651	30	
1652	56	
1653	7	
1654	18	
1655	17	
1656	26	
1657	37	
1658	44	
1659	37	
1660	47	
1651–60	319	31.9

Source: Hart, "Amsterdam," p. 6; Amsterdam, Gemeente Archief, Notarial Archive.

and Denmark in the prosperous years of the 1630s and 1650s. This is, of course, not a great deal compared to the 1500–2000 Dutch ships passing the Sound every year to the Baltic in the seventeenth century, but it is still an impressive sum for so arduous a route. Furthermore, the ships going to Archangel were large by the standards of the time, and increased in size from the end of the sixteenth century by about 25 percent. This conclusion is borne out by Hart's findings, shown in Table 3.3, on the average cargo capacity of the Dutch ships to 1640. (After that date, statements of cargo capacity are rarer.)

The Dutch and Russian records agree in revealing a dramatic increase in the volume of trade at Archangel. The Dutch records also provide some indication of the path of Russia's exports to Western Europe. The charter parties in the notarial records usually indicate the main ports at which the ship is to call. Most of the Dutch ships were to go directly from Amsterdam to Archangel and back. A few were to stop in Russian Lapland at various small harbors along the Kola Peninsula and load the products of Arctic sealing and fishing, as well as going to Archangel. Another small but constant number went from Amsterdam to Archangel and rather than returning to the Netherlands, took their cargo directly to Genoa or Livorno. The number of Lapland ships (included in the yearly totals of Table 3.2) is shown in Table 3.4. The stops at Lapland were clearly a subsidiary part of the Archangel trade. Undoubtedly a few Dutch ships went only to Lapland, but it seems that the attraction of the northern route was Archangel and the products of Russia, and not the products of the Arctic fisheries that first brought the Dutch north in the late sixteenth century. The ships going from Archangel directly to the Italian ports are

Table 3.3. *Cargo capacity of Dutch ships, 1594–1640*

Years	Cargo (lasts)[a]
1594–1600	95.5
1601–10	109.0
1611–20	101.0
1621–30	113.0
1631–40	119.5

[a]The last, the usual measure of weight in Northern European shipping, was equal to two tons.
Source: Hart, "Amsterdam," p. 6.

of greater interest for the history of the Archangel trade. Hart gives numerous examples of such voyages for the period up to 1640. The figures for the middle of the century are given in Table 3.5.

The Dutch kept up a small but fairly constant direct-export trade from Russia to Italy that followed the ups and downs of the Archangel trade for the most part. The long absence of such voyages from 1651 to 1655, however, is harder to explain. The Anglo–Dutch War of 1652–4 explains part of it, especially because an English squadron was cruising off Livorno, but it cannot explain this drop entirely. In any case, the late 1650s seem to have made up for the earlier decline. The most consistent exporters of Russian goods directly to Italy were two brothers, Amsterdam merchants of Italian origin, Jean Andrea and Ottavio Tensini. Every year they chartered one or two ships for this voyage, although they also generally chartered a ship to stop in Lapland and a larger number to make the usual voyage from the Netherlands to Archangel and back. In 1642 one of their ships was captured by Provençal pirates, and the Tensinis valued the cargo at 10,000 Flemish pounds, broken down as follows:

124 barrels of tallow	4,200
40 ½ bundles of Russian leather (jucht)	4,300
10 bundles of dried pork (schevinken)	500
83 casks of salmon	400
150 casks of tar	200
520 puds of dried cod	300
242 bundles of hides (kip huiden)	100
Total	10,000

Source: Amsterdam, Gemeente Archief, Notarial Archive, books of Jan Warnaertsz, 683, p. 163 (April 11, 1643).

Over 90 percent of the cargo was thus made up of the products of Russian stock raising, with the fisheries and forest products playing a very minor

Table 3.4. *Archangel ships stopping in Lapland*

1641	1	1646	0	1651	1	1656	1
1642	1	1647	0	1652	6	1657	2
1643	1	1648	1	1653	0	1658	1
1644	2	1649	1	1654	0	1659	2
1645	1	1650	4	1655	1	1660	3

Source: Amsterdam, Gemeente Archief, Notarial Archive.

role. Flax, hemp, and furs, otherwise important Russian exports, were absent.

These Dutch and Russian records of shipping to Archangel provide valuable information about the trade at that port. Because they give us an opportunity to check two independent sources of information, they are the most reliable sources we have for finding a trend, and the trend is extremely clear: Russian trade with the Dutch increased nearly four times between the end of the sixteenth century and middle of the seventeenth, measured in volume. Considering that the English were still important in the 1590s, the total increase in shipping was probably less, about three times. As we shall now see, this trend was matched by a similar trend in the overall value of the goods bought and sold there.

Gross value of Archangel trade

Another index of the trends in the trade at Archangel is provided by the records of toll collections at the Archangel market, the "summer collection" (*letnii sbor*). The account books of the Novgorod Quarter, which in large part survive, provide us with records that have been published in a little-known article by A. Iziumov.[3] Table 3.6 shows the revenue collected on the trade at Archangel. The value of such data lies not so much in the specific figures, but in the general confirmation of the trends revealed by the figures for ship traffic. According to Hart's data for Dutch

Table 3.5. *Dutch voyages from Archangel to Italy, 1641–60*

1641	0	1651	0
1642	2	1652	0
1643	1	1654	0
1644	1	1654	0
1645	1	1655	0
1646	0	1656	2
1647	0	1657	3
1648	1	1658	3[a]
1649	0	1659	2
1650	1	1660	2

[a]In this year one ship went from Archangel to Cadiz.
Source: Amsterdam, Gemeente Archief, Notarial Archive.

Table 3.6. *Summer collection of tolls at Archangel*

Year	Total sum (rounded to nearest ruble)
1614	9,228
1615	6,206
1621	20,278
1625	15,567
1626	17,263
1627	18,635
1628	16,654
1629	20,425
1631	22,786
1633	24,192
1634	23,865
1634–5	34,435[a]
1635–6	31,658[a]
1636–7	30,354[a]
1637–8	30,460[a]
1638–9	31,719[a]
1639–40	31,442[a]
1640–1	32,979[a]
1641–2	17,893[b]
1643	24,082
1644	30,140
1645	26,213
1653	43,950
1654	54,032[c]
1655	51,586[c]
1656	63,225[c]
1657	76,959[c]
1658	91,742[c]
1659	78,323[c]
1660	89,355[c]
Decennial averages	
1661–70	68,666
1671–80	70,693
1681–90	78,570

[a]The figures for 1634–5 through 1640–1, being the total collection of the Dvina district winter and summer, should be lowered by 20–25 percent to eliminate the collections from Kholmogory and the winter collection of Archangel.
[b]Dvina district: 22,003.
[c]The figures for 1654 to 1660 (and the average of the 1660s) are high by about 10 percent because they include the *pischie denigi* (registration charges collected by the clerks and other minor charges).
Source: Iziumov, "Razmery," pp. 250–8.

ships, the average number roughly doubled between the decade 1601–10 and in the 1630s. The same is true in Table 3.6, so that the two sources complement one another. In general, we can conclude that there was a great expansion of trade at Archangel between 1590 and 1650, perhaps by as much as three times the value of that trade in 1590.

The records of the toll collection can also be used to arrive at a rough estimate of the value of trade (imports and exports) at Archangel because the rate of taxation is known. However, a number of methodological problems immediately arise.

The most obvious problem is that the rate of taxation increased after 1646, as explained in Chapter 2, by a little more than twice the original rate, at least for foreign merchants. Because the Russian merchant did not share this rate increase until 1667, some of the increase in toll collections over the period 1630–45 must be attributed to this increase of rates. Thus, about one-third of the collection of 1653 must be eliminated in order to make a comparison with the earlier period. If this fact is taken into account, then the revenue figures reflect a virtually constant volume of trade from the 1630s, except for the depression of the 1640s, with only a gradual increase over the last half of the seventeenth century.

The second problem is the value of the ruble over the course of the seventeenth century. There is no price history of that century similar to Man'kov's work on the sixteenth century, and therefore it will be necessary to describe the history of prices after 1600 in some detail. Until recently, the historian of the Russian economy of the seventeenth century had to rely for information on the history of prices on the 1884 essay of V. O. Kliuchevskii. Kliuchevskii based his price index on the grain prices of the sixteenth through the eighteenth centuries, and compared these prices to the grain prices of 1881 in order to have a standard of comparison. This method was extremely clumsy, but can be converted into a more common index with the result shown in Table 3.7. Thus, goods worth 100 rubles in 1551–1600 were worth 560 rubles in 1610–12 and 480 in 1613–36. (In each period data are the averages from the years for which prices are available.)

Kliuchevskii concluded that there was a sharp inflation in the second half of the sixteenth century lasting through the Time of Troubles, followed by a gradual deflation lasting to about 1700. Then, as a result of Peter the Great's wars, the treasury was forced to inflate the currency to cover its expenses, and this inflation continued through the rest of the century. When Kliuchevskii compiled his index, very little was known about price history in Western Europe. The only detailed history was the work of Thorold Rogers on wages and prices in England and this effort was not matched on the continent until the 1920s and 1930s. Since then there has been considerable interest in the problems of price history and the impact of prices on the European economy. Generally, it may be said that (apart from temporary fluctuations due to wars or other disturbances and certain national and regional differences for particular decades) both Eastern and Western Europe show the same pattern: a precipitous rise in prices in the sixteenth century, followed by a stabilization or even a fall starting sometime in the first half of the seventeenth century. This fall continued into the early eighteenth century in most countries, followed by another sharp rise increasing in speed toward the end of the eighteenth century. From Kliuchevskii's data it would seem that Russian prices follow the general European pattern of these three centuries. However, recently B. N. Mironov has questioned this conclusion. Mironov's research was directed at the history of the eighteenth-century prices, and he asserted that the real "price revolution" in Russia took place in the eighteenth rather than in the sixteenth century. When he made this assertion in 1971, it was difficult to refute his point of view because little was known beyond Kliuchevskii's article about prices in the seventeenth century. However, recent research on seventeenth-century grain prices by Iu. A. Tikhonov shows that Kliuchevskii's price index is roughly correct in showing the basic trend over the centuries, even if his results for certain decades are not without flaw. Mironov, in contrast, is very selective in his use of data for the period before 1700, and consequently produces a picture that is fundamentally incorrect. He repeatedly states that the price revolution in Russia took place in the eighteenth century rather than earlier, but offers no proof beyond a single table that appears to demon-

Table 3.7. *Value of the ruble, 1551–1715*

	Base years		
	1551–1600	1601–12	1637–1700
1551–1600	100	—	—
1601–12	560	100	—
1613–36	480	86	—
1637–1700	395	70.5	100
1701–15	745	133	189

strate a uniform level of grain prices from 1551 to 1701.[4] An integration of
the data in the work of Man'kov and Tikhonov, however, reveals quite a
different picture. Table 3.8 is constructed from the raw data of Man'kov
and Tikhonov, and deals only with the rye prices of Central Russia,

Table 3.8. *Prices of rye in Russia, 1573-1680*
A. Nominal prices of rye in Central Russia, 1573-1600

Year	Price (den'gi)	Year	Price (den'gi)
1573	23	1585	43
1574	30	1586	82.5
1575	27	1587	83.3
1576	20	1588	83.3
1577	20	1589	65.5
1579	27	1591	50
1580	34	1593	30
1581	38.6	1594	20
1583	40	1598	72.5
1584	58	1600	40

B. Nominal and real prices of rye in Central Russia, 1627-80

Year	Price (den'gi of the 17th century)	Price (den'gi of the 16th century)
1627-8	196	137
1629-30	132	92
1634-5	224	156
1637-8	215	150
1639-40	—	—
1640-1	150	105
1641-2	125	88
1643-4	85	60
1644-5	105	74
1648-9	120	84
Averages:		
1664/5-1672/3	203	142
1673/4-1679/80	133	93

Note: Rye was chosen because it was the chief grain of Russia and because the most continuous
series of prices exists for rye. Prices are given per *chetvert'* of grain.
Source: Man'kov, *Tseny*, pp. 106-11; Tikhonov, *Krest'iane*, pp. 110-12.

eliminating the North and Novgorod. For years in which there are more than one example the arithmetic average is given.

Thus, in comparison to the last thirty years of the sixteenth century the level of rye prices had tripled by the 1620s and remained at that level throughout the century. Only in the 1640s did the price of rye drop by a third to a half, then to return to the previous level in the 1660s. A smaller decline in the 1670s confirms the picture of the seventeenth century as one alternating relative stability with occasional deflation. Because Man'kov established a price rise in the latter half of the sixteenth century over the first half, it is evident that there were two price revolutions in Russia: one starting about 1550 and lasting to about 1620, followed by nearly a hundred years of stability, and one in the eighteenth century correctly identified by Mironov. It is important to note that this pattern of prices is exactly the same as in Western and Eastern Europe, which in turn means that the Russian market must have been to some degree part of the common European market. This is especially clear because these Russian prices are grain prices, and Russia did not participate in the international grain trade to any significant extent before the very end of the eighteenth century. From the point of view of weighing the value of the toll returns at Archangel, this conclusion is also of the first importance. Grain prices usually show greater fluctuations than prices of other commodities, so that for the seventeenth century we can presume a rough stability of prices in Russia. This conclusion is borne out by the exchange rate of the ruble to the guilder over the course of the century, shown in Table 3.9.

Table 3.9. *Rates of exchange: ruble to guilder*

Year	One ruble =	Year	One ruble =
1606	f. 7.50	1645	f. 5.25
1607	f. 7.50	1648	f. 5.60
1613	f. 7.10–7.50	1650	f. 5.30
1625	f. 6.00	1651	f. 5.40–5.50
1626	f. 6.00	1656	f. 5.35
1629	f. 6.00	1661	f. 4.50
1634	f. 5.50	1663	f. 4.25
1640	f. 5.20–5.25	1674	f. 5.00

Note: After 1674 the exchange rate fluctuated between f. 4.70 and f. 5.10, until the outbreak of the Northern War, when the exchange rate of the ruble began to drop.
Source: Hart, "Amsterdam," p. 30.

The final problem is presented by the relation of the sums of revenue collected to the few existing figures of the total value of either imports or exports at Archangel, and particularly the data offered by de Rodes. For the first half of the seventeenth century there are only three documents that give some idea of the gross value of trade at Archangel. For the year 1604, there is Floria's figure: 148,849 rubles.[5] This figure is calculated by Floria from the itemized records of the goods brought to Archangel by each Western merchant, and thus deserves considerable credence. On the assumption that the value of exports exceeded that of imports slightly (a fact that is borne out by the repeated references to bullion carried as ballast to Russia) the total value of the trade at Archangel should be estimated at 300,000–350,000 rubles in 1604. The next figure is the value of Russian exports cited by Attman for the year 1642 from an anonymous Swedish report on Russian trade: 430,000 rubles.[6] Here we should estimate the total at between 800,000 and 850,000 rubles. In the first case (1604) the total toll collection at the pre-1646 rate should be about 4,500–6,000 rubles, which is approximately correct if in 1614 it was about 9,000. In the case of 1642, at the same pre-1646 rate, the toll collection should be 12,000–16,000 rubles, although in fact it was 17,893 rubles. (It should be remembered that the totals included a small amount of fixed charges for docking, warehouse charges, etc.) Thus, the estimated totals for 1604 and 1642 must be taken as approximately correct.

The difficulty is presented by de Rodes's figure of the value of Russian exports as 1,164,676 rubles.[7] De Rodes's total is deceptively exact, and his assertion that it comes from the Archangel toll books seems to lend authority to his figures. However, even Kurts, the editor of de Rodes's tract, was skeptical about the total, pointing out that the toll collection for 1653 was too small for such a great volume of exports. Kurts also noted that de Rodes lists 3,000 barrels of potash sold for 120,000 rubles, whereas in fact only 500 barrels were sold in 1653 and scarcely more the next year.[8] Thus, 100,000 rubles must be eliminated immediately. Furthermore, grain was not sold every year, although there were some sales in the 1650s, but very few in 1653; de Rodes, however, valued it at 250,000 rubles. The same is true of Persian silk, which he valued at 13,500 rubles. Nevertheless, it is difficult to bring his figure below 750,000 rubles, which is surely too high for such a bad year as 1653. Clearly the problem is that de Rodes simply guessed at some of the more important items such as *iuft'*, which he gives as amounting to "750,000 Rollen," and his total is of little value. The best that can be said is that de Rodes did give a roughly accurate picture of the

selection of goods exported. If we assume the rate of taxation after 1646 to
be 3–5 percent (because of the differential rate), then the value of trade
(imports plus exports) at Archangel in a good year would have been over a
million rubles, perhaps closer to one and one-half million. This estimate
means that the total value of trade increased two to three times compared
to 1604, and thus the evidence of the shipping statistics is confirmed.

The most important fact to emerge from the remaining records of trade
at Archangel is the great increase in its scale from the 1580s to the middle
of the seventeenth century. This increase was two to three times the value
of the trade at Archangel in the first years of the seventeenth century.
Both the Russian and the Dutch merchants were operating at a time of
greatly expanding opportunities that the disasters of the Time of Troubles
could not destroy. The tremendous economic expansion of the Netherlands in this period was certainly one of the main reasons for this growth
of trade. However, the Dutch could not have sustained this expanded
commerce without an adequate market in Russia. In the Russian market
the dominant commercial force was the Russian and especially the
Moscow merchants, as we shall now see.

The Russian merchants at Archangel (1630)

The only comprehensive document to survive for the first half of the
seventeenth century is the list of passes (*proezzhie gramoty*) of 1630. This
document, TsGADA, f. 141, 1630, no. 68, records the goods shipped to
the interior of Russia, and has a number of lacunae, the main one being the
prices of the goods. It is also possible that it has certain other omissions,
the most obvious being any references to the trade of the treasury, which
other sources indicate was going on. The *d'iak* and former *gost'* Mikhailo
Smyvalov sold silk for the treasury that summer,[9] and there was some
state trade in grain that year. However, even the large government purchases of munitions for the Smolensk War amounted to only 28,893 rubles, and could not greatly affect the trade in Archangel.[10] (As will be
demonstrated in Chapter 9, the trade of the treasury was not nearly as
great as has been assumed, and perhaps was less than 50,000 rubles in
most years.) Only a few merchants from the northern towns are listed,
and those only from Tot'ma and Vologda. There are no merchants from
Sol' Vychegodsk or Ustiug. However, two of the "Ustiug group" of
Moscow merchants are listed as Muscovites in the document, and were
probably the chief merchants connected with Ustiug at Archangel that

year. Although we can suppose that there may have been some half-dozen merchants from the northern towns who are not included in the list, this omission does not change its general value. Finally, only one English merchant appears on the list. Clearly, the Muscovy Company does not appear because of its privileged position. However, in view of the predominance of the Dutch, this is also an omission of limited importance.

In spite of these limitations it is possible to draw a number of interesting conclusions. First of all, as shown in Table 3.10, the relative proportion of the various Russian cities in the Archangel trade can be determined. The most notable fact revealed by Table 3.10 is the leading role of the city of Moscow. This is partly because this list reflects the weight of the various towns on the market of Moscow itself, the office in Moscow having only asked for a list of those merchants going to Moscow. Nevertheless, a

Table 3.10. *Merchants at Archangel, 1630*

City	Category	Number	Percent
	Moscow *gosti*	4	3
	Moscow merchants	73	56
	Moscow Germans	11	9
Moscow		88	68
Yaroslavl		9	
Shatsk		4	
Vologda		3	
Voronezh		2	
Murom		2	
Suzdal'		2	
Uglich		1	
Kostroma		1	
Nizhnii Novgorod		1	
Galich		1	
Tot'ma		1	
	Total Russians (exc. Moscow)	27	21
	Gollandskoi zemli *gosti*	4	
	Dutch (not *gosti*)	10	
	Total Dutch	14	
	English	1	
	Total foreign merchants	15	11
	Total all merchants	130	100

Source: TsGADA, f. 141, 1630, no. 68.

comparison with Kozintseva's figures for 1710 is revealing. Of the value of foreign goods bought at Archangel, Moscow accounted for 40 percent, Yaroslavl 15.7 percent, and Vologda 7.9 percent, the same order of magnitude as in 1630.[11] In 1630 Yaroslavl sent 7 percent, and Vologda 2.3 percent of the merchants. In 1630, as in 1710, Moscow, Yaroslavl, and Vologda were the three best-represented Russian cities. (Shatsk is a curious exception to this rule; it and Voronezh were not even represented in 1710. Clearly their role in 1630 was the result of the special conditions of the colonization of the steppe in the first half of the seventeenth century.)

Among the Muscovites it is difficult, if not impossible, to assess the role of the various categories as a whole. Only the *gosti* were assigned to a specific legal status, yet it is possible to identify individual merchants of the *gost'* hundred (Isaak Reviakin, for example) or *kadashevtsy* (Aleksei Ragozin, the Zolotovs). One interesting group that does not seem to appear later in the century was the "Muscovite Germans" (such as Paul Westhoff, or Pavel Vestov), who were clearly distinguished from the real foreigners, the latter being definitely called Dutch or English. In number of merchants this group was nearly as large as the true foreign group, and larger than the Russians of any town outside of Moscow. It is a mistake to identify the Moscow Germans with the other foreign merchants in Russia because the former were real merchant immigrants, identical in character to the German and Italian merchants who continued to settle in the cities of Poland until the middle of the seventeenth century. Of Dutch, German, or English origin, the Moscow Germans lived in Moscow and formed a distinct group among the Moscow merchants, tied to both the Russian and foreign residents of the capital. Vestov, whose descendants still traded at Archangel in 1710, was a good example of this group. However, the West European immigrants among the Moscow merchants did not acquire the domination of the merchant class in Moscow that they acquired in Poland or the rest of Eastern Europe. We shall see that their share in the trade of the total Muscovite group was not greatly out of proportion to their share in the merchant population of Moscow (12.5 percent). The same is true, although not quite to the same extent, of the English and Dutch merchants operating in Russia. Indeed, because they comprised only 11 percent of the merchants going to Moscow from Archangel, they would have had to display an enormous concentration of wealth to have "dominated" the Russian market in any sense. Such a concentration of wealth they did not display. As among the Russians and the Moscow Germans, some of the Dutch were quite wealthy (chiefly the

Gollandskie zemli gosti), such as Georg van Klink and Mark de Vogelaar.[12] Others, however, were only able to import rather modest quantities of goods to Russia. (Among the foreign group it should be noted that the predominance of the Dutch is perhaps greater in our document than it was in fact because the one Englishman registered may be an interloper, and the Muscovy Company may not be recorded at all.) In general, the Archangel market was dominated by Russian merchants from the city of Moscow.

The leading role of the Muscovites in Archangel is also shown by the distribution of imported goods among the various groups. The most important imported commodity was cloth throughout the seventeenth century. In 1604, cloth amounted to 38.21 percent of all imports (by value). In 1710, cloth was 47.8 percent of all imports.[13] The extract from the toll records of 1630, of course, does not give prices, but it is clear from the frequency with which the merchants had bought cloth that the approximate proportions were the same. In order to analyze the purchase of cloth by the various groups of merchants, it is necessary to compare quantity rather than ruble value, which presents certain difficulties. Various types of cloth were brought to Russia, and not all types were of the same length; the basic unit of measurement was the *postav*, which was a natural unit related to the size of the loom. However, the *postav* was usually twenty to thirty *arshins* long, and so for the sake of simplicity, the cloth has been reduced to *postavs* of twenty five *arshins* (two *polovinki* are equal to one *postav*). No measurements were used besides *postav*, *polovinka*, and *arshin*. The results of such a calculation appear in Table 3.11.

Table 3.11. *Purchase of cloth at Archangel*

City/group	*Postavs* cloth	Cloth (%)	Merchants (%)
Moscow *gosti*	274.0	12.0	3.0
Moscow merchants	900.2	40.0	56.0
Moscow Germans	413.4	19.0	9.0
Moscow total	1,587.6	71.0	68.0
Russian merchants (not Muscovites)	377.6	17.0	21.0
Foreign merchants	254.4	12.0	11.0
Total	2,219.6	100.0	100.0

Source: TsGADA, f. 141, 1630, no. 68.

The Moscow merchants had the largest share of the cloth trade, but this share was in proportion to their number among the merchants trading at Archangel. They have by no means eliminated the Russian merchants from cities other than Moscow, although they have a slight advantage over them. This advantage is due entirely to the high proportion of the trade in the hands of the *gosti* and the Moscow Germans. These two groups together comprise 12 percent of the merchants, but they imported 31 percent of the cloth. It is notable that the foreign merchants' cloth trade was almost exactly proportionate to their share in the merchant population. Indeed the comparison between the *gosti* and Moscow Germans on the one hand, and the other Muscovites on the other, is not entirely fair because the *gosti* and the Moscow Germans were to some extent an elite group, whereas the *gost'* hundred and *kadashevtsy* were concealed in the category "Muscovites." Nevertheless, Table 3.11 shows that although an elite of Russians and immigrants from Western Europe had clearly formed, it by no means monopolized the trade in cloth, which was the most important single item imported into Russia at that time.

Another commodity was copper. The results of Table 3.12 point to a clear predominance of foreign merchants in the purchase of copper (even greater than indicated because a part of the copper imported by the foreign community was not measured in puds). This was also a concentration in the hands of the Dutch because the only Englishman did not import copper. Thus, the Dutch, the Moscow Germans, and the Russian *gosti* had the greater share of the copper trade, shipping over 51 percent of the copper with only 23 percent of the merchants. The extremely low amount of copper shipped by non-Muscovites is striking. This fact may result

Table 3.12. *Purchases of copper*

City/group	Puds copper	Copper (%)	Merchants (%)
Moscow *gosti*	288.00	9	3
Muscovites	1,465.25	46	56
Moscow Germans	279.25	9	9
Moscow total	2,032.50	64	68
Russians (not Muscovites)	95.00	3	21
Foreign merchants	1,065.00+	33	11
Total	3,192.00+	100	100

Source: TsGADA, f. 141, 1630, no. 68.

from a concentration of the brass and copper trade in Moscow or from the needs of the state for coinage. (Fifty of the ninety-five puds were shipped by a merchant from Shatsk who could have sold it in Moscow. The rest went with merchants from Vologda, Uglich, and Suzdal', where there was also a copper and brass-working industry.) Metals were the second largest Russian import, being 15.28 percent of imports in 1604 and 18.5 percent in 1710.[14] It is important to note that in 1604 the English virtually monopolized the importation of metals into Russia, but by 1630 the trade was entirely in the hands of the Dutch.[15]

Another item of some interest is pepper. Floria and Kozintseva include it under the category of "spices" or "foods" but the important thing about pepper was that it was a colonial ware, brought largely from the East Indies. In 1604, 854 puds were imported, making 4.15 percent of the total imports, and 70 percent was brought by the Dutch. The amount of pepper imported in 1710 cannot be determined from Kozintseva's figures. Foods in 1604 were 10.36 percent and 10.7 percent in 1710.[16] In 1630 the amount of pepper remained virtually the same, 875.5 puds, but its importance among the colonial goods had surely risen because the amount of pearls had fallen off sharply. In 1604 pearls (from the Persian Gulf and the Indian Ocean) accounted for 25 percent of all imported goods (by value) and nearly all of these pearls were brought by the Dutch.[17] Pearls were still an important item in 1613–14, but by 1630 they had clearly fallen off significantly. Their preeminent place among the precious stones and metals was taken by gold and silver thread, for what reason it is not known. Because pepper was in 1630 one of the main colonial goods, its distribution, shown in Table 3.13, has some interest.

Table 3.13. *Purchases of pepper*

City/group	Puds pepper	Pepper (%)	Merchants (%)
Moscow *gosti*	44.0	5	3
Muscovites	403.5	46	56
Moscow Germans	194.0	22	9
Moscow total	641.5	73	68
Russians (not Muscovites)	22.0	3	21
Foreign merchants	212.0	24	11
Total	875.5	100	100

Source: TsGADA, f. 141, 1630, no. 68.

Evidently, the pepper trade was marked by a sharp predominance of the two foreign groups. They shipped to Moscow 46 percent of the pepper and formed 20 percent of the merchants. It is notable that the *gosti* did not play an important role in this trade, and that the amount shipped by non-Muscovite Russians was small. Pepper must have mainly gone to the tables of the court and the aristocracy in Moscow, and must have been brought there in large part by the foreign and immigrant merchant groups. However, even in the case of pepper, the Russians of Moscow had a slight edge over the foreigners and Moscow Germans (51 percent to 46 percent by weight).

As mentioned earlier, gold and silver thread (and some gold bullion) replaced pearls as the main precious commodity imported into Russia. In 1604 the Dutch seemed to have had the lead. In 1630 the main importer is more difficult to determine because the only gold or silver was brought by the one Englishman, and it is impossible to judge who sold it to the Russians before it left Archangel. Table 3.14 shows the distribution among merchants of gold and silver purchases. In this case there is a strong concentration in the hands of the merchants from the city of Moscow, and especially in the hands of the Moscow Germans. The importance of gold and silver thread and bullion was not great in the total amount of goods imported, as only 282 *litry* were imported in 1604 (1.35 percent of the value of all imports). Most of it was brought by the Dutch. In 1710 all precious metals were 1.5 percent of the value of all imported goods.[18]

Finally, one of the most important items brought into Russia by the trade with Western Europe was silver coins, the *efimki* (Joachimsthaler).

Table 3.14. *Purchases of gold and silver* (litry)

City/group	*Litry* gold/silver	Metal (%)	Merchants (%)
Moscow *gosti*	198	11	3
Muscovites	578	32	56
Moscow Germans	676	37	9
Moscow total	1,452	80	68
Russians (not Muscovites)	340	19	21
Foreign merchants	10	1	11
Total	1,802	100	100

Source: TsGADA, f. 141, 1630, no. 68.

This was an extremely important item, for Russia had at that time no native sources of gold or silver. In this period Russia greatly benefited from the fact that the value of the goods exported from Russia was usually greater than the value of the goods imported, and the difference was made up by the importation of silver bullion (especially in the sixteenth century) and of the *efimki*. In 1604, 111,104 *efimki* were imported, equal in value to 39,997 rubles,[19] that is, somewhat over 25 percent of the value of the goods imported into Russia in that year. In 1630 only 47,571 *efimki* were shipped from Archangel to Moscow, the equivalent of 23,785.5 rubles.[20] It does not follow, however, that altogether fewer *efimki* came into Russia in 1630 because the foreign merchants had to pay tolls in *efimki*. Also, any sales by the treasury were for *efimki*, so many of the *efimki* are probably not included in this document. The distribution is shown in Table 3.15. It should be noted that of the sum brought by *gosti*, about half (7,200 to 7,300) was brought by only one man, the *gost'* Grigorii Leont'ev Nikit-nikov, who thereby accounted for 15 percent of the total by himself. On the whole, Table 3.15 shows a concentration in the hands of the *gosti* (not just Nikitnikov) and the same lack of silver imported by foreign merchants that appeared in the case of the gold and silver thread.

The goods that have been chosen and analyzed here do not represent the full range of goods imported into Russia and shipped south to Moscow in 1630. The usual variety of goods – playing cards, glasses, wines, paper, and so on, were sent south by many merchants. These few, however, were some of the most widespread (and easiest to count), and represented a fair proportion of the total amount of imported goods, especially the cloth, copper, and *efimki*. Consequently, it is possible to draw some limited

Table 3.15. *Purchases of* efimki

City/group	Number	*Efimki* (%)	Merchants (%)
Moscow *gosti*	14,855	31	3
Muscovites	16,239	34	56
Moscow Germans	4,400	10	9
Moscow total	35,494	75	68
Russians (not Muscovites)	11,277	23	21
Foreign merchants	800	2	11
Total	47,571	100	100

Source: TsGADA, f. 141, 1630, no. 68.

conclusions about the role of the various groups in the Archangel trade. The most obvious conclusion is the relatively modest role of the foreigners (leaving aside for the moment the Moscow Germans). In spite of the fact that all of the goods that have been described were brought in Dutch and English ships to Archangel, and by Dutch and English merchants, the foreign merchant community was not able to exploit this advantage sufficiently to dominate the trade in the imported goods once they left Archangel for the interior of Russia. This fact is clearly demonstrated by the comparatively modest share of the foreign merchants in the cloth trade, one of the few imported items that could be said to have a "mass" market. If the Dutch and English could not control the trade in cloth (which they had themselves brought to Russia), they could not be said in any sense to control the Russian market. The case of copper was somewhat different because more than a third was in foreign hands, and metal (chiefly copper) amounted to perhaps 15–20 percent of the imported goods. However, even in this case there was no question of overwhelming predominance. The city of Moscow (excluding the Moscow Germans) contributed about half of the copper. The extremely low amount of *efimki* and gold and silver thread in the hands of the English and Dutch is also important. Most of the thread was sent to Moscow to be bought by the palace officials, and the *efimki* were taken in by the Novgorod Quarter in exchange for the equivalent in rubles. Evidently the Russian regulations on gold and silver at that time had the effect of keeping the cash not only in the treasury, but also in the hands of Russian merchants, which to some extent must have compensated for the lack of ready cash in the Russian market.

In this situation the Moscow Germans occupied a position somewhere between the Russian and foreign merchants. In the case of cloth and copper they behaved like the Russians, shipping proportionately more cloth and less copper. The same is true of the gold and silver thread. In the case of pepper, however, they behaved like the foreign merchants, and shipped proportionately more pepper. In the importing of silver coins they fell somewhere between the Russian and foreign merchants. These facts suggest that they were not by and large able to exploit their foreign connections to gain an advantage over the Russian merchants. Rather, they blended into the Russian landscape and behaved like Russian, rather than Western European merchants.

The group that did "dominate" the Archangel market was the Muscovites, but as Tables 3.10–3.15 uniformly show, not out of proportion to the size of the Moscow merchant community. They dominated simply by being the largest group. Among the Muscovites it is notable that, although there was clearly an elite group among the merchants that had an unusually large share of the market, there did not exist a situation in which a few great merchants dominated the scene. It is in fact remarkable to what an extent, given the existence of the *gosti*, the trade was spread among a large group. It is evident that the *gosti*, although on the average richer than their brother merchants, were not a dominant group in any sense. Kozintseva observed the same situation in 1710.[21] What did change by 1710 was the degree of predominance of Moscow: In 1630 over half of the merchants were Muscovites, but in 1710 only about 16 percent were Muscovites. In 1630, Muscovites bought normally more than half of the foreign goods for sale, and in 1710 about 40 percent. The notable change by 1710 is the great increase of non-Muscovites at Archangel, especially merchants from small villages and towns. The size of their purchases, however, was small (and may be due to the great increase in trade at Archangel after 1700). In spite of this relative decline, the merchants of the city of Moscow remained the most important single group in the Russian merchant class throughout the course of the seventeenth century. They led, but did not dominate, the Russian merchant class.[22]

Russian exports through Archangel

Russian records have few, if any, indications of the size, value, and composition of Russian exports through Archangel. De Rodes's data of the 1650s are usually cited as evidence, but as we have seen, de Rodes is not very reliable. Rather than being used as primary evidence, de Rodes must himself be analyzed by the use of other accounts of Russian exports. In view of the inadequacy of Russian records, the London Port Books must be used to gain some idea of the goods exported from Russia at the end of the sixteenth century. T. S. Willan has extracted the relevant figures,

Table 3.16. *English ships from Archangel, 1587–9*

Year	Ships	Tonnage	Value of cargo (London)
1587	10	1,151	£ 13,530 13s. 4d.
1588	6	610	£ 6,249 3s. 2d.
1589	5	—	£ 3,813 8s. 2d.

Source: Willan, *Russia*, pp. 182–3.

Table 3.17. *English imports from Archangel, 1587*

Commodity	Quantity	Value	% of total
(I) tallow	227,000 lb.	£ 1,690	12.5
cordage	484,400 lb.	£ 2,811	21.0
flax	305,700 lb.	£ 1,819	13.0
		sum of above (I)	46.5
(II) wax	135,700 lb.	£ 3,340	25.0
train oil	186¼ tons	£ 931	7.0
		sum of above (II)	32.0
goatskins	1,750	—	—
dry cow hides	3,440	—	—
rough bristles	700 lb.	—	—
sealskins	2,430	—	—
elk hides	893	—	—
beaver bellies	900	—	—
beaver backs	120	—	—
squirrel skins	1,200	—	—
coarse sables	300	—	—

Source: Willan, *Russia*, pp. 182–3.

Table 3.18. *English imports from Archangel, 1588*

Commodity	Quantity	Value	% of total
(I) tallow	178,700 lb.	£ 1,330	21.0
cordage	357,400 lb.	£ 2,127	34.0
flax	142,800 lb.	£ 850	13.5
		sum of above (I)	68.5
train oil	84½ tons	£ 423	7.0
dry cow hides	1,000	—	—
cow hides	4,800	—	—
elk hides	1,180	—	—
beaver bellies	160	—	—
beaver backs	80	—	—
beaver wool	20 lb.	—	—
squirrel skins	11,000	—	—
isinglass	250 lb.	—	—

Source: Willan, *Russia*, pp. 182–3.

shown in Table 3.16, for the 1580s, when the Muscovy Company was still ahead of the Dutch in importance.[23] Tables 3.17 and 3.18 show the detailed cargo for 1587 and 1588, with the official values (from the customs rates of 1583). Unfortunately, values cannot be calculated for the goods other than tallow, cordage, flax, train oil, and wax, so that we cannot be sure of the relative importance of the other goods. However, it is clear even from the data we have that the export of the products of agriculture (flax and hempen cordage) and stock raising (tallow), which have been put together as Group I, were predominant over forest products (furs and wax), which form Group II in the above tables. Indeed, the extremely modest role of furs at this time is quite striking. Either they were being exported largely by the Livonian towns, or else there must have been a decrease in the fur trade at the end of the sixteenth century, at least in the fur trade to Western Europe. In any case, the results given in Tables 3.17 and 3.18 can be claimed to represent the great majority of the Russian exports through Archangel because in 1587–9 the Dutch were just beginning to come there to trade: Only four Dutch ships came in 1589, two of them small.[24] Willan's account is thus a fairly complete picture of the situation at the end of the sixteenth century.[25]

Finally, we must turn to the very fragmentary data for the first half of the seventeenth century. For this period we have only the records of the goods sold at Archangel by two of the wealthiest Moscow merchants, the *gost'* Grigorii Nikitnikov and the *kadashevets* Aleksei Zolotov. Both these records cover the latter part of the 1620s and are thus some twenty years earlier than any other such records. Unfortunately, they only give the sum of the value of all the goods sold at Archangel, and not the price of each commodity. Consequently, only yearly totals can be given:

Grigorii Nikitnikov's sales at Archangel, 1626–30

1626	10,941 rubles
1627	15,650 rubles
1628	11,892 rubles
1629	8,148 rubles
1630	37,620 rubles

Aleksei Zolotov's sales at Archangel, 1628–31

1628	1,716 rubles
1629	6,206 rubles
1630	9,900 rubles
1631	6,376 rubles

Source: TsGADA, f. 141, 1633, no. 41, pp. 126–66; f. 210, no. 37, part 1, pp. 192–205.

Because it is impossible to determine the relative worth of the various goods, there is little point in a detailed enumeration, and we shall only give an example – Nikitnikov's sales for 1630; 3,060 *iufti;* 3,163 salted cow hides; 575 dry cow hides; 360 goatskins; 1,104 *Bukhara* cow hides; 195 elk hides; 10,000 squirrel skins; 23 korsak (a kind of fox) skins; 160 puds of wax; 785.5 puds of raw silk. Zolotov's sales in 1630 were the following: 1,800 dry goat skins; 150 calf skins; 2,667 puds of hemp; 615 puds of wax; 680 elk hides; 8 puds 20 funt beaver bellies; and 100 of mink.[26] It should be noted that in spite of considerable overlap there is some degree of specialization that is the result of the merchants' regional connections outside of Moscow. Nikitnikov, who came from Yaroslavl, clearly retained his connections there because Yaroslavl was the most important center of leather production, and the silk came from his connections in Astrakhan. Zolotov, by contrast, had his chief agents in Kaluga, which accounts for the hemp and wax. Elk hides, squirrel skins, to a certain extent wax, and beaver could be purchased either in the north or in Moscow or any other large town of Central Russia. This degree of specialization, limited as it is, can be found in the other years for which records exist of the trade of Nikitnikov and Zolotov. The complete absence of sables and other Siberian furs is striking, and is borne out in other years, when the two merchants only sold small quantities of such furs. Evidently the merchants of the Russian North, who were the main buyers of furs in Siberia (see Chapter 7), were also the main sellers at Archangel.

The lists of Russian goods sold by Nikitnikov and Zolotov in 1630 confirm the general picture that emerges from the Muscovy Company's exports in the 1580s. De Rodes's figures, if taken not as precise data but as rough estimates, show the same selection of goods. Finally, the records of 1710 reveal the same types of exports. It was not until the middle of the eighteenth century that leather, tallow, flax, hemp, and furs began to give way to other goods. In the seventeenth century, grain was usually sold by the treasury as part of Russia's foreign policy, as in the case of the sales to Sweden in the 1630s. In certain years the quantity of grain sold could be significant, as in 1652 when nearly all the Dutch ships going to Archangel intended to return with either grain or the usual goods. (There is no way of knowing how many actually did return with grain.) On the whole, little if any grain left the Archangel port, and when it did, it was invariably the result of special circumstances in Russia or the West. Indeed, various Dutch merchants did have plans to start companies to trade in Russian grain, but none of these plans ever came to fruition. Although Russia's main exports were agricultural, grain was not among them until late in the eighteenth century.

Conclusions

The most striking conclusion from the history of the trade at Archangel is the very rapid increase in its importance, both to the Dutch and to the Russians. Between 1590 and 1650 Archangel changed from a small trading post on the White Sea to one of the major commercial centers of Northern Europe. Consequently, the Moscow merchants who were active in that period were operating with greatly increased possibilities for enrichment and the expansion of their activities. Evidently the merchants of Moscow responded adequately to the possibilities because, in spite of the enormous distance to the mouth of the Northern Dvina, the Muscovites were the largest group present by 1630 and remained so throughout the century. Also, they did not succumb to the greater commercial potential of the Dutch and English merchants who traded in Russia. The modest role of the foreign merchants is clear, as is the equally modest role of "Moscow Germans," merchants of foreign origin settled in Moscow. In view of this fact, the conventional picture of the Russian merchant crushed by foreign competition cannot be sustained. Nor can the idea of the monopolistic role of the *gosti*, derived from Kilburger, be considered applicable to the situation before 1650 (if at all). An elite of wealthy merchants, among whom were the *gosti* and "Moscow Germans," had certainly formed, but its relative weight in the commerce of Russia has been greatly exaggerated. Later we shall see that in other respects the *gosti* did play an important role (although never a monopolistic role) in the Russian economy of the seventeenth century, but at Archangel their role was quite modest.

4

Russia and the Baltic trade

The growth of the trade at Archangel since the 1550s overshadowed the trade that Russia continued to maintain through the Baltic for the greater part of the sixteenth and seventeenth centuries. The volume of the trade was much less than that of Archangel, and there were many serious obstacles to the Baltic trade, the main problems being the absence of a significant port in Russian hands before 1609, and the Swedish control of Ingermanland after the Time of Troubles. As Shaskol'skii rightly points out, it was not so much the Swedish Crown but the Reval patriciate, which steadfastly adhered to its traditional right of staple for Russian goods, that formed the "Baltic barrier."[1] In the seventeenth century the Swedish government tried to impose its own commercial policy on the burghers of Reval and Riga, but only began to have success after the return of Count Axel Oxenstierna from Germany in 1636. However, Oxenstierna was not trying to make things easier for the Dutch or Russian merchants, but was trying to fill the Swedish treasury; thus the trade between Russian and Western merchants remained encumbered by the Swedish-German middleman.[2] The problem of an adequate port with ready access to the Russian interior remained unaffected by Oxenstierna's policies, and only the founding of St. Petersburg made it profitable for a large part of Russian commerce with the West to flow through the Baltic.

Nevertheless, the small scale of the trade through Narva does not make it insignificant in the history of Russian trade. The relative abundance of sources makes it possible to construct a more detailed analysis of the Baltic trade than that of Archangel, and to show that Archangel was, in fact, an integral part of the Baltic trade. These sources, which have been exploited by Artur Attman and Elisabeth Harder, are primarily the toll records of

Narva and the records of the Novgorod Kontor in Lübeck.[3] Attman had at his disposal the records of the Swedish toll collectors at Narva, which he fully exploited for the years 1580–1610. These records give the name and price of the goods (at Narva), as well as the origin of the ships that brought them to the Narva port. Aside from missing years, these records also do not record the actual sales and purchases in Narva. In theory they could be attacked on the grounds that they do not differentiate goods going to Russia and those going to parts of Estonia, but in fact this is not a serious problem. The hegemony of Reval over the Estonian hinterland was considerable, and its rivals were Pernau and the small ports of the Estonian islands, not Narva. Even Attman's severest critics (Nilsson and Heckscher) did not question the validity of Attman's conclusions for the trade at Narva.

From 1638 on, there exist the records of the Novgorod Kontor at Lübeck, which registered the yearly coming and going of ships and goods to Narva and Reval. The Lübeck records have the advantage of giving the amount of Russian goods even if they came from Reval, so that on the side of exports the problem presented by the Narva records is eliminated. Indeed, the Lübeck records suggest that in the case of Narva almost all trade was intended for Russia, in addition to part of Lübeck's trade with Reval.

Finally, the Sound Toll Registers[4] allow us to fill in the years between the information of the Narva and Lübeck records (roughly 1615–38). The Sound Tolls have the defect of only recording ships that passed the Sound so that any trade of Narva with the Baltic ports is eliminated. Because the trade of Lübeck did not begin in 1638, as the records do, a fairly large part of the trade of Narva for those years is absent. Unfortunately, no attempt has been made to systematically compare all three types of records for simultaneous years in our period to determine their relative accuracy. Consequently, it is not possible to make an absolute determination of the size and value of Narva's trade, although it would seem likely that the data from the Narva records would give the most complete view of the trade. In any case, the possibility of mapping certain trends and patterns in the Narva trade is not excluded because the three sources of information complement one another in a number of ways.

The Narva trade was distinct from the trade of the other ports in the east Baltic only in that it was smaller in value. Indeed the importance of the Narva trade as being representative of the Baltic trade caused one of the fundamental controversies about the nature of the Baltic trade, a con-

troversy that was sparked by the publication of Attman's book in 1944.
What excited the controversy was Attman's statement that the Baltic
countries (including Russia) had a very large active balance of trade and
that this balance was made up by the export of silver coins and bullion to
the Baltic ports. This statement provoked sharp opposition from the
Swedish historians Sven Nilsson and Eli Heckscher, who maintained that
Attman had not taken into account the possible role of land routes and
bills of exchange in channeling money back into Western Europe.[5] In 1949
C. H. Wilson came to Attman's defense by arguing that bills of exchange
were irrelevant because the Baltic trade was not multilateral. Bills of
exchange could not be drawn on any third trade route where treasure was
moving from Eastern to Western Europe.[6] Wilson may have overstated his
point because Baltic trade was not as completely bilateral as he maintained. In general, however, he and Attman were correct, as has been
clearly demonstrated by the work of Bogucka and Mączak on Danzig and
Elbing, and that of Jensch, Doroshenko, Soom, and Piirimäe on the ports
of Riga and Reval.[7] In particular the findings of the Polish historians
decide the argument because Danzig and Elbing were the chief ports of
call for the Dutch and English respectively. Finally, it should be noted
that in the petitions and statements of the merchants from Holland and
England, and in the writings of publicists of the time, it was assumed that
the merchant going to these countries was in need of a large supply of
silver coin.[8] Mączak and Bogucka show that in the second half of the
sixteenth century the surplus of silver coming into Poland was continuous
and large, whereas in the first half of the seventeenth century the size
decreased and years of passive balance for Poland appeared. Thus, they
both substantiate and extend Attman's conclusion.

The importance of these disputes lies not only in their relevance to the
Narva trade. A mere glance at the structure of imports and exports shows
that Archangel and the Baltic traded in goods of the same type (often
exactly the same goods) and roughly in the same proportions. Moreover,
as was shown in Chapter 3, silver was being brought into Russia at Archangel in large quantities. Archangel and Narva thus share the same
problems in the history of Russian trade.

After Ivan III closed the Hansa yard in Novgorod in 1494, the trade
shifted to the Livonian towns that in turn were now trading largely with
the Dutch, rather than the Hansa.[9] Until the destruction of Antwerp by
the Duke of Parma in 1585, this meant trade with Dutch shippers (from
Amsterdam and other ports in the province of Holland, such as En-

khuizen), who in turn shipped for Antwerp merchants. In the 1560s and 1570s several companies were formed in Antwerp for the purpose of trading with Russia. One such company was already formed in 1562 and a successor was formed in 1565 that included several prominent Antwerp financiers and representatives of the Genoese banking house of Spinola.[10] More is known about the *Compagnie opter Nerve ende Zweden* of 1573–6, for which the account books of an expedition to Riga and Pskov survive. These are the accounts of Isidor Dalz, the company's agent who traded mostly in cloth, gold, and silver, which he sold in exchange for tallow and hides, including *iuft'*. Practically all of his wares were sold in Dorpat and Pskov to Russians, and the tallow was shipped out of Narva in English ships. Dalz sold 2,615 Reichsthalers worth, but among his sales were 549 Reichsthalers worth of gold and silver.[11] Thus the Antwerp company confirms the picture of bullion exported to Russia during the "Narva Navigation," although in this case Narva itself played a minor role.[12]

General statistics are available only after 1582, and are provided by Attman, based on the records of the Swedish toll collectors at Narva. The value of imports and exports for the years where data survive is given in Table 4.1. For the years 1605–8 an accurate account of the value of the cash and bullion imported into Narva has been preserved for the first time:

Year	Import or cash and bullion (in Reichsthalers)
1605	121,186
1606	66,464
1607	71,839
1608	84,163
Total	343,652 or an average of 85,913 per year

Source: Attman, *Ryska*, p. 87.

In other words, Narva was taking in the equivalent of about 43,000 rubles a year in cash and bullion. Certainly some of this remained in Narva because Narva merchants did a good business as intermediaries, but because most of Narva's trade was with Russia, a great part of this must have been passed on to Russian merchants. It is also notable that in the years 1606 and 1607 the import of treasure was greater than the active balance in trade. In 1608, a passive balance for Narva of 22,005 Reichsthalers still brought 84,163 Reichsthalers in treasure. However, it must be pointed out that the excess of exports over imports gradually fell in the period 1583–1608, which indicates that the flow of money to Narva and Russia

Table 4.1. Narva trade (imports and exports given in Reichsthalers)

Year	Import	%Im.	Export	%Ex.	Surplus/deficit	% Surplus or deficit
1583	29,865	36.2	52,586	63.8	+22,721	+27.6
1584	32,581	26.7	89,362	73.3	+56,781	+46.6
1585	68,469	39.6	104,555	60.4	+36,086	+20.8
1586	38,983	31.4	85,153	68.6	+46,170	+37.2
1587	34,674	23.0	115,954	77.0	+81,280	+54.0
1588	10,928	58.7	7,701	41.3	-3,227	-17.4
1595	45,275	53.4	39,573	46.6	-5,702	-6.8
1596	110,094	33.9	214,332	66.1	+104,238	+32.2
1597	60,378	46.0	70,862	54.0	+10,484	+8.0
1598	87,146	23.5	284,271	76.5	+197,125	+53.0
1605	162,685	34.4	309,239	65.6	+146,554	+31.2
1606	167,956	42.1	229,969	57.9	+62,013	+15.8
1607	197,139	44.0	250,547	56.0	+53,408	+12.0
1608	231,036	52.5	209,081	47.5	-21,955	-5.0

Source: Attman, Ryska, pp. 87–8.

must have decreased somewhat as Russian imports grew. Attman has calculated the percentage of the value of the average export surplus to the value of the total turnover of goods at Narva for the years of surviving data:

Years	Percentage
1583–8	35.8
1595–8	33.6
1605–8	13.6

Source: Attman, *Ryska*, p. 88.

Unfortunately, it is not possible to make such a calculation for later years, and hence the overall trend from about 1580 to 1650 must escape us, although the data of the Lübeck trade suggest a continued surplus of exports on the Russian (Narva) side.

The years 1605–8 were clearly high points of the Narva trade. In comparison, the figures for 1612 and 1613 are quite low.

Year	Import	Export	Balance
1612	26,479	21,050	− 5,429
1613	40,615	19,937	−20,678

Source: Piirimäe, "Narvskoi," p. 104. Amounts in Reichsthalers.

A comparison with Table 4.1 shows the effect of the collapse of the Russian market in the Time of Troubles. Although the imports in 1612–13 are about the same as the lower years in the period 1583–1608, the fall in the value of exports is much greater. Except for the extremely bad year in 1588, the lowest registered exports from Narva were in 1595 at 39,573 Reichsthalers, which is twice the value of exports in 1612. From 1605–8 the drop in imports is about 75 percent, whereas the drop in exports is more than 90 percent. This fact illustrates the dependence of the Narva trade on Russian exports.

Unfortunately there are no reliable statistics for the period 1613–38, when the series of statistics for the trade of Lübeck in Russian goods begins. Therefore we must turn to the far less helpful records derived from the Sound Toll Registers, which, it should be remembered, only record trade between Narva and Ingermanland and Western Europe. Table 4.2 does not give a complete picture of the scale of the trade because the Lübeck data reveal that Lübeck sent the majority of the ships to Narva after 1638, and probably since about 1630.

The ships listed in the Sound Toll Registers as sailing west from Narva are almost all Dutch (over 75 percent), whereas the rest are English and a scattering are from German and Scandinavian ports. It would therefore be

Table 4.2. *Ship traffic at Narva and the Ingrian ports*

Year	Narva	Year	Narva	Ingermanland (Nyen)
1595	3	1620	0	1 (Nöteborg)
1596	3	1621	0	1 (Koporje)
1597	1	1622	2	1 ("Rusland" for Jacob de la Gardie)
1598	1	1623	2	1
1599	0	1624	0	0
1600	6	1625	0	0
1601	15	1626	0	0
1602	16	1627	0	0
1603	18	1628	0	0
1604	5	1629	2	2
1605	10	1630	2	0
1606	8	1631	13	1
1607	14	1633	8	2 (1 Koporje)
1608	10	1635	4	0
1609	1	1636	4	0
1610	2	1637	7	1
1611	0	1638	15	4
1612	0	1639	10	3
1613	1	1640	6	3
1614	0	1641	9	8
1615	2	1642	6	1
1616	0	1643	5	3
1617	0	1644	1	1
1618	1	1645	0	0
1619	0	1646	5	1
		1647	8	5
		1648	9	6
		1649	11	9
		1650	9	4
		1651	12	7
		1652	12	7
		1653	8	2
		1654	25	8
		1655	24	7
		1656	15	0
		1657	1	0

Source: N. Bang, ed. *Tabeller over skibsfart*, I.

expected that the fluctuations in the ship traffic at Narva bore some relationship to the general curve of Dutch ship traffic in the Baltic. However until 1631 it is difficult to relate the pattern of Narva's ship traffic either to the pattern of Dutch trade in the Baltic or to the patterns of good and bad years in Russia. In 1620-4, some of the best years of the era for the Dutch, the trade at Narva was either absent or very small. The situation grew worse in 1624, with the intensification of the Polish–Swedish War of 1617-29 that did such harm to Dutch commerce. This lack of coordination at Narva with the patterns of Dutch trade is in sharp contrast to the patterns of ship traffic at Reval, which do follow the general evolution of the Dutch commercial activities in the Baltic. At Narva it seems that there was a period of general prosperity from the time of Ivan the Terrible's capture of the town to 1608, a prosperity that survived numerous shifts of political rule and fortune. After 1609, however, the crisis in Narva trade to the West brought on by the Time of Troubles, revealed both by Piirimäe's data and the shipping figures in the Sound Tolls, continued until 1631. No explanation has been advanced for this long depression of 1609-30 at Narva; at Archangel the expansion continued during these years. The Sound Toll Registers suggest that Reval was the beneficiary, if not the cause, of Narva's temporary decline. In the period 1602-8 the yearly average of ships passing the Sound from Narva was 9.6, whereas the yearly average from Reval was only 5. In the 1620s by contrast, when Russia was already recovering from the Time of Troubles, the yearly average of ships passing the Sound westward from Reval was 32.4, and from Narva and Ingermanland together only 1.3. In the 1630s, the corresponding figures are an average of only 16.4 ships from Reval, and 6.7 ships from Narva alone. This change was not merely the result of Swedish commercial policy, for the new Swedish policy came into effect only after the trade at Narva began to recover: The privileges given for Russian trade in 1629 to Abraham Duquesne and others achieved little.[13] Nyen was legally founded as a town outside the fortress of Nyenskans in 1632, but Reval had the staple and the guest-right in Russian trade (and the right to charge an extra 6 percent toll on ships going to Narva but not Reval) until 1643. The influence of Count Axel Oxenstierna's mercantilist policies were not felt until he returned from Germany in 1636.[14] We must conclude that the reason for the increase of trade at Narva was the general expansion of Russian trade with Holland. That is, recovery after the Time of Troubles brought no recovery in Narva because of the dominance of Reval and the greater costs that resulted from the presence of the Reval

and Narva middlemen. The Dutch shifted their whole attention to Archangel. In the 1630s, however, a general increase in Russian trade at
Archangel had the effect of "overloading" the White Sea route, and some
Dutch ships began to return to Narva, followed by the Lübeckers. It was
this expanding trade that Oxenstierna unsuccessfully tried to exploit, and
that the city of Lübeck did exploit with great profit.

For it was not only Russia that was having a revival of trade. In the
1630s Lübeck was increasing its trade with Spain and France, as a result of
the continuing war between Spain and the Dutch Republic.[15] From 1638
on, there are data for ship traffic between Lübeck and Narva/Nyen that
come from the city records of Lübeck. The data, shown in Table 4.3, refer
only to trade in Russian goods because they come from the Novgorod
Kontor of Lübeck. In 1657, 1658, and 1659 there continued a sharp decline, and in 1660 the trade recovered. This short-lived drop was the result
of the Russo–Swedish War in those years, but it is notable that the recov-

Table 4.3. *Lübeck–Narva/Nyen shipping*

Year	Entering Lübeck from:			Leaving Lübeck for:		
	Narva	Nyen	Total	Narva	Nyen	Total
1638	17	0	17	16	0	16
1642	4	8	12	6	6	12
1643	7	4	11	4	2	6
1644	6	5	11	6	2	8
1645	3	4	7	5	1	6
1646	15	5	20	11	5	16
1647	22	9	31	22	9	31
1648	12	7	19	7	3	10
1649	16	2	18	13	3	16
1650	12	6	18	12	5	17
1651	15	8	23	13	11	24
1652	26	16	42	22	7	29
1653	22	7	29	15	9	24
1654	19	6	25	13	6	19
1655	14	8	22	12	11	23
1656	15	6	21	1	0	1
1657	1	0	1	2	0	2

Source: Harder, "Seehandel," 41, p. 103.

ery after 1600 was not quite to the high point of 1652, which seems to have been the best year of the century in Narva and Nyen for the Lübeckers.

As the century advanced, there was a great increase in the value of Lübeck trade in Russian goods, but it was the result of the rise of Lübeck's trade in Russian goods at Reval. In 1638, seventeen Lübeck ships returned from Narva with 72.5 percent of Russian goods imported that year. In 1690, sixteen ships returned from Narva and seven from Nyen, but together they accounted for only 52 percent (Narva 42 percent and Nyen 10 percent) of the Russian goods imported that year. Reval accounted for 42 percent in 1690, and 16.8 percent in 1638. The absolute amount of the value of imported goods from Narva increased by less than one-third, whereas the total value of Russian imports increased threefold.

The combined data from the records of Narva and Lübeck all indicate a definite increase in Russian trade with Western Europe (mainly Lübeck and Holland) through the Baltic. This trade recovered successfully from the Livonian War and the Russo–Swedish conflicts of the 1590s to become an important outlet for Russian trade in the years just after 1600. The Time of Troubles, however, led to a serious drop in the volume of Narva's trade, which did not recover until the 1630s. By this time, the main trading partners of the Narva and Reval merchants who dealt in Russian

Table 4.4. *Proportion of exported goods at Narva*

Goods	1583–8	1595–8
Linen	22.1	19.6
Hemp	21.6	13.1
Tallow	16.7	23.5
Wax	6.1	6.4
Leather	19.2	15.8
Iuft'	2.3	0.6
Sheepskin	2.7	1.4
Hides (elkhides)	1.2	2.5
Squirrel skins	1.7	1.7
Other furs	2.5	3.4
Gloves	—	1.2
Rye	2.0	7.4 (grain)
Other commodities	1.9	3.4
	100.0	100.0

Source: Attman, *Ryska*, pp. 54-5.

goods were Lübeck, followed by the Dutch. In the 1680s the English were to replace both.

An important advantage of the data of the Baltic towns is the possibility of determining the structure of Russian exports, from the 1580s onward. The first data, shown in Table 4.4, come from the Narva records.

The years 1605–7 and 1640 give the results shown in Table 4.5, unfortunately not altogether comparable to the earlier years. A comparison of Tables 4.4 and 4.5 shows a number of trends. The proportion of linen and hemp has increased, and that of tallow has slightly declined. The great variable is the role of grain exports, which were not a regular commodity, but were exported only in certain years such as 1640, giving the proportions among the exports a certain distortion.

The data on this point from the Lübeck, shown in Table 4.6, are not more illuminating, although they include a small number of Russian exports through Reval and even Riga. The problem is that grain was again exported in 1638. If we put flax and hemp together for all years from Tables 4.4–4.6 we obtain the following result:

$$
\begin{array}{ll}
1583\text{–}8 & 43.7 \\
1595\text{–}8 & 32.7 \\
1605\text{–}7 & 45.5 \\
1638 & 36.0 \\
1640 & 52.3 \\
\end{array}
$$

That is, flax and hemp fluctuated between one-third and one-half of all exports. Hides and furs added together (with hides the main part) give:

$$
\begin{array}{ll}
1583\text{–}8 & 29.6 \\
1595\text{–}8 & 25.4 \\
1605\text{–}7 & 39.9 \\
1638 & 7.0 \\
1640 & 8.1 \\
\end{array}
$$

It is notable that the fluctuations of flax and hemp were not related to the size of the exports of grain because the two high grain export years of 1638 and 1640 showed a low and a high proportion of flax and hemp. Hides and furs (of which the main part were hides), on the contrary, were always low in proportion when grain exports were high. It is hard to tell whether this fact was the result of difficulties in shipping or the state of Russian agriculture. In any case, by the end of the seventeenth century, this problem was

Table 4.5. *Proportion of exported goods at Narva*

Goods	1605-7	1640
Linen and hemp	45.5	52.3
Tallow	13.1	7.1
Wax	—	—
Hides and furs	39.9	8.1
Grain	—	26.5
Other commodities	1.5	6.0
	100.0	100.0

Source: Attman, *Ryska*, p. 56.

overcome because in 1690 *iuft'*, leather, hides, and furs accounted for 40 percent of exports and grain for 23 percent. This shift in the second part of the century was achieved at the expense of hemp and flax, which together accounted for only 10.5 percent.[16] This would indicate a certain increase in grain and stock raising, at least in that sector of agriculture that was export oriented. It could also indicate a shift in the demand for Russian products on the side of the Lübeckers.

Attman has shown that in the years 1583-1608 Russia had a very favorable balance of trade through Narva. Harder has also shown that such a favorable balance of trade existed for Russia in the entire period from 1638

Table 4.6. *Proportion of Russian goods brought to Lübeck, 1638*

Goods	%
Flax	31
Rye	26
Tallow	18
Wheat, barley, oats	11
Furs, hides, leather	7
Hemp	5
Other	2
	100

Source: Harder, "Seehandel," 41, p. 108.

to 1780. In the mid-seventeenth century the balance was especially favorable, as is demonstrated by Table 4.7 from Harder's work. The high point of 1653 was then not regained until 1696, although the value of Russian exports never fell below the pre-1646 level.

The other and newer branch of Russian trade on the Baltic was the trade with Stockholm. About this trade little is known. The main Russian exports were cheap cloth such as *sermiaga*, the cheap Russian woolen, and leather and leather goods. Some flax, hemp, tallow, and furs were also sent to Stockholm. In return the Russians brought back iron and copper, the latter both in the form of money and of copper plates. The export of copper from Sweden caused problems because much of it was in the form of currency, which could not be legally taken from Sweden, although in fact it was. This copper was in part sold to the state to be minted as Russian coins, and in part used in industry. The trade balance seems to have been heavily favorable for the Russians. Unfortunately, it is not possible to give estimates of the volume of this trade.[17]

For our purposes one of the major questions is the extent to which Muscovites participated in this trade, both in the Stockholm trade and in the more general Baltic trade. On the whole the answer is that they did not participate directly to any large extent. In the Stockholm trade we can arrive at an impression only for the period after 1648. It seems that the

Table 4.7. *Balance of Russian trade with Lübeck (amounts in Lübeck marks)*[a]

Year	Russian goods to Lübeck	Lübeck goods to Russia	Diff.
1642	173,750	79,525	+ 94,225
1643	217,550	53,875	+163,675
1644	419,125	95,425	+323,700
1645	170,750	60,275	+110,475
1646	426,075	61,175	+364,900
1647	548,675	119,800	+428,875
1648	377,325	105,975	+271,350
1649	521,000	188,800	+332,200
1650	568,150	170,550	+397,600
1651	676,175	196,225	+479,950
1652	990,175	280,875	+709,300
1653	998,250	422,025	+576,225

[a]One Reichsthaler is three Lübeck marks.
Source: Harder, "Seehandel," 41, p. 113.

first place was held by the merchants of Novgorod, and the second place was held by the town of Tikhvin, giving way to Olonets by the end of the seventeenth century. In addition to these towns, certain rural settlements in the area to the northeast of Lake Ladoga, Lake Onega and (by the end of the century) the western shores of the White Sea sent groups of traders every year. The cities of Central Russia, such as Moscow or Yaroslavl, only sent occasional merchants to Stockholm.[18]

In general, this pattern seems to be true of the Baltic trade as a whole. Most of the trade was carried on by merchants from Pskov and Novgorod, and Muscovites only came to those towns to buy from the Russian merchants of the towns. The Pskov toll book of 1624 shows only fourteen Pskov merchants and no Muscovites trading with the Baltic merchants.[19] In fact, the Muscovites did not even play a major role in the Russian towns of the Northwest. For 1670–1 we have the following figures, showing the value of the transactions of merchants of various towns at the Pskov market:

Total	29,230 rubles	
Pskov	7,400	25.00%
Yaroslavl	4,530	15.50%
Toropets	2,433	8.40%
Uglich	1,947	6.70%
Ostashkov	1,419	4.80%
Rzhev	1,207	4.10%
Novgorod	1,111	3.80%
Moscow	366	1.25%

Source: E. V. Chistiakova, "Pskovskii torg v seredine XVII v.,"
Istoricheskie zapiski, 34 (Moscow, 1950): 206–9.

It is evident from these figures that Moscow could not have played an important role in Pskov's trade. It is also striking that the goods sold by Muscovites were cotton prints (*sittsy*), silk, and pepper, the first two evidently brought from Persia. The toll book of 1624 cannot be a perfect guide, but it seems that for most of the seventeenth century the Baltic route cannot have been more than a minor route for the Muscovites. Only a few isolated Muscovites traded in this area before 1650. In 1627 Ofonka Karpov, a *kadashevets*, received a pass to go from Moscow to Korela (Kexholm) "i do inykh Sveiskich gorodov," apparently via Novgorod.[20] His wares were not enumerated. In 1650, the Swedish customs in Nyen recorded the sales of "Gavrilla Gavrilloff," who was apparently the agent of the Muscovite (of the *gost'* hundred) A. Luzin.[21] He dealt in silk, *iuft'*, slippers, leather soles, soap, spice cakes, bridles, and leather straps. During the whole period from 1617 to 1653 these are the only recorded Muscovites, whereas Novgorod, Pskov, and the other towns of the Northwest were sending merchants to Stockholm regularly. The same was true of the treasury's trade with Sweden. The grain trade, more a political subsidy than a real commercial transaction, was handled by Dutch or Swedish agents of the Swedish crown, and the trade of the Russian treasury in silk and furs was conducted by Novgorodians in 1629–30, 1639, and 1650, and in 1653 by a merchant from Yaroslavl. The only instance of a Muscovite in the state's trade with the Baltic powers is the case of the Moscow German Grigorii Faldergei's (van den Heijden's) sales of grain and caviar to Sweden and Denmark in 1632.[22] Apparently even the treasury bowed to the economic realities of the Baltic and did not try to push the *gosti* of Moscow into the forefront. Novgorod carried the field, both in its own trade and in contracts with the treasury.

Because the Muscovites did not play an important role in the Baltic, the importance of the Baltic for the history of the Muscovite merchants lies in the realm of theoretical problems. We know enough about the trade of the Baltic to show that Moscow played a very minor role. The connection between the regional markets of the Northwest and Central Russia was largely in the hands of merchants of Yaroslavl and other upper Volga towns rather than in those of the Muscovites. However, the Baltic provides a more general context for the history of the development of Russian trade with the West. This is in spite of the fact that the scale of trade at Narva was inferior to that at Archangel, perhaps only a fifth as great. The Russian exports through Nyen, Narva, or the Russian exports to Lübeck show that the same assortment of goods went out to the Baltic as was sold at Archangel. The same is true for imported goods. Even copper, an important Swedish export, entered Russia at Archangel also. A discussion of the Baltic trade in the seventeenth century is thus relevant to the trade at Archangel. Archangel, like Poland, Prussia, or Livonia, had, by and large, a favorable balance of trade, which is shown by the continuous flow of silver coins into Russia through the port. Ships going to Archangel came with ballast and silver, in addition to the cloth and other wares. For the Russian economy, which had no silver sources of its own, this flow of coins was of critical importance. However, further research must be done on the problem of the terms of trade at Archangel. The Hungarian historian Zsigmond Pach has argued that in the trade between Eastern and Western Europe in the seventeenth century, the middle of the century witnessed a shift in the terms of trade. The prices of agricultural exports fell on the Western European markets, and those of the products of Western European industry rose or remained stable, which ultimately reduced or eliminated the flow of bullion to the East.[23] Did any of these processes affect Russian trade, and to what extent? The curve of prices in seventeenth-century Russia is roughly the same as in the rest of Europe, which implies that the Russian market was integrated into the general European market and price structure. The price of *iuft'* began to fall on the Amsterdam Bourse in 1669, and there was an analogous fall in the price of *iuft'* in Russia. There also seems to have been a fall in the flow of silver to Russia by the end of the century: In 1710 all precious metals accounted for 1.5 percent (18,542 rubles) of the goods imported at Archangel, in sharp contrast to the much larger sums imported in 1604 and 1630. The collection of the tolls at Archangel in *efimki*, and the silver entering Russia at Narva in 1710 were probably not large enough to change the situation.[24]

Pach's hypothesis was an attempt to explain the decline of towns, trade, and industry in Poland, Hungary, and the Habsburg lands in the course of the seventeenth century. Yet no such decline occurred in Russia, in spite of the fact that the terms of trade should have turned against Russia. Russian trade may not have expanded as rapidly in the period 1650–1700 as in the half century before, but it did not decline. The Russian towns and industry grew rather than declined: If the salt industry fell into decline in the 1690s (see Chapter 8), it was replaced by iron. Why did Russia fare better than its neighbors, especially considering that Russia was more backward than Poland or the Habsburg lands? Part of the answer lies in the new demand for naval stores in England at the end of the seventeenth century, which benefited Russia as a supplier of hemp and linen to make sailcloth.[25] This new demand, however, only seriously affected Russia after 1700, and does not account for better relative position of Russia in the late seventeenth century. Another part of the answer lies in the selection of goods exported from Russia. Leather had to be manufactured from the raw hides of animals in Russia, so that even if it was used as a raw material in the West, it was a manufactured product in Russia, and leather was the largest single export from Russia by 1710: With tallow (also processed in towns) it made up 50 percent of exports. Poland and Hungary, in contrast, exported agricultural products raw: grain and cattle on the hoof.[26] In Russia, the urban economy benefited from the leather and tallow trade because the town was not merely a middleman for the countryside, but also a producer. Some of the profits of this trade must have stayed in the town and not gone primarily to the nobility as in Poland. The export trade strengthened the whole urban economy, not just the elite of import–export merchants.

The Archangel trade was not unique, but was an integral part of the Baltic trade, the trade between England and the Dutch Republic on the one hand and the Baltic countries of Eastern Europe on the other. The same countries, even some of the same merchants, sent ships to Archangel and Riga or Danzig. Many of the same goods went to the West as from the Baltic: especially the naval stores that formed such a great part of the export of Sweden and Finland, Riga and Königsberg. The terms of trade evolved in similar ways, the pattern of the flow of silver was the same. On the whole, Archangel was part of the Baltic trade. Insofar as Russia differed from the Baltic pattern, the difference was wholly to Russia's advantage.

5

The trade with Poland

The trade with Poland was the other route by which goods from Western and Central Europe reached Russia. There is indirect evidence that this route was quite significant in the second half of the sixteenth century in the growing prosperity of Mogilev and in the fact that the *smol'niane* were evidently one of the most successful groups among the Russian merchants (see Chapter 1). Not enough is known about the trade of Wilno, which was at that time the main market of the Russian merchants in the Polish-Lithuanian state. Polish historians have concentrated on the flow of goods to Poland and the few Russians who came as far west as Lublin or Poznań.[1] The historians who have discussed the Russian merchants in Lithuania have concentrated on the "Belorussian" cities.[2] Only the records of the passes given to Russian merchants going to the Commonwealth give some idea of the total flow of goods and of the merchants involved. To some extent these records make up for the lack of information on the trade at Wilno itself.

The trade of Russia with Poland and Lithuania was quite significant from about the middle of the fifteenth century. Much of the diplomatic correspondence, which is well preserved for this period, contains references to merchants going back and forth between Moscow and Wilno. The building of a *gostinnyi dom* for Russian merchants in Wilno in 1503 suggests that it was at about that time that trade between Moscow and Wilno became important. From the instances of merchants appearing in the diplomatic correspondence it seems that the Russians were trading in furs in order to buy Western cloth, mostly from Central Europe, and some other products such as knives and other small metal items from Krakow. From the Polish side this trade was largely a transit trade, although naturally some of the Russian fur remained in Poland. The rest went to Leipzig and other markets farther west.[3]

This pattern of exchange continued into the early years of the seventeenth century, although it is impossible to arrive at more than a general idea of the trend in Russo-Polish trade. By the 1550s the trade was extensive enough that Wilno merchants borrowed money from a number of Russian treasury officials, although the circumstances are not known. More revealing is the rise of Mogilev, a town whose trade with Russia provided the basis of its prosperity. Mogilev was first mentioned in 1503–5, and does not seem to have even existed before then. However by 1577, when it was granted the Magdeburg law, it had a population of 7,000 so that in the Grand Duchy of Lithuania (the post-Lublin boundaries) it was the third-largest city, only Wilno and Polotsk being larger. By 1609 Mogilev's population had grown to ten thousand and so it was larger than Polotsk. From Russia, according to the records of Mogilev's trade at Poznań in April 1607, the Mogilev merchants bought mainly furs and hides, including 248 *iufti*, and brought to Russia woolen cloth and ironwares. That is, Mogilev was typical of the trade between Russia and the Polish state, and its rapid rise to importance in the second half of the century suggests an expanding trade along the route that ran from Moscow to Poznań.[4]

Some idea of the size of Russian trade in Poland can be derived from the data of the Brest and Grodno toll registers, which survive in a fragmentary state for the years 1583 (Brest) and 1605 (Grodno and Brest). These registers have been studied in detail by Kopysskii, but unfortunately Brest and Grodno were minor routes for Russian merchants. Neither the Grodno toll register nor the Brest register of 1583 show any Russian merchants at all. Fryderyk Paczek of Krakow was the only merchant who was trading in Russia via Brest in that year, and he was sending his servant to Moscow with thirty-two wagon loads of sickles and knives, made in Poland and Hungary. The goods were worth 1700 *kop groszy*, a considerable sum, but Paczek was the only man definitely trading in Russia that year. In 1605, two Moscow merchants passed through Brest, out of a total of 337 merchants who passed through that year (not counting 236 more from Brest itself). Obviously the number of Russian merchants who traded anywhere other than Wilno, Mogilev, and Vitebsk was minimal. In Vitebsk, where there was more trade of a purely over-the-border type, in addition to merchants going on to Wilno from Smolensk, twenty-nine wagon loads of goods were registered as belonging to Russian merchants, out of a total of 100 registered in the last five months of 1605.[5]

Numbers of this size provide some standard of comparison when we turn to the Russian sources, which are chiefly the passes issued in Moscow to the merchants going to the Commonwealth in 1588–9 and 1603–4. In the earlier group of passes (1588–9), ten men received the documents to go to Poland, of whom six were from Moscow, one from Smolensk, and one from Viaz'ma (two did not list their place of origin). In 1603–4, three Muscovites went to Poland and eleven merchants of Smolensk made the trip.[6] The scale of the numbers in the Polish sources suggests that these groups of Russian passes can be regarded as complete. What is missing from them is probably the merchants of Toropets and other border towns, who got passes on the spot or simply went illegally and smuggled their wares across the border. The number of cases that can be found is too restricted to allow any far-reaching conclusions, but it does seem that the amount of trade between Moscow and Wilno or Moscow and Mogilev was rather small in this period.

Some idea of the scale of Russo-Polish trade can also be gleaned from a comparison of the amount of imported Russian furs with the amount of furs traded in the main Polish fur market, Poznań. It was mainly at Poznań that Polish furs were sold to the Germans, and Russian furs were reexported. Furs make a useful item of comparison because the Polish sources distinguish Russian squirrel furs from those produced in Poland, and squirrel was the fur most widely used and sold. Sables are also useful in comparisons because they only came from Russia. For Poznań, data on sables after 1554 are lacking, but in 1519–20 sixty "forties" (*soroka*) were registered, and in 1533–4 seventy-one were registered. In 1605, 140 sables were shipped to Poland through Brest, and only one sable through Grodno. In 1603–4 the Russian merchants took ninety forties to Poland.[7] Clearly, the trade in sables had increased only slightly, and the shipments through Brest and Grodno represented only a small part. The figures of squirrel skins are even more instructive because they were traded in larger numbers, and thus are apt to be more significant as statistics. Rybarski found that in 1519–20 about 500,000 squirrel skins were sold in Poznań and in 1547–8 and 1585 about 1,000,000. In 1603–4 the Russian merchants shipped 200,000 squirrel skins to Poland. In 1605, 201,760 Russian squirrel skins passed the toll office in Brest, and 67,679 through Grodno.[8] In other words, about 270,000 squirrel skins from Russia were shipped west to Poznań and other towns, about the same number of squirrel skins as were produced in the Grand Duchy of Lithuania. The two together would then represent about half of the amount sold in Poznań. The extreme sketchiness of this comparison is obvious, but it is all that is possible with the available sources. The only solid conclusion that can be drawn is that the number of Russian merchants going to Poland was fairly small, and the importance of Russian commerce to Poland was not great, except for the specific item of furs. The only goods shipped to Poland by Russians in 1603–4 besides furs were small quantities of *iuft'* and cheap woolen cloth (*sermiaga*).

The type of trade of the individual merchants does reveal a pattern of some interest. The three Muscovites who went to Poland in 1603–4 went by themselves (or with servants), whereas the eleven Smolensk merchants went in groups, making five parties with two or three merchants each. Moreover, the three Muscovites only took furs to Poland, and the *iufti* and other commodities went with the merchants of Smolensk. The three Moscow merchants were: Mikhailo Smyvalov (*gost'* hundred), Andrei Kotov (*gost'* hundred), and Grigorii Bogdanov (woolen drapers' hundred).[9] Thus, we have virtually the ideal picture of the traditional historiography: the Moscow merchant from the privileged ranks trading in expensive luxury goods, and the provincial merchant trading in cheaper goods with a wider appeal. However, the history of trade at Archangel shows that this was not normally the case, so that it must be that this feature was a peculiarity of the trade with Poland. Of course, the available information is quite sparse, but general considerations would seem to confirm this possibility. Russian trade with Poland began to expand mainly at the end of the fifteenth century, and (paradoxically) reached its height in the second half of the sixteenth century, in spite of the Livonian War. When this trade grew up, it was primarily an exchange of furs and other forest products, destined for the luxury markets of Europe, for Western cloth. Evidently this pattern persisted in the trade with Poland, after it had begun to alter at Archangel and along the Baltic route.

The only solid evidence of Russo-Polish trade in the seventeenth century is the results of Mitiaev's analysis of the toll records of the 1670s, unfortunately twenty years after our period.[10] The main trading partner of Smolensk to the east was not Moscow, but Viaz'ma, as the following figures show:

Year	1673 – 4	1676 – 7	1677 – 8	1678 – 9
Trade	52,359	57,190	61,102	56,178
(in rubles)				
Viaz'ma	2,311	3,350	3,886	3,140
Moscow	663	275	792	311

Source: Mitiaev, "Oboroty," pp. 57, 73, 79.

The trade of Toropets at Smolensk was about the same as that of Viaz'ma, and the trade of Rzhev was about the same as that of Moscow. Clearly Smolensk had become the center of a regional market that in turn directed its main export (hemp) to Riga in return for salt and silver coinage (Smolensk had a strong active balance of trade with Riga). The trade with Vitebsk, whose merchants seem to have served as middlemen between Smolensk and Riga, was much larger than the older trade with Mogilev:

Year	1673 - 4	1676 - 7	1677 - 8	1678 - 9
Mogilev	1,973	2,232	1,577	1,232
Vitebsk	5,392	3.469	7.074	3,287

Source: Mitiaev, "Oboroty," pp. 80–1.

The trade with Mogilev continued in the old pattern of furs and Western European cloth and luxury items, whereas Riga had become a major exporter of hemp from the whole Grand Duchy of Lithuania.[11] Although this situation was probably not typical of the period 1618–54, it does show a weakening of commercial ties in the second half of the century, one that may have begun in the 1630s or 1640s.

Before the Time of Troubles, the Russian merchant sold furs and some hides to the Polish merchant in return for cloth and other smaller manufactured goods such as metalwares. This trade expanded modestly throughout the sixteenth century, and brought prosperity to the merchants of Wilno and Mogilev in Poland-Lithuania and Smolensk and Moscow in Russia. This was roughly the same exchange that took place at Archangel and Narva, and thus was susceptible to the competition of the Dutch. Clearly the rise in importance of Archangel undercut the Russo-Polish trade of the sixteenth century, and a new situation emerged after 1617. The now Polish Smolensk joined Vitebsk and Wilno in exporting grain and naval stores (timber and hemp) through Riga and Königsberg. Trade with Russia was mainly with the border towns of Viaz'ma and Dorogobuzh rather than Moscow. Although the older trade persisted on a much reduced scale, the basic commercial tie between the two states was weakened. Viaz'ma and Dorogobuzh were also the centers of hemp-producing regions, but from there products passed to the West through Moscow to Archangel or Pskov to Narva, not through Poland. The Russian reannexation of Smolensk did not change this situation, it merely added to the total Russian production of hemp and did not lead to a renewal of ties with Poland. Russian trade with Poland did not revive until after 1750 when Russian merchants began to appear at the Leipzig fairs, reflecting increased activity all along the route from Moscow to Leipzig.

6

The trade with the South: The Ottoman Empire and Persia

The commercial relations of Russia with its Muslim neighbors to the south has traditionally been an area of unfounded speculation. The reason for this is the relative paucity of sources, both in Russia and in the other countries concerned. For the entire period before 1700, there exist only two important studies of these problems, that of Syroechkovskii on the *gosti-surozhane* (which falls before our period) and the work of Fekhner on the sixteenth century. The seventeenth century is handled only in general accounts and in a few articles on the trade of the second half of the seventeenth century. By and large the period 1580–1650 has not been discussed in any detail. Furthermore, Fekhner and other historians suffer from an exclusive use of illustrative evidence, and make only the most elementary efforts to determine whether the illustrations that they adduce are representative. The problem of Russian merchants going to these countries is very complicated: There are numerous references, but mostly in connection with diplomatic missions, and it is difficult to determine if Russian merchants regularly traveled to these places. In general, it may be said that until about 1530, Syroechkovskii's evidence showed that Russians (mostly Muscovites) regularly went to Kaffa, and some even got as far as Tokat in Asia Minor. Trips to Istanbul were apparently not as common.[1] After 1530 the picture becomes quite vague. According to Berindei, in the mid-sixteenth century, the importation of furs in the Ottoman Empire was organized by Süleyman II as a monopoly of the treasury, so it is possible that after this time it was no longer profitable (or possible) for Russian merchants to make the journey to Kaffa.[2] About this time the overland route through Moldavia and Poland seems to have become the main route by which Russian and Ottoman goods were exchanged. From about 1580 to 1630 Russo-Ottoman trade was generally in a deep decline. By the 1630s and 1640s, we no longer hear of Russian merchants going regularly to Turkey; they seem to trade with the Greeks and Armenians in the Svinsk fair (near Briansk), Putivl' (after 1675), or Nezhin. The trade seems to be entirely in the hands of Greek and Armenian merchants living in a series of towns stretching from Istanbul through Moldavia to Kamenets-Podol'skii, Lwow, and Nezhin. By this time the Ottoman treasury had abandoned its monopoly of the fur trade. Thus it would seem that after about 1530 the Russians gradually withdrew from direct trade with Turkey, not to reenter it until the eighteenth century.

The volume of the trade between Russia and the Ottoman Empire is extremely difficult to determine. Bennigsen and Lemercier-Quelquejay write that, "The balance [of trade] must have leaned heavily toward the Russian side; for it was mainly with precious metals, gold and silver coins, or more rarely in golden jewelry, that the Ottoman merchants paid for their furs."[3] This statement is based on the recurrent mention in the Ottoman records of money being brought by Ottoman merchants going to Russia. Estimates of the amounts are hard to come by, but in 1570 the Ottomans registered complaints with the King of Poland that the Cossacks stole from Ottoman merchants on one occasion 60,000–70,000 gold pieces and on another 40,000–50,000 gold pieces (*altïn*). Fekhner gives the exchange rate at 20 gold pieces for 16 silver rubles, which would mean that in 1570 at least 80,000 to 96,000 rubles worth of currency was moving toward Russia. This amount could, however, be the result of exaggeration, or a particularly good year.[4]

It is not until the 1640s that the Ottoman sources begin to allow Berindei to give some figures of the purchases of sables in Russia. The numbers are:

	Amount (rubles)	Sables (forties)
1643	1,600	40
1645	6,000	40
1646	4,500	30

Source: Berindei, "Contributions," p. 408.

A rough estimate of the importance of this trade with the merchants of the Ottoman Empire can be made by comparing these figures with what is known of the scale of fur production and trade in Russia. The data of the trade in sables to Poland (along the Smolensk-Wilno route) suggest numbers two or three times greater than the sales to the merchants of the Ottoman Empire (see Chapter 5). In the period from about 1630 to 1660 the yearly export of sables to European Russia from Siberia was approximately 20,000 to 25,000 sables from Mangazeia and Eniseisk *each*. Because these two towns were the two main centers of the sale of Siberian sables, the yearly production of Siberia at mid-century must have been about 50,000 sables at the very least.[5] If Berindei's figures are at all accurate, the merchants of the Ottoman Empire purchased an insignificant proportion of the total product of Russia. De Rodes, who is not absolutely trustworthy, asserted that 579 forties of sables or 23,160 skins were sold at Archangel in 1653. In 1649 the treasury sold 153 forties or 6,120 skins. It is evident that the 1000–2000 skins purchased by the merchants from the Ottoman Empire were not a very large part of the sales of Russian sables abroad. This was even true of the Svinsk fair, where in 1648 the treasury sold 136 forties or 5,440 skins.[6]

The importance of Russian trade with the Ottoman Empire should not be exaggerated: Even the importance of Russian importation of cloths such as brocade and taffeta from Anatolia can be overestimated because the Archangel records show that much of Russia's market for these types of cloth was supplied by the Dutch or the English, who shipped them around Europe from Smyrna or sold European imitations of Oriental cloth. Furthermore, Bennigsen, Lemercier-Quelquejay, and Berindei consider the overland route to Russia via Moldavia only in terms of Russian trade, but many of the merchants traveling on that route may have done most of their trade in Lwow or Kamenets, and only then gone on to Russia. As noted previously, all instances of Russians trading at the Svinsk fair or at Nezhin must not be regarded only as trade with the Ottoman Empire. Lwow had a large and prosperous guild of furriers who largely worked sables and other furs brought from Russia.[7] It is difficult to escape the conclusion that the trade between Russia and the Ottoman Empire was an affair of secondary importance for the Russians as well as for the Turks.

The trade of Russia with Persia was another matter, and has left more traces in Russian archives. By 1570 the main entrepôt was Astrakhan, and the travels of Persian merchants up the Volga or Russian merchants to Persia were less significant.[8] What the Russians sold at Astrakhan we can only guess, but for the late 1590s there are records of purchases by merchants accompanying the Persian diplomatic missions to Moscow: in 1595, 200 *iufti;* and in 1601, 150 *iufti.* The impression is that leather and especially the more expensive and finely worked *iuft'* was one of the main items of export. Fekhner also mentions furs but gives no idea of the amounts likely to be exported to Persia.[9] It should be noted that the amounts of *iuft'* purchased by the diplomatic agents are very modest, and it is unlikely that the merchants going on such missions conducted a large part of the trade between the two countries.

The most important source for Russo-Persian trade, and one that makes possible an evaluation of the role of the Moscow merchants in that trade, is the records of the *Astrakhanskaia prikaznaia izba,* preserved in the archive of the Leningrad Section of the Institute of History, and a unique source not only for Russo-Persian trade but for the history of the Volga region, in view of the almost complete loss by fire of the documents of the Kazan palace.[10] The documents of this collection are unfortunately not those of the toll collection and thus do not indicate prices; rather they are passes for the trip up the Volga, and give the name, place of origin, and goods of each merchant. Thus, they do not directly show purchases, but rather shipments of purchased goods. They come from the years 1622–3, and are earlier than most documents from Archangel. Documents concerning shipments of salt from the salt marshes of the lower Volga, and of fish from the fisheries have been excluded. The figures in Table 6.1 relate only to shipments of Persian goods from Astrakhan to Kazan. This table shows a total of seventy-five merchants, of whom ten, or 13 percent, were Muscovites. Practically all of these merchants, including the five Moscow

Table 6.1. *Number of merchants shipping from Astrakhan (by town), 1623*

A. Central Russia		B. Upper Volga		C. Nizhnii Novgorod/Oka	
Moscow	10	Yaroslavl	8	Nizhnii Novgorod	12
Vladimir	4	Kostroma	8	Murom	2
Suzdal'	1	Iurevets	1	Pavlovo	1
Rostov	1	Tver	1	Gorokhovets	1
Kashira	1				
Total	17		18		16

D. Middle/Lower Volga		E. North		F. Peasants	
Kazan	12	Viatka	1		
Astrakhan	5	Galich	1		
Sviiazhsk	2				
Samara	1				
Total	20		2		2

Source: LOII, fund 178, 1622–3.

gosti, sent only one shipment of Persian goods. Only a half-dozen of the seventy-five shipped jointly with other merchants, although the number who shipped by the agency of their clerks was very large.

In order to arrive at an estimate of the economic importance of this route to the Muscovite merchants, a mere statement of the number of merchants involved is insufficient. Nevertheless, it is notable that only about 13 percent of the merchants dealing in Persian wares in 1623 were Muscovites, whereas seven years later at Archangel, 68 percent of the merchants came from the city of Moscow. To measure the significance of the Persian trade we must follow the procedure used in the case of Archangel, the analysis of the distribution of goods among the various towns and merchants, in the absence of information on the prices of the goods. The shipments of the most valued commodity of the Persian trade, silk (forty-seven merchants), are shown in Table 6.2. In this table, there are a number of surprises. The high figure for Galich is partly deceptive because it represents a single shipment described as *plokhoi* (poor), and thus in value was probably closer to that of Vladimir or Sviiazhsk.[11] A greater surprise is the absence of Yaroslavl, which is the result of a certain

Table 6.2. *Silk shipments from Astrakhan, 1623* (*in* ansyrs *of weight*)

Town	Ansyrs	Percent
Moscow	883	20.0
Kazan	1,260	28.0
Galich	500	11.3
Nizhnii Novgorod	477	11.0
Kostroma	421	9.5
Suzdal'	220	5.0
Vladimir	143	3.2
Sviiazhsk	180	4.0
Pavlovo	88	2.0
Astrakhan	79	1.8
Samara	75	1.7
Kashira	64	1.4
Gorokhovets	40	0.9
Viatka	10	0.2
Total	**4,440**	

Source: LOII, fund 178, 1622–3.

specialization of the Yaroslavl merchants in *zenden'* rather than silk. Nizhnii Novgorod has, in general, a lower proportion of merchants trading in Persian goods, as opposed to salt and fish, than the other large towns of the period: Twelve merchants traded in Persian goods and eight in salt and fish (one in both: Tikhon Minin). In contrast, all Moscow merchants traded in Persian goods as did eight of eleven Yaroslavl merchants. The result is that Moscow imported a large proportion of the silk, although not as much as Kazan. The two towns sent 28.5 percent of the merchants and brought back 48 percent of the silk. In Table 6.3, a slightly different picture is revealed by the imports of raw silk (*sholk-syrets*) (eleven merchants). The extreme predominance of Moscow in the raw silk trade suggests some special factor, such as the use of the raw silk in the cloth-working industries of Moscow, very likely by the *khamovniki* and other groups working for the palace. Merchants from Kazan and Nizhnii Novgorod imported no raw silk at all. It is striking that Kostroma played such a large role in the silk trade for such a comparatively small town. In Archangel in 1630 there was only one merchant from Kostroma.

One final consideration is the grouping within the Moscow merchants. The *gosti* Vasilii Lytkin, Ivan Sverchkov, and Vtoroi Ozerov contributed 208 *ansyrs* of finished silk (23 percent), whereas the merchant Aleksei Pankrat'ev contributed the other 675 *ansyrs*, or 77 percent. This Aleksei Pankrat'ev was probably a *kadashevets*, a group known for their extensive trade and contacts with the Volga. Among the dealers in raw silk, on the other hand, 101.5 puds were contributed by *gosti*. Thus, it is evident that in the silk trade at least, the *gosti* played a more important role than at Archangel.[12]

Table 6.3. *Shipments of raw silk 1623 (by* pud*)*

Town	Puds	Percent
Moscow	110½	61.0
Kostroma	40⅛	22.0
Yaroslavl	15	8.3
Vladimir	14½	8.0
Tver	1½	0.6
Total	181⅝	

Source: LOII, fund 178, 1622–3.

On the whole, however, Moscow was distinctly not in the front rank of the silk trade. Aleksei Pankrat'ev did own the largest shipment made that year, with 675 *ansyrs* of finished silk and nine puds of raw silk, but in almost every other respect Kazan overshadowed Moscow. Not only was the amount of finished silk imported by Kazan greater, but the proportion of Kazan merchants involved in the trade was greater. In all, fifty-one merchants of seventy-five, or 68 percent, were involved in the shipment of either raw or finished silk. In the case of Kazan, of twelve merchants dealing in Persian goods, eleven were shipping silk (92 percent). In the case of Nizhnii Novgorod, all twelve merchants engaged in the trade in Persian goods were importing silk. In the cases of both Moscow and Nizhnii Novgorod, the degree of concentration of the trade was higher: Not only did Pankrat'ev provide 77 percent of the finished silk, but the *gost'* Ivan Sverchkov provided 90 puds out of 110.5 (78 percent) of raw silk. In Nizhnii Novgorod, Ivan Shubin shipped 258 *ansyrs* of 477, or 54 percent. By contrast, the greatest shipment by a merchant of Kazan, Dorofei Alferov's 400 *ansyrs* (the second largest shipment of that year), made only 32 percent of the total.[13]

Besides silk, Persia exported to Astrakhan a variety of textiles, mostly cotton or silk or some combination of different fibers. One was a cotton cloth called *zenden'*, or *zenden' semendi*, which can be taken as representative of the less expensive sorts of Persian cloths shipped north by Russian merchants from Astrakhan. *Zenden'* was shipped north by thirty-five of the seventy-five merchants, and was distributed among the merchants of various towns as shown in Table 6.4. In the case of *zenden'*, Yaroslavl had a commanding lead. Of eight Yaroslavl merchants shipping from Astrakhan that year, seven shipped *zenden'*. Of the total of 3,790 pieces, 1,200 were shipped by the merchant K. Krisant'ev (32 percent). The next largest shipment was 830 pieces, or 22 percent.[14] In Moscow, by contrast, the two *gosti* Nadeia Sveteshnikov and Vasilli Lytkin shipped practically all the *zenden'*. Of the ten Moscow merchants active that year, only three shipped *zenden'*:

	Number of pieces	Percent
Chetverka Vasilev	21	2
N. Sveteshnikov	800	42
V. Lytkin	1,070	56
Total	1,891	

Source: LOII, fund 178, 1622–3, nos. 717, 638, 689.

The shipment of *zenden'* by Moscow merchants was concentrated almost entirely in the hands of two *gosti*.

The only other towns besides Yaroslavl so heavily involved in the shipment of *zenden'* were Astrakhan (five out of five merchants) which was third in importance, and Nizhnii Novgorod (six out of twelve merchants). The second biggest shipper in the latter town was the same Ivan Shubin so prominent in the Nizhnii Novgorod silk trade, who shipped 400 pieces (39 percent), and the largest shipper was one Ivan Fedorov at 420 pieces (41 percent), the two controlling 80 percent of the shipments of *zenden'*. This pattern is more like that of Moscow than of Yaroslavl: a smaller proportion of merchants involved in the trade in *zenden'*, and among them, two who controlled most of the shipments of that year. (Astrakhan shows a pattern like Yaroslavl: The largest shipment was 350 pieces, or 32 percent, the second largest was 300 pieces, or 27 percent.)[15]

A third item imported from Persia and one of considerable importance was *saf'ian*, a finely worked goatskin. This item was a Persian specialty, and later in the century the Russian merchants reexported it to the West. In the 1660s it was so highly valued that attempts were made by the treasury to set up workshops near Moscow to make it in Russia. It was also one of the few items among the regular imports from Persia that was not a

Table 6.4. *Shipments of* zenden' *by town, 1623*

Town	Number of pieces	Percent
Moscow	1,891	16.5
Yaroslavl	3,790	33.0
Astrakhan	1,105	9.6
Nizhnii Novgorod	1,028	9.0
Vladimir	777	6.8
Murom	600	5.2
Sviiazhsk	600	5.2
Kazan	536	4.7
Pavlovo	360	3.1
Gorokhovets	200	1.7
Tver	150	1.3
Suzdal'	145	1.3
Kashira	100	0.9
Peasants	100	0.9
Rostov	30	0.3
Iurevets	4	—
Total	11,416	

Source: LOII, fund 178, 1622–3.

textile. In 1623, twenty-nine merchants shipped it north from Astrakhan. The distribution is shown in Table 6.5. Moscow here played a much more insignificant role than it did in the cases of *zenden'* and silk. At least in those two cases, Moscow was the second largest shipper of the year, whereas in the case of *saf'ian* it had been outdone even by Murom, and stood in fifth place. The role of the *gosti* among the Muscovites is exactly the opposite of their role in the case of *zenden'*. For Moscow the figures are:

	Pairs	Percent
Aksen Vasil'ev Klimshin	200	90.0
gost' G. Nikitnikov	12	5.5
gost' V. Ozerov	10	4.5
Total	222	

Source: LOII, fund 178, 1622-3, nos. 667, 654, 732.

This trade, however, was in general highly concentrated. In Kazan, Druzhina Karpov shipped 480 pairs, or 50 percent, and the monastery serf of Kazan Chernopyl'skii shipped 350 pairs, or 37 percent. Thus, out of the six Kazan merchants shipping *saf'ian*, two of them shipped 87 percent. Indeed, Karpov owned 22 percent of all the shipments that year, and Chernopyl'skii owned 16 percent, the two having 38 percent of the shipments of *saf'ian* on the whole Volga route. Altogether, the two Kazan

Table 6.5. *Shipments of* saf'ian, *1623*

Town	Pairs	Percent
Moscow	222	10.2
Kazan	958	44.0
Kostroma	352	16.2
Nizhnii Novgorod	272	12.5
Murom	230	10.6
Pavlovo	103	4.7
Astrakhan	10	0.4
Peasant	10	0.4
Suzdal'	7	0.3
Rostov	4	—
Viatka	4	—
Samara	1	—
Total	2,173	

Source: LOII, fund 178, 1622-3.

merchants, Klimshin, and one merchant each from Kostroma and Murom (five men) shipped 70 percent of the *safian* in 1623.[16]

These results of the shipping records of the Volga of 1623 create a picture of the trade of the Moscow merchants that is quite different from the situation in Archangel seven years later, in 1630. The most striking difference is in the number and proportion of Muscovite merchants. On the Volga there were 75 merchants in all, and at Archangel 115 Russian merchants, but whereas on the Volga only ten were Muscovites, at Archangel eighty-eight were Muscovites. Another striking difference is in the proportion of *gosti*. Half of the Muscovites on the Volga were *gosti* (five), whereas only four of the Muscovites at the Archangel were *gosti*. Nor are these the same *gosti:* Only Grigorii Nikitnikov and Vasilli Lytkin were represented at both places. Clearly, from the point of view of the merchant of Moscow, the trade in Persian goods on the Volga and the trade with the Dutch and English at Archangel were two different sorts of trade, whose economic significance was different. The trade with the Persians at Astrakhan drew mainly a small number of Muscovites, among whom *gosti*, or a few very rich non-*gosti* such as Klimshin or Aleksei Pankrat'ev, were extremely prominent. The mass of the Moscow merchants did not go to Astrakhan or deal in Persian goods. The bulk of the trade (on the side of imports) was in expensive luxury goods such as silk and *safian*, and was concentrated to a large extent in the hands of a few merchants from Kazan and (to a lesser extent) Moscow. The cheaper Persian cloths, which can be assumed to have had a wider circulation, were to a great extent a specialty of Yaroslavl. Moscow's trade with Persia was highly concentrated, dominated by *gosti*, and played a small role in the total trade with Persia at Astrakhan, where the Russian merchants of the Volga towns played the major role. In contrast with Archangel, it cannot be said that the trade in imported Persian goods was significant for the Muscovite merchants as a whole, and thus it can be said that Moscow's trade was definitely oriented toward the Dutch and English markets by way of Archangel as early as the first years of the seventeenth century. It is probable that this situation already existed by the 1580s.

7

Moscow and the internal market

The relationship of the great merchants of Moscow to the internal market of Russia in the period 1580–1650 is one of the central problems in the history of Russian trade. Unfortunately the sources for this period are very limited because the great majority of the toll books of provincial towns (as well as of Moscow!) are lacking for the whole of the seventeenth century (Novgorod, Yaroslavl, Nizhnii Novgorod) or for the first half of the century (Pskov). A complete series exists only for the northern towns of Ustiug Velikii, Tot'ma, and Sol' Vychegodsk and the monastic town of Tikhvin near Lake Ladoga. These documents begin in the 1620s and in the case of the northern towns have been published for a number of years in the first half of the century. The scarcity of sources is compounded by the lack of interest in the problem until fairly recent times. In the immediate postwar years Soviet scholars occupied themselves with the demonstration of the existence of an "all-Russian market" in the seventeenth century, that is, of a single national market connecting all regions of the Russian state. However, many basic questions went unanswered because their own proof of the existence of a national market was not enough to convince Soviet historians that the tradition stressing the primitiveness of the seventeenth-century Russian economy was misconceived. Consequently, attention has turned away from trade in recent years toward industrial and agrarian history. Nevertheless, the existence of a national market was not the only major change in Russian trade in the seventeenth century: An equally significant change was the shift in Russian exports from the forest products that prevailed in 1500 (furs, wax, and honey) to the agricultural products that prevailed by 1600 (hemp, linen, leather) and remained the chief Russian exports for more than a hundred years. This

shift alone would have been enough to change the relationship of the
Moscow merchants to the internal trade of Russia. The growth of a large
city like Moscow, the spread of handicrafts in the villages, the conquest of
Siberia, and other events also radically changed the nature of internal
trade in the Russian state. Most of these problems are beyond the scope of
this work and indeed would require exhaustive research in the surviving
records of the time. It is possible here only to consider a limited number of
problems, concentrating on the North and Siberia, with some attention to
Central Russia. In the history of the Moscow merchants, the main questions are: What goods did they trade in the small cities and towns? How
great was their share in such trade? Were there any regions within the
national market that were especially the preserve of the Muscovites?

The list of goods exported at Archangel in the late sixteenth and early
seventeenth centuries shows the predominance of certain goods: leather,
hemp, linen, and tallow. All were agricultural products and (except linen)
all were grown in the Central Russian region. The problem, then, is
by what route did they reach Moscow in order to be shipped to Archangel?
K. N. Serbina, both in her work on Tikhvin and in her work on peasant
iron working around Ustiuzhna Zhelezopol'skaia, maintains that there
was a hierarchy of *skupshchiki* – small-scale merchants who bought their
wares in the villages, and sold to merchants of larger villages or small
towns, until the wares finally reached Moscow or some other major town.
This observation is undoubtedly true for the iron-working industry but it
is not certain that all goods reached Moscow by such a hierarchy of
skupshchiki. [1]

Central Russia and the steppe

The most interesting and extensively documented example of a merchant
trading both in Central Russia and at Archangel in this period is that of the
kadashevets Aleksei Zolotov and his son Pantelei Alekseev Zolotov. The
Zolotovs were two of the most prominent merchants among tbe
kadashevtsy of Moscow. Both father and son were trading in Archangel in
1630, shipping English cloth, copper, herring, and paper to Moscow. The
father Aleksei traded in Ustiug Velikii in 1635–6 (or rather his clerk,
Prokopii, who stopped in Ustiug on his way from Siberia to Vologda
traded there). Prokopii stopped in Sol' Vychegodsk on the same trip in late
1635. [2] The Zolotovs' trial for smuggling, for which we are indebted for
the extensive information about their enterprises, occurred in 1632 and

resulted in a short period of exile in Siberia. By 1642, however, they were again in Moscow and in good enough favor for Pantelei Zolotov to apply to farm the tavern, tolls, and other duties at Pavlov Perevoz on the Oka for the two coming years.[3] The Zolotovs continued to trade for some years after their return in 1642.

The Zolotovs had a number of bases for their operations: Moscow itself, where they lived; Kaluga, where they had close relations with a number of local merchants; and Vologda, where they maintained a warehouse to store their goods on the way to Archangel. The goods that they shipped to the North came from Kaluga, as the excerpts from the Moscow toll station's records show for 1629 and 1630:

September 26, 1629: A. Zolotov, 26 puds wax (104 rubles).

January 11, 1630: A. Zolotov from Kaluga to Vologda in two sleds, 36 puds wax (140 rubles).

January 31, 1630: A. Zolotov, on 25 sleds, hemp and 6 elk hides.

February 14, 1630: A. Zolotov, on 21 sleds, 220 elk hides, 1,200 goat skins, 194 puds wax (1,800 rubles).

February 17, 1630: 33 carts of hemp.

March 1, 1630: A. Zolotov, 8 carts of hemp.

March 2, 1630: A. Zolotov, 14 carts of hemp, and on 3 sleds, 70½ puds wax. Wax worth 280 rubles.

March 7, 1630: on 2 sleds, 150 puds wax, 24 elk hides (460 rubles). In Moscow 28 elk hides were sold from the sleds.

April 19, 1630: A. Zolotov in a boat declared 37 puds wax and 6 elk hides (170 rubles).

May 16, 1630: Pantelei Zolotov, in four carts, 100 puds wax (400 rubles).

May 29, 1630: A. Zolotov, on three carts, 49 carts wax (200 rubles). In the fall of 1629 the elder Zolotov was selling English cloth in Moscow, and in January 1630 shipped herring to Kaluga.[4]

However, Zolotov was not simply an intermediary between Archangel and Kaluga: Nizhnii Novgorod was also part of his commercial network. In January 1630, he shipped 300 sturgeons from Nizhnii Novgorod to Kaluga. Even more extensive were his shipments of salt from Nizhnii Novgorod to Kaluga. In March 1626, A. Zolotov together with the Kaluga merchant Ivan Petrov declared 13,999 puds of salt (from the lower Volga) in Kaluga, valued at 1,594 rubles.[5] In August 1630, Pantelei Zolotov declared in Kaluga 3,904 puds of salt worth 494 rubles, 21 altyn, 2 dengi. Apparently the 14,000 puds of salt brought to Kaluga in 1626 were bought in Nizhnii Novgorod from the Stupins (Yaroslavl merchants) in 1624. Sometime between 1626 and 1630 Zolotov bought in Kaluga, from the *gost'* Nadeia Sveteshnikov, another 10,000 puds of salt in the name of his mercantile colleague of Kaluga, Ivan Petrov Kuchin, and his son Sofronii. Zolotov's name did not appear in the Kaluga toll books, and apparently Zolotov was keeping this purchase secret for some reason.[6] Perhaps Kuchin, as a native of Kaluga, paid lower taxes on his purchases, or perhaps Zolotov was really smuggling this salt into Poland-Lithuania, as was claimed in the suit brought against him. (Although Poland-Lithuania as a whole was well supplied with salt, Belorussia was not, and there was a considerable border trade in Russian salt.)

Aleksei Zolotov was a merchant of considerable wealth, as the sketch above suggests. Also revealing is the yearly value of the goods he sold at Archangel, personally, through his son, and through his slave Vasilii Larionov:

1629	6,206 rubles
1630	9,900 rubles
1631	6,376 rubles

Source: TsGADA, fund 210, no. 37,
part 1, pp. 190–5, 201.

This scale of operations is only slightly smaller than the dealings of the *gost'* Grigorii Nikitnikov at Archangel in the years 1626–31, so that the elder Zolotov must have been one of the richest merchants in Moscow. This fact did not prevent his conviction in the smuggling case, however, and among other things it was shown that Zolotov had secured for one of his relatives the position of farmer of the tavern and tolls in Meshchevsk, at that time on the Lithuanian border, so as to allow him to trade across the border unobserved and untaxed by the government. In January 1633, he was banished to Siberia, but very quickly allowed to return; evidently he reestablished his economic position because his agents were trading in the North in 1635–6, and his sons continued to prosper.[7]

Zolotov and his family's activities do not allow us to solve the problem of the relationship to the internal market entirely. It is clear that the center of Zolotov's purchases of hemp, wax, and other Russian products for the export market was Kaluga and not Moscow. Undoubtedly Ivan Petrov Kuchin, his "junior partner," did most of the actual buying around Kaluga, but whether in the Kaluga market or from peasants cannot be known. Zolotov did not entrust this buying to him entirely because his son Pantelei and even Zolotov himself on occasion seem to have been in Kaluga. The strategic importance of salt in Zolotov's dealings is quite evident. His purchases of hemp and wax in Kaluga were financed by sales of salt. Given this orientation, it is clear that for Zolotov the crux of his dealings was this exchange in Kaluga, and the shipment of the hemp and wax to the Dutch and English merchants at Archangel. (In Siberia he used his clerk; in Kaluga he used his sons.) Zolotov thus had a sort of "triangular trade": He sold hemp and wax to the Dutch for the money to buy the salt in Moscow, Nizhnii Novgorod, or Kaluga, and then sold the salt to buy hemp and wax. From the point of view of both Kaluga and the salt trade, the Moscow merchant in the person of Aleksei Zolotov and his family was a vital link. Without being a "monopolist" (about twenty merchants sold salt in Kaluga) or even a *gost'*, Zolotov played an important role in the development of a provincial market.

An attempt to determine if the pattern of Aleksei Zolotov's transactions is typical is severely hampered by the lack of sufficient information for the early years of the seventeenth century. With few exceptions, series of toll books start after 1650, and the majority of those are from the North and Siberia. Thus it is virtually impossible to give an account of the relations of Moscow with such towns as Yaroslavl or Suzdal' before the very end of the seventeenth century. Nevertheless, some approximation to a picture of the situation can be made.

For the Northwest, we have the evidence of Tikhvin since 1629 and Pskov in the 1650s. The origin of merchants from outside of Tikhvin itself is reflected in Table 7.1, which shows that over 50 percent of the merchants coming to Tikhvin each year were from Novgorod or the towns of the western part of the Russian North. The large town in the Tikhvin market was clearly Novgorod, not Moscow or Yaroslavl. The role of Moscow was in fact quite minor, even if it is kept in mind that merchants who came all the way from Moscow to Tikhvin must have been fairly wealthy and thus their share of the market may have been somewhat larger than the 1-2 percent of their share in the number of merchants. Tikhvin was largely a center for the distribution of the products of the peasant metal working of the northwest of Russia (Ustiuzhna Zhelezopol'skaia, Karelia), and to a lesser extent a place where the goods imported from Sweden (copper, higher-quality iron) could be purchased by the artisans of the Northwest. Moscow's needs for iron were largely supplied by Tula and the northern iron-working areas stretching to the east from Beloozero, so that it is logical to expect little activity by merchants from Moscow. It is important to note, however, that in Pskov in the 1670s the figures were not much different: Moscow had only 1.25 percent of the transactions, although the Central Russian area as a whole was better represented. Yaroslavl, Moscow, Uglich, Ostashkov, and Rzhev together accounted for about one-third of the trade at Pskov.[8] In general, the impression is created by such evidence, sparse as it is, that the connection between the regional markets of Central Russia and the Northwest (including Karelia) was made by merchants from the North-

Table 7.1. *Origin of out-of-town merchants in Tikhvin, 1629–54*

	1629		1637	
	Number	%	Number	%
Novgorod	86	35.0	57	30.0
Ustiuzhna Zhelezopol'skaia	28	11.0	37	19.5
Ladoga	52	25.0	16	8.5
Yaroslavl	11	4.4	13	7.0
Moscow	5	2.0	7	3.7
Total	248		190	

	1648		1654	
	Number	%	Number	%
Novgorod	90	33.0	69	20.0
Olonets	0	—	56	16.0
Ustiuzhna Zhelezopol'skaia	38	14.0	39	11.0
Ladoga	13	5.0	26	7.5
Yaroslavl	29	11.0	36	10.0
Kostroma	14	5.0	18	5.0
Moscow	4	1.5	4	1.1
Total	269		349	

Note: Only the largest groups are given.
Source: Serbina, *Tikhvinskii posad*, pp. 195–6.

west. For example, Serbina was able to trace a number of families of
blacksmith-merchants from Ustiuzhna Zhelezopol'skaia who became merchants by shipping iron to Tikhvin and Moscow (not to Novgorod).[9]
Thus, the Northwest constituted not only a regional market, but a regional merchant class, based in several different towns and cities.

In the case of Central Russia (the *Zamoskovnyi krai*), there are only
general considerations to back up the case that Moscow exerted a dominant influence. The most important is the very high proportion of Moscow
merchants from towns in this district, as indicated in Chapter 1. In
particular, Yaroslavl was the birthplace of practically all of the richest
Moscow merchants: Grigorii Nikitnikov, Nadeia Sveteshnikov, Nazar
Chistoi. The exports by Moscow merchants (at least of the richest, such as
Zolotov and Nikitnikov) at Archangel were the result of the stock raising,
leather working, and hemp growing of the rural areas of Central Russia.
Other than these products, the Moscow merchants traded mainly in furs
and salt, so that their livelihood was dependent on their ability to acquire a
good proportion of the produce of Central Russia.

Closely related to the regional market of Central Russia in this period
was the market of the gradually expanding southern steppe. It should be
remembered that during this period the southern border was still thinly
populated and not self-sufficient, even in grain. The Don cossacks had to
import grain from the north even in the second half of the seventeenth
century, as well as the products of leather working. This fact may come as
a surprise, given the possibilities of trade with the Nogais and the nature
of the terrain, but throughout the seventeenth century, the Don cossacks
imported even *iuft'* and calfskin from Central Russia, mainly from
Moscow or Voronezh merchants. (The cossacks shipped north the skins of
elks, aurochs, goats, beavers, otters, and horses, but not cattle.) Obviously, the Don cossacks did not exploit the economic possibilities of the
region.[10]

Farther north than the Don, the steppe was still dependent on Central
Russia. For example, in the Belgorod district, the town of Belgorod in
1626 had only 884 households.[11] Clearly the steppe had to be supplied
from farther north, and not solely by shipments of grain to the soldiers as
part of their salary. In this situation the fragmentary evidence for Voronezh is significant. In December to February 1623-4 (winter was a very
active trading season), of ninety two deals by merchants (including peasants) the largest numbers by town were:

Elets	14	*Source:* E. V. Chistiakova,
Voronezh (district)	11	"Remeslo i torgovlia na
Voronezh (town)	7	Voronezhskom posade v seredine
Moscow	7	XVII v.," *Trudy Voronezhskogo*
		gosudarstvennogo universiteta 25
		(Leningrad, 1954): 55.

Because most of the sales by peasants from the Voronezh district and a large part of the sales by merchants from Elets (a more settled agricultural region) were probably food, the presence of the Muscovites is significant. They sold metalwares, weapons, cloth, silk, leather, furs, soap, paper, and *moskatel'nyi tovar* (general merchandise) in Voronezh, and thus were the main suppliers of the town with the products of Central Russia and the West, along with the merchants of Voronezh itself. An important supplier of food in this area by the 1640s, if not earlier, was the Ukraine, still part of the Polish Commonwealth.

The towns of Kasimov (1650s) and Belev (1660s–1670s) provide a somewhat different example from Voronezh, and deserve to be considered although there is no information from before 1650. Both of these towns even in the early seventeenth century were not really border towns in any sense because the rural areas around them had been fairly well settled in the last years of the previous century. Kasimov had been founded on the middle Oka River as the center of the autonomous Tatar khanate of Kasimov in about 1450, and many of the local gentry were still Tatars, although the autonomy was only a formality. Around 1650 the town had only some 300 households, making it quite a small town. The toll records of 1654–5 recorded only one Moscow merchant, the member of the *gost'* hundred, Semen Cherkasov. Significantly, his business in Kasimov was selling salt. Together with the clerks of D. M. Stroganov, Cherkasov sold over 75 percent of the salt sold in the town, and this salt trade made up about a third of the whole trade of Kasimov.[12] Salt was an important item on the northern fringe of the steppe because the vast, open areas between settlements supported many cattle whose meat had to be salted. Cherkasov was a natural supplier because he owned important salt works in Solikamsk.[13] The trend in the trade in salt to the steppe is revealed by the market of Belev. This was also a secondary town because it was close to Kaluga on the Oka and Briansk, site of the Svinsk fair. Furthermore, its earlier role as the gateway to the steppe had been replaced by Orel after 1650. In particular, the most important market for the exchange of steppe grain for salt had shifted to Orel. Belev's merchants, however, did not languish: In the years 1664–79 salt was sold in the town mainly by local merchants, who had from 20 to 50 percent of the trade depending on the year. The role of Moscow in the Belev market was quite modest: Its merchants' trade ranges in importance from none to 4.2 percent.[14] The merchants of Belev, in contrast to those of Kasimov, were no longer dependent on the great merchants of Moscow for the most basic commodities, and by 1710 the Belev merchants ranked thirtieth in value of goods sold at Archangel, practically all of their wares being hemp or hemp products.[15]

As the examples of the Don, Voronezh, and Kasimov show, Moscow merchants played an important role in the steppe and the towns of the Oka basin just to the north of the steppe. This role was founded on the supply of food to newly colonized territories and on the supply of salt to the saltless areas to the south of Moscow. However, the merchants of the smaller steppe towns like Belev became important in their own right in the second half of the century, controlling the markets of their native towns and trading in Archangel.

No important town appeared in the entire district between Moscow and Voronezh, and even Voronezh did not become a large town until after 1800. No southern Yaroslavl appeared in the south before 1800 who could act as a rival to the Moscow merchants.

The North

The Russian North reached the apogee of its economic (and cultural) importance to Russia in the seventeenth century, for the seventeenth century saw the high point of several types of trade vital to the survival of the North. The most ancient was furs. The most valuable types, such as sable, were already extinct in most of the North, except in a few remote river valleys. However, throughout the century the North was the route to Siberia, where the hunting of sables flourished, so that the North kept its traditional role in the fur trade. The presence of Archangel, and its increasing importance, helped to keep the fur trade in the northern towns, because of the proximity to the mouth of the Dvina. The Archangel trade also stimulated the commerce of all the northern towns, especially those such as Ustiug Velikii that lay along the river route from Vologda to Archangel. Finally, almost all the smaller towns (Tot'ma, Sol' Vychegodsk) and the shore of the White Sea were rich in salt, which was another important item of northern commerce. Because the problem of salt production and trade will be considered separately, the main problem to be considered here is the fur trade and the role of the Moscow merchants in that trade.

The history of the fur trade inside Russia is the story of the gradual shift of the main centers from the North to Siberia, and then farther and farther east in Siberia. In the period 1580–1650, the northern town of Sol' Vychegodsk was still one of the main places where merchants from Moscow and other towns outside the fur-producing areas bought furs. (The other centers were in Siberia by this time, Tobol'sk and Mangazeia being the major ones.) Consequently, an analysis of the fur trade at Sol' Vychegodsk has considerable importance in determining the significance of Moscow in the internal market of Russia, and especially in the buying up of exportable commodities.

The fur trade in Sol' Vychegodsk was discussed in some detail by I. S. Makarov in 1945, using the whole series of toll books for that town from 1625 to 1679. In addition, the publication of the toll books by Iakovlev includes two of the toll books of the first half of the century (one is not for the full year). Makarov found that the 1640s were the high point of the fur trade at Sol' Vychegodsk (measured in ruble value of furs). The role of Moscow was characterized by Makarov in the following terms:

> Already in the 20s and the 30s the Moscow merchants dominated the market. In the 40s, in the time of the highest peak of the fur trade in Sol' Vychegodsk, the Muscovites stood ahead of the representatives of other cities not only relatively, but absolutely. By the 60s and 70s, when the trade in furs sharply fell, the stream of provincial merchants almost stopped completely, and there were years when only Muscovites were buying furs.[16]

This conclusion is borne out by Table 7.2. Thus, Makarov's conclusion that Moscow merchants dominated the trade in furs at Sol' Vychegodsk can be accepted as valid. Of the twenty-one Muscovites trading at the town in 1634–5, there was only one *gost'* and only two merchants that can definitely be identified as being in the *gost'* hundred.[17] Those merchants of the twenty-one who purchased more than 100 rubles worth of furs are listed in Table 7.3. Of the twenty-one Moscow merchants, thirteen merchants (two with partners) accounted for 3,994 rubles, or 90 percent of the total of 4,464 rubles spent by Muscovites at Sol' Vychegodsk. Sveteshnikov and Pankrat'ev by themselves accounted for 1,140 rubles or about 25 percent of the trade of all Muscovites. The other eleven merchants accounted for only about 65 percent of the trade of Muscovites at the town that year. Consequently, it can be said that the trade at Sol'

Table 7.2. *Sol' Vychegodsk fur trade*
(values are in rubles spent on fur trade surchases)

Year	Moscow	Yaroslavl	Vologda	Ustiug	Total
1625–6	1,255	0	360	0	1,615
%	77.0	—	23.0	—	
1634–5[a]	4,464	830	1,408	810	7,512
%	46.5	8.6	14.6	8.5	
1635[a]	4,450	1,416	280	30	6,439
%	70.0	22.0	4.4	0.5	
1638–9	6,317	1,656	814	613	9,500
%	66.5	17.5	8.5	6.5	
1640–1	11,472	1,497	1,555	400	15,779
%	72.7	9.5	10.0	2.5	
1642–3	15,906	290	920	0	19,256
%	82.6	1.5	4.8	—	
1643–4	14,850	1,050	1,896	1,200	22,010
%	67.5	4.5	8.6	5.5	
1644–5	10,840	500	2,650	3,720	20,390
%	53.2	2.5	13.0	18.0	
1646–7	8,945	0	115	0	11,329½
%	79.0	—	1.0	—	
1647–8	24,990	1,120	800	1,898	32,118
%	77.8	3.5	2.5	6.0	
1648–9	8,759	2,852	2,750	130	16,241
%	53.9	17.5	17.0	0.8	
1651–2	10,666	3,350	3,770	1,050	21,908
%	48.7	15.0	17.0	4.8	

Note: Minor towns are omitted.

[a] The figures for 1634–5 and 1635 have been recalculated and substituted for Makarov's figures, on the basis of the published toll books for those years. The recalculation reveals that although Makarov's results are on the whole accurate (within four percentage points in the case of the proportion of Muscovite trade), they are somewhat arbitrary. The problem is that they are based on the declarations of cash held by a given merchant when he came to Sol' Vychegodsk. In some cases, the book states that the cash was "na sobol'nuiu pokupku" and in some cases says nothing about the use intended for the cash. However, it is obvious from the records of the same books, that practically all merchants not from the town itself were there to buy furs. (The number of salt purchases was one or two, and in both cases for less than 100 rubles.) Clearly, when a Moscow merchant declared 600 or 700 rubles, all or most of it was going to buy furs. Moreover, salt was more likely to be carefully noted because the tax was higher. The logical way to deal with the source would be either to exclude all nonspecified declarations of cash, or include them all as furs, given the nature of trade in Sol' Vychegodsk. Makarov did neither, and arbitrarily included some nonspecified declarations of cash as intended for furs. In recalculating, I have included all cash specified for furs and all cash not specified for a given commodity. In the case of Moscow, where the number of merchants and the sums involved were large, this makes little difference. The same is probably true for Yaroslavl and the total of

Vychegodsk was relatively concentrated in the hands of Muscovites as opposed to merchants from other towns, and that among the Muscovites the *gosti* and merchants of the *gost'* hundred were the largest traders. Nevertheless, about 65 percent of the furs were purchased by what might be called the middle group of Moscow merchants, who were not *gosti* or even in the *gost'* hundred, but who were also operating on a fairly large scale. That some of these "middle rank" merchants must have had fairly large-scale operations can be judged also from the fact that four of them were represented by agents, as were Pankrat'ev and Sveteshnikov.

Because the figures for 1635 are incomplete, any conclusions drawn from them must necessarily be more tentative. Of the 4,450 rubles spent on furs, the *gost'* hundred merchant Bogdan Filat'ev accounted for 1,100 rubles (25 percent). However a partnership of two other Moscow merchants of ordinary rank, M. Sergeev and I. Ivanov, accounted for 1,300 rubles, or 29 percent of the total, so that it was not only the *gosti* who had large-scale dealings. In general, the distribution in 1635 is about the same as in the previous year.[18]

The problem of the participation of the merchants of Moscow in the fur trade will be continued in connection with the activities of Muscovites in Siberia, but for tbe present a few words should be said about the Muscovites in the market of Ustiug Velikii, who are the subject of the well-known monograph of Tikhonov and Merzon. Both authors were more interested in the Ustiug market from the bottom rather than from the top, and thus devoted a great deal of attention to the "trading peasants" from Vetluga who supplied the town with grain, and little attention to the Muscovite merchants and their dealings. In general, however, they did

---

Notes to Table 7.2 (*cont.*)

the money spent on furs in a year. In the case of minor towns, where the sums are small and few merchants came to Sol' Vychegodsk, the results are necessarily more uncertain. For the sake of comparison, Makarov's figures are reproduced below, with the minor towns of the north and center, and Kazan (which did not appear in most years) omitted:

Fur Trade in Sol' Vychegodsk 1634–5 and 1635:

Year	Moscow	Yaroslavl	Vologda	Ustiug	Total
1634–5	2,954	1,330	1,340	388	7,971
%	37.0				
1635	3,960	1,106	230	0	5,296
%	74.7				

Source: Makarov, "Pushnoi rynok," p. 164. Makarov gave percentages only for Moscow. It should be noted that the records for 1635 are incomplete because they cover only Sept. 1–Dec. 1, 1635. However, well over half of the fur trade had been completed by the end of December because the autumn was the period of intense fur trading in Sol' Vychegodsk.

find that Ustiug was for the Muscovites largely a secondary market for ikons, leather, and other manufactured goods of the Central Russian towns, and was also a fur market, although unimportant in comparison with Sol' Vychegodsk. In view of this fact, we shall merely present the size of the total transactions of Muscovite merchants, comparing them with Vologda, Yaroslavl and the *gost'* hundred merchants of Ustiug itself (the Bosois, Reviakins, and Usovs):

Towns	1633–4	1635–6
Moscow	723	1,839
Vologda	2,673	2,582
Yaroslavl	1,577	3,501
Gost' hundred of Ustiug Velikii	4,930	3,857½

Source: A. I. Iakovlev, ed. *Tamozhennye knigi* ɪ, pp. 312–32, 383–92; Merzon and Tikhonov *Rynok*, p. 330.

Moscow was clearly a poor fourth in the market of Ustiug Velikii, compared with Vologda or Yaroslavl. The leading merchants in the town were the three families of the *gost'* hundred who, although they were in theory members of the Moscow *gost'* hundred, continued to live in Ustiug and keep the base of their operations there. Of course, if they were counted as Muscovites (and they usually declared themselves as such to the customs

Table 7.3. *Muscovites as Sol' Vychegodsk, 1634–5 (fur purchases in rubles)*

Nadeia Sveteshnikov (*gost'*)[a]	640
Ignatii Pankrat'ev (*gost'* hundred)[a]	500
Bogdan Filat'ev (*gost'* hundred)[a]	50
Aleksei Markelov (with 3 partners)	300
Matvei Sverchkov	160
Mikhail Evdokimov (with 1 partner)	400
Ivan Fillipov[a]	400
Zakhar Leont'ev	314
Mikhail Sergeev	320
Grigorii Oblezov[a]	320
Vasilii Dmitr'ev[a]	320
Semen Ivanov	120
Ivan Tomilov	200

[a] Actual purchase made by clerk or slave.
Source: A. I. Iakovlev, ed. *Tamozhennye knigi*, vol. 1, pp. 312–32.

officials in other towns, e.g. Archangel), Moscow would stand first in the Ustiug market. However, they were a special case, and the customs officials in Ustiug gave them a separate charter of their records, apart from both the *"ustiuzhane"* and merchants from towns other than Ustiug (this section included *gosti* not from Ustiug). Ustiug may thus be considered an exceptional case because Moscow merchants undoubtedly had great difficulty competing with rivals who both stood first in Ustiug and were members of the Moscow *gost'* hundred with all the access to Moscow markets that such membership entailed.[19]

Siberia

Siberia was only added to the possessions of the Russian state beginning in 1581, when the cossack Ermak and his band defeated the last of the Tatar khanates that formed the remnants of the Golden Horde. By 1700 Russian rule stretched to the Pacific Ocean and the Amur River, so that the history of seventeenth-century Siberia is in large part the history of this Russian expansion to the East. The Russians inherited from the Siberian Tatars the suzerainty over most of Western Siberia, that is, the valleys of the Ob' and its tributary, the Irtysh. As the century advanced they moved east, occupying enormous but thinly populated territories, and building a chain of small forts along the main river valleys. Settlement by Russian peasants began very early in the century, but it was not widespread and was confined to certain river valleys on the eastern slopes of the Urals. Farther to the east, the numerous native populations remained, becoming subject to a small and thinly spread Russian administration, which relied on tiny units of cossacks and musketeers for its strength. Until the 1680s (when the trade with China began), the value of this huge acquisition lay almost entirely in the furs of the sables, foxes, and other fur-bearing animals that abounded in the vast Siberian taiga.[20]

The small numbers of Russian settlers and the great distance from European Russia gave Siberian life a quality distinct from that west of the Urals, and required the administrative structure of the state to conform to some extent to local conditions. Siberia was subject to a separate administrative office, the Siberian Office (*Sibirskii prikaz*), but this separate office had not been created in 1581. Originally, Siberia was administered by the Foreign Office, followed by the Novgorod Quarter, then the Kazan Palace. In 1637 the Siberian Office was formed from a subdepartment of the Kazan Palace. The Siberian Office was one of the most important

Russian offices, and also one whose records have been very well preserved and catalogued. As a result, it is possible to obtain information about Siberia of a kind that is difficult or impossible to obtain about European Russia.[21]

Everywhere in Russia the chief administrative officer of a district was known as a *voevoda*, who was a nobleman of appropriate rank. The distinct feature of Siberia was the enormously greater power of the *voevoda*, owing both to the great distance from Moscow and his long term (about four years). Until the 1620s, all of the collections of taxes, including that of the tolls, was in the hands of the *voevodas*, in contrast to the system of elected townsmen described in Chapter 1. The power of the *voevoda* also derived from the absence of any other social or political force. Although Siberia's Russian population consisted in large part of black land peasants, the system of local self-administration found in the Russian North did not exist. Because there were no gentry landowners, there were no *gubnye starosty*, the local judges elected by the gentry to try criminal cases. Even the church lacked wealthy and powerful institutions like the great monasteries of the North. The *voevoda* had virtually a free rein over the native population and the Russian settler alike.[22]

One new force in the Siberian administration was introduced in the 1620s, when the collection of tolls (but not, apparently, tavern revenues) was taken out of the hands of the *voevodas* and handed over to elected toll chiefs and their assistants. Normally the assistants were elected from among the merchants of the nascent Siberian towns, but the chiefs were elected in the towns of the Russian North and then confirmed and sent out by the Siberian Office. Occasionally merchants from Moscow fulfilled this task, but more often northerners. The toll system administered by these northern merchants differed fundamentally from that in practice in European Russia. The tolls in Siberia were not paid in money but in furs, and in the most valuable fur, the sable. This was greatly to the advantage of the treasury because the furs were worth much more when they were brought to Moscow and sold. Furthermore, the rate was much higher than in European Russia: 10 percent. This was 10 percent of the value of the furs in a given transaction, extracted in the form of sables to that value. Goods imported from European Russia were also taxed at the 10 percent rate. Other goods were taxed at the rate of 5 percent of the value, a bit higher than the Russian norm.[23]

The importance of the Siberian toll system was very great – greater than was assumed by the older Russian historiography. Lantzeff and Fisher, following this tradition, conclude that the greater portion of the state's income in Siberia came from the *iasak*, the tribute paid in sables by the native populations. This conclusion was inevitable because little investigation was made of the abundant Siberian toll records until the 1950s. The results of these investigations prove that the great majority of the state's income did not come from the *iasak* alone, but about equally from the 10 percent toll extracted from Russian fur merchants and the *iasak*. It was only in the 1680s, when the depletion of the Siberian furs became serious, that the *iasak* began to supply the state with the overwhelming majority of its furs. As the fur trade declined, it became more and more a state enterprise based entirely on the *iasak* collections.

Fisher and the older Russian writers on Siberia stressed the fact that the state had the largest single supply of sables under its control, and therefore was the largest "businessman" in Siberia. This fact is undoubtedly true, in the sense that no one merchant or group of merchants shipped as many sables to European Russia as the treasury. However, the aggregate shipment of the merchants from Siberia was far greater. In 1627, about 72,000–92,000 rubles worth of furs were shipped from Siberia to European Russia, about 12,000 rubles worth were collected as tolls, and about the same or slightly more (18,000 rubles) were collected as *iasak*. This means that the state had in its control 30,000 rubles worth of furs, and the merchants two to three times that amount. In 1631, 115,000 to 131,000 rubles worth of furs were shipped west by merchants, and 18,000 rubles worth were collected in tolls. Added to 24,000 rubles worth of *iasak*, the state could command 42,000 rubles worth, and the merchants two to three times that amount. However, the amount of furs shipped west by the merchants is certainly too low. The *iasak* system was relatively easy to organize: The natives were simply told to supply a certain number of furs at a certain place once a year, so that even small *iasak* collections worth a few hundred rubles are recorded. To collect all the tolls legally due the state along the thousands of miles of the rivers and pathways of Siberia was another matter, and the number of merchants who got back to European Russia without paying a single kopeck can only be guessed.[24]

The uncertainty in the results caused by the relative simplicity of toll evasion in Siberia must be kept in mind in all discussions of Siberian trade. Nevertheless, this factor does not invalidate the conclusions that can be drawn from the existing work based on the Siberian toll records. In recent Soviet writing on trade in Siberia two opinions have been put forward on the role of the merchants. V. A. Aleksandrov, following Bakhrushin, asserted that a small group of *gosti* and members of the *gost'* hundred were the leaders in the fur trade, and also in the actual hunting of the fur-bearing animals.[25] O. N. Vilkov, however, denies that the *gosti* were the dominant force in trade because the nonprivileged merchants of European Russia bought the overwhelming mass of Siberian fur.[26] In this controversy, Aleksandrov would appear to have the better data because his article is based on the fur trade at Mangazeia, which (at least to 1650) accounted for the lion's share of the trade in Siberian furs. However, his use of the data is inferior to that of Pavlov, Vilkov, and Kopylov because the latter attempt to arrive at a global picture of the trade in each town that they discuss, whereas Aleksandrov's methods are merely illustrative. When he asserts that "large" purchases accounted for 152 of 307 forties of sable sold at Mangazeia in 1653, he does not explain his definition of "large," and it is clear that he has not proven his point.[27]

Aleksandrov also fails to make his point with his own statistics, that merchants had the leading role in the hunting of fur-bearing animals. It is certainly true that the great merchants of Moscow and Ustiug Velikii did organize on the basis of *pokruta* (a combination of wages and loan of equipment and money), expeditions of hunters (fifteen to twenty men, for the most part) in various parts of Siberia. Among others, the *gost'* Nadeia Sveteshnikov took part in the organization of such expeditions.[28] However, Aleksandrov himself gives figures for Eniseisk in 1630 and 1631 that tell the opposite (hunters is a translation of *promyshlenniki*; sables are in forties):

	1630			*1631*		
	sables		*men*	*sables*		*men*
Hunters	490	(78%)	c. 400	517	(66%)	c. 400
Merchants	89	(14%)	8	204	(26%)	13
Pokruchenniks	37	(6%)	88	35	(4.5%)	61
Total	625		c. 500	788		c. 500

Source: Aleksandrov, "Rol' krupnogo kupechestva," p. 178.

These figures, which represent the number of animal skins brought to Eniseisk and sold there (and who sold them), show that all of the merchants, from whatever part of Russia, and of whatever degree of wealth, had a very modest place in the total product of the year's hunt in Eniseisk, and probably in all of Siberia. The merchants bought furs from the hunters rather than organizing the hunts themselves.

On the question of trade, we must accept the conclusion of Vilkov and Kopylov: The leading role was played by the merchants of European

Russia, from the very beginning of the records of trade in Siberia (1626) to the end of the century. As we shall now see, the first place among those merchants was held by the Muscovites, although not necessarily only by the *gosti* or other very wealthy merchants. Fairly detailed work has been done on the trade at three cities: Mangazeia, Eniseisk, and Tobol'sk. Of these three, Mangazeia was before 1650 the place where the greatest volume of furs was traded in all of Siberia. In 1627–8 Surgut and Berezov were the second and third largest depots, but by 1631–2 the center of the fur trade outside of Mangazeia had shifted to Eniseisk. Whereas the trade at Surgut and Berezov has not been studied, that of Eniseisk has been analyzed by Kopylov. Tobol'sk, by contrast, although an important administrative center and close to the emerging grain-producing areas in Western Siberia, was a relatively unimportant trading center, ranking, out of fifteen towns, eleventh (1627–8) and tenth (1631–2).[29] Thus, some element of uncertainty remains in our findings because the most important centers (Mangazeia, Berezov, Surgut) have not been as well studied as the others.

The importance of Mangazeia in the early period of Siberian colonization was based on two factors. One was that the historic trade route into Siberia was much farther north than the route used by peasant settlers (and later merchants). This route ran up the Vychegda (hence the importance of Sol' Vychegodsk) to the Urals and across to the Northern Sos'va, and thence by way of Berezov to the Ob'. The merchant then turned south, going up the Ob' to Surgut, or turned north, going down the Ob' to its estuary, and then turning south up the Taz to Mangazeia. This route had been used long before any part of Siberia was Russian, because the main areas supplying furs were in the northern part of Western Siberia. As this area was gradually hunted out in the first half of the seventeenth century, the center of gravity of the fur trade shifted south and east, as the Baikal region and even Dauria (the transbaikal region) became the main centers of the hunting of sable. Thus the main route to Siberia shifted south to the Kama River–Verkhotur'e–Turinsk–Tiumen'–Tobol'sk route, especially because the settlers came by this route, which was more convenient to the Tiumen'–Tobol'sk area where they settled. Finally, the Kama–Chusovaia–Irbit route became important at the very end of the century, and with the founding of Ekaterinburg in 1721 and the growth of the Irbit fair, it became the main route from European Russia to Siberia, and remained so until modern times. The towns along the older routes, Verkhotur'e and Mangazeia, fell into decline. Indeed, Mangazeia was abandoned in 1670–72 for Turukhansk, a hundred miles or so to the east, on the Enisei. This geographic and commercial change explains the shifting fortunes of the Siberian towns in the early centuries of Russian settlement.

Because Mangazeia was the most important of the centers of the fur trade until 1650, it should be considered first. In 1627–8 this town accounted for 85.5 percent of the fur sent to Russia, and in 1631–2 it accounted for 76.2 percent. In these years the total value of furs shipped west from Siberia was 72–90,000 rubles and 115–131,000 rubles, respectively.[30] (These values are local Siberian prices.) Table 7.4 shows Pavlov's yearly estimate of the value of furs declared for shipment west, based on the revenue of the toll collectors (one-tenth of the value of the furs, taken in sables of equivalent value). The trend is clear: a sharp rise to the end of the 1630s, followed by an equally sharp drop by the 1650s, and by the end of the century Mangazeia ceases to exist.

The role of the Muscovites in Mangazeia varied from year to year, but some idea can be obtained from Table 7.5, also from Pavlov's calculations. But first of all the role of the merchants in the fur trade must be made

Table 7.4. *Fur trade at Mangazeia, 1624–57*

Year	Value of furs in rubles (Siberian prices)
1624	33,000
1626	63,200
1627	63,700
1628	62,500
1629	57,800
1630	47,800
1631	27,700
1632	42,500
1633	55,700
1634	61,600
1636	104,200
1637	91,600
1642	79,000
1656	29,400
1657	29,300

Source: P. N. Pavlov, "Vyvoz pushniny iz Sibiri v XVII v.," *Sibir' XVII–XVIII vv.*, Sibir' perioda feodalizma 1 (Novosibirsk, 1962), p. 128.

clear. The great majority of the sables declared in Mangazeia were declared by hunters who had come there from the Russian North (the production of the native population was absorbed by the *iasak*), not by merchants or by Russian hunters settled in any part of Siberia. This fact is illustrated by the year 1642, when of the 62,882 sables declared, 51,141 (81 percent) were declared by hunters, 8,135 (13 percent) by merchants, 683 (1.1 percent) by *sluzhilie liudi* (officials and soldiers), and 2,923 (4.6 percent) by others.[31] Thus Aleksandrov's contention that the merchants played the leading role in the trade and hunting of furs in Mangazeia is clearly wrong, and it is for this reason that Sol' Vychegodsk remained such an important center of the fur trade as long as it lasted: The hunters brought the furs over the Urals themselves. For the years from 1642 on it is possible to identify the place of origin of the merchants and to thus determine the place of the Muscovites among them (minor towns are omitted in Table 7.5).

It is evident that Moscow played an important and perhaps leading role among merchants in Mangazeia. However, it was certainly not a large enterprise, as the number of Muscovite merchants at Mangazeia in those years was: 1642, nine; 1648, three; 1654, two; 1647, one. In 1642, an unusually good year for the Muscovites at Mangazeia, they declared 80 percent of the sables declared by merchants, but this was in turn only 13 percent of the sables declared that year. Clearly, both the merchants as a

Table 7.5. *Origin of merchants at Mangazeia, 1642–57 (values are number of sables declared)*

Town	1642	%	1648[a]	%	1654[a]	%	1657	%
Moscow	6,497	80	1,758	24	1,307	12	1,800	27
Yaroslavl	0	0	0	0	1,337	12	1,347	20
Sol' Vychegodsk	0	0	363	0.5	170	1.5	150	2
Ustiug	108	1	383	0.5	673	6	1,016	15
Kazan	1,530	19	779	1	1,880	17	0	0
Others	0	0	4,162	74	5,761	51.5	1,376	36

[a]In 1648, one merchant from Kineshma declared 1,544 sables, or 21 percent. No merchants from Kineshma appeared in any other year. Also, an unusually large proportion of the merchants' place of origin was not indicated (2,422 sables, or 33 percent). In 1654 Tobol'sk, which like Kineshma appeared only in this year, accounted for 2,318 sables, or 21 percent, and Kholmogory, an unusual place of origin, for 1,306 sables, or 12 percent.
Source: Pavlov, "Uchastie," p. 34.

whole, and the Muscovites in particular acted mainly as buyers of the furs, and buyers who rarely ventured into Siberia itself at that.

None of the historians who have dealt with the trade at Mangazeia completely identify the particular Muscovites who traded there. Aleksandrov cites only the *gost'* V. Fedotov-Gusel'nikov (Skoraia Zapis'), who declared 2,240 sables in the Mangazeia district in 1653, and 920 in 1656. The *gost'* A. Almazov, by contrast, declared only 240 sables in 1656. No other Muscovites appear in his lists of the merchants with the largest dealings, but there may have been other Muscovite merchants with smaller dealings. Pavlov gives only similar examples. The *gost'* Nadeia Sveteshnikov registered in Mangazeia the following numbers of sables: 1629, 368; 1630, 1,220; and in 1636 in the Mangazeia, Eniseisk, and Iakutsk districts, 6,151 sables. The *gost'* Vasilii Shorin together with Semen Zadorin (*gost'* hundred) declared 810 sables in 1648, and 2,820 in 1659.[32] Considering the very small number of merchants from Moscow at Mangazeia, it is very difficult to draw any conclusions. In 1648, Shorin and Zadorin accounted for 46 percent of the total purchases by merchants from Moscow, but such an isolated example does not allow one to make many generalizations. Still, if there are at least four *gosti* in a period in which four of the years produced a total of fifteen merchants from Moscow, then the importance of the Moscow *gosti* at Mangazeia was considerable. If one keeps in mind the importance of the Bosoi-Reviakin group of Ustiug *gosti*, then the role of the *gosti* as a group at Mangazeia was considerable, among the few merchants who did manage to send agents that far into the Siberian hinterland. However, as we have seen, merchants did not play an important role at Mangazeia, where the hunters from the Russian North controlled the supply of furs.

At Eniseisk, which was an increasingly important center of the fur trade after about 1630, the situation was quite different. In 1642, the hunters declared 14,467 sables, or only 40 percent of the total of 36,360. The merchants accounted for 15,285 sables, or 42 percent, and the *sluzhilie liudi*, the officials and soldiers, for 4,868 sables, or 13 percent. In 1647, of 36,030 sables declared in the Eniseisk district, the hunters declared 18,036, or 50 percent, the merchants declared 13,360, or 37 percent, and the *sluzhilie liudi* declared 2,517, or 7 percent. Furthermore, the sables declared by the merchants were over 95 percent the result of purchase rather than of their own organizations of hunters. (At Mangazeia, some merchants organized their own hunts with *pokruchenniki*.)[33] Therefore, at Eniseisk the merchants played a far more important role than at Mangazeia; so much more so that the number of sables declared at Eniseisk by all merchants is on the average more than twice the number declared by all merchants at Mangazeia, even though Mangazeia was at that time by far the most important center of the fur trade. Table 7.6 shows Kopylov's breakdown of the various towns for the year 1645–6 in Eniseisk (smaller towns have been omitted). Moscow stands definitely in first place among the other towns in Table 7.6, although not by very much. The four most important towns together only accounted for 65 percent of the trade of Eniseisk, and the other 35 percent was spread among twenty other towns and districts. The reason for Moscow's supremacy is made clearer by a look at the makeup of the 16,503.09 rubles of trade. Of this, 10,811.64 rubles was the value of the "Russian goods" brought to Eniseisk from European Russia, which makes 34 percent of the total value of Russian goods (32,065.00 rubles). Of the 4,329 rubles in cash brought to Eniseisk, Muscovites accounted for 2,850 rubles, or 66 percent. In contrast, Muscovites brought back from Eniseisk only 2,841.45 rubles worth of furs, or 15 percent of the total (18,810.00 rubles). Consequently, the importance of Moscow was not nearly as great in the fur trade as in the shipping to Siberia of the products of European Russia and Western Europe, and in the supplying of Siberia with currency.[34] It is in this respect interesting that the Muscovites brought exactly as much currency as they bought furs, which was not true of the other groups who brought coins (Yaroslavl,

Table 7.6. *Trade of Eniseisk with European Russia, 1645–6*

Town	Rubles	%
Moscow	16,503.09	30.0
Ustiug	11,326.03	20.5
Sol' Vychegodsk	4,992.15	9.0
Yaroslavl	3,279.40	6.0
Peasants	2,828.50	5.0
Vaga area	2,429.02	4.4
Lal'sk	1,436.65	2.6
Pezhemskaia *volost'*[a]	1,166.16	2.3
Total	55,304.00	

[a]One of the so-called Ust'ianskie volosti near Ustiug Velikii.
Source: Kopylov, *Russkie na Enisee*, p. 244.

for example). Many of the smaller towns and districts (fourteen of them, to be exact), did not bring any Russian goods to the Eniseisk market, and simply bought furs to take to some point along the route to European Russia. Moscow's ascendancy in the Eniseisk market was in large part due to its ability to supply Siberia with the necessary products from the markets of Central Russia.

Kopylov has also given us the names, listed in Table 7.7, of the Moscow merchants who traded in Eniseisk in 1645–6. In this year the fur trade was much more concentrated than the trade in Russian goods. Chanchikov contributed 43 percent of the furs shipped west from Eniseisk, whereas the largest importers of Russian goods, Shorin and the combination of Balezin and Chanchikov, each contributed about 35 percent. However, it is difficult to generalize from one year about the nature of the Muscovites' trade because we have only seven merchants to deal with.

Finally, the case of trade at Tobol'sk is necessary to round out the picture. Tobol'sk was not a town of great importance in the fur trade, although furs were bought there; rather it was with Tiumen' one of the centers of Russian colonization in Siberia, and for this reason is important to Siberian historians. Vilkov's extremely detailed account of the trade at Tobol'sk presents a somewhat different picture from Eniseisk as is clear from the sales of Russian goods in the town. In Tobol'sk, unlike Eniseisk, the chief sellers of Russian goods were the merchants of Ustiug Velikii and Kazan. In 1639–40, out of 34,935 rubles worth of such goods, the following percentages were sold by merchants of the various towns: Ustiug Velikii, 35 percent; Kazan, 23.9 percent; Viatka land, 14 percent; Sol-

Table 7.7. *Muscovites in Eniseisk, 1645–6*

Merchant	Russian goods	Currency	Furs
Gost' V. Shorin	3,821.70	1,700	513
Gost' hundred:			
B. Balezin			612.50
S. Chanchikov	3,830.77	1,250	1,210.50
I. Usov (Grudtsyn)	1,335.12	655.70	66
I. Zerkal'nikov	673	0	0
Woolen drapers' hundred:			
D. Kurilov	1,158.77	0	0
S. Gneznikov (?)	0	0	439.45

Source: Kopylov, *Russkie na Enisee*, p. 244, note 2.

ikamsk, 8 percent; Sol' Vychegodsk, 7 percent; Moscow 2.7 percent. Data for later years show the same approximate trend, with Moscow playing a relatively unimportant role. It is also revealing that whereas Ustiug was represented by nineteen parties of merchants and Kazan by twelve, only seven parties of Moscow merchants came to Tobol'sk in 1639-40.[35]

In the fur trade, Moscow had the same modest role because in 1639-40 Moscow merchants traded only slightly less than 5 percent of the furs traded at Tobol'sk. The largest fur traders in Tobol'sk were the merchants of Tobol'sk itself (a sharp contrast to Eniseisk), because they accounted for 29 percent of the fur trade. Ustiug Velikii came first among the cities of European Russia, with 10 percent, followed by Viatka (7.7 percent) and Kazan (7 percent).[36]

Taking Siberia as a whole, a contrast can be seen. At markets like Mangazeia or Eniseisk, where the fur trade was concentrated, the Muscovites stood first among the merchants, perhaps partly because of their superior ability to supply Siberia with needed products, or because of their greater resources of capital and numerous clerks. In a town like Tobol'sk, it is evident that the towns with which trade was most active were the main towns from which the settlers of Siberia were drawn: the Russian North, and the Kama river valley. Trade seems to have followed colonization. In Mangazeia, where trade was longer established, but few settlers were attracted, Moscow was more important than any single northern town, although the North as a whole had an edge over the Muscovites. However, the most striking fact is the secondary role played by all Russian merchants in the Siberian fur trade until the 1650s, compared with the role of the hunters from the villages and towns of the Russian North. Furthermore, the number of Moscow merchants who were involved in the fur trade east of the Urals was quite restricted. At any given Siberian town in any given year, the number of Moscow merchants rarely exceeded a dozen, and was usually closer to half a dozen. Fewer still maintained continuous operations in Siberia. Compared with the eighty or so Moscow merchants going to Archangel each year, this number is small indeed. For the Moscow merchants, the fur trade was an affair almost entirely confined to a few towns in the Russian North.

The role of the internal market

Any conclusion about the role of the internal Russian market in making the fortunes of the Moscow merchants is seriously hampered by the extremely uneven distribution of the available data. Whereas the exact share of Moscow merchants in the trade of secondary centers in the North and Siberia can be determined, little can be said about the relations of Muscovites with Yaroslavl or Nizhnii Novgorod, to say nothing of Moscow's agricultural hinterland in central Russia. Consequently, the conclusions must be rather tentative. One clear result of the latest research on Siberia and the analysis made here of the fur trade in Sol' Vychegodsk is that the role of the fur trade must not be exaggerated in the history of Russian trade, and especially not in the history of the Moscow merchants. The fur trade was largely responsible for the great prosperity of the Russian North in the seventeenth century, not only of towns like Ustiug but of hundreds of obscure villages and districts that sent, yearly, a few dozen hunters each to the wilderness of Siberia. Undoubtedly Moscow merchants traded in furs, but furs were not the main products sold to the West. In any case, Moscow merchants bought the furs only after they had been brought out of Siberia. Moscow was vital to the fur trade, but the fur trade was not vital to Moscow. The example of Zolotov's dealings in Kaluga, and what other scraps of information can be collected with reference to Central Russia, suggest that the Muscovites probably had a leading role in the purchase of hemp, wax, leather, and other products of the countryside, in particular for shipment to Archangel. Thus, the role of connecting link between the internal market of the Russian state and the merchants of Holland, England, and Persia was undoubtedly one of the Moscow merchant class's greatest sources of wealth. Another major source was the production and distribution of the one commodity that was needed almost everywhere in Russia, and was neither exported nor imported from abroad – salt. To the vital role of this commodity in the commercial history of the seventeenth century we must now turn.

8

Salt production and the internal market

Discussions of the beginnings of Russian industry in the seventeenth century have concentrated on the history of iron production at Tula and a few other places, and have created two impressions that have persisted in the literature of the period. One is that the metal industries were the most significant of the seventeenth century, and the other is that the foreign merchants and the state played the main role in the development of Russian industry. Such a view was encouraged by the Soviet historian, P. G. Liubomirov, in his account of the early history of Russian industry, if only because for the seventeenth century he dealt only with metal-working industries. When Liubomirov was called upon to give a more general view of the role of merchant capital in the economy of the seventeenth century,[1] he was careful, however, to include the merchants as one of the three groups responsible for early industrial development (with the state and foreigners). E. I. Zaozerskaia, in a recent work, looks mainly for evidence of "manufactures," that is, large-scale (but pre-factory) enterprises, and not surprisingly finds once again that the state, the monasteries, and boyars were the main forces. She also finds that the monasteries and the *gosti* who had "feudal" privileges were the other groups that were important in Russian industry. This general tendency of Russian historiography has also been in large part accepted in the West, where the state and the foreign merchants have been considered the leading forces in Russian industry.[2]

It is not possible within the scope of this chapter to discuss the problem of the development of Russian industry as a whole even for the limited period 1580–1650. Therefore, we will confine ourselves to a few remarks on iron production and then turn to the salt industry. In the literature an unconscious or conscious assumption is made that the iron industry is the standard by which Russian industry of this period should be judged; if iron production was small, primitive, and dominated by foreigners, then this condition must have been typical of all of Russian industry. As will be shown, the iron industry was not necessarily typical. Furthermore, it is not at all certain that the iron industry should even be considered important for the seventeenth century. Here we become entangled in the problem of Russian industrialization, and later developments in the eighteenth century, and with the idea (suggested by Sombart, among others) that the state-run iron industries were an important stage in the process of industrialization and the growth of capitalism. However, in Northern and Eastern Europe in the seventeenth century, the iron industry did not play this role in leading up to industrialization, except perhaps in Sweden. Certainly in the seventeenth century, in most of Eastern Europe, there was a retreat of entrepreneurial and merchant capital from iron production, and the state and the foreign merchants moved in to take their place, as in Russia. In Sweden, the iron industry was dominated by Louis de Geer and other Dutch financiers. In Poland, the small iron producers who had held the field before 1570 were largely replaced by 1650 by Italian merchants who depended on contracts with the Polish artillery works and the army.[3] In the Habsburg lands, the Styrian iron industry became a state enterprise in 1625 and remained so into the eighteenth century.[4] The production of silver, copper, and mercury in the Habsburg territories (Inner Austria and Hungary) passed from local merchants, small producers, and the Fuggers first to Italian subcontractors, and later to the state backed by Dutch and Oppenheimer capital.[5] In other words, Russian iron production was in no way different from that of any other Eastern European state of the seventeenth century. In Russia, as elsewhere, we will not find early or protocapitalism in large-scale enterprises of the iron or other metal industries; rather, we must look for an industry dominated by merchants or by entrepreneurs among the producers, as in the case of the Bohemian-Silesian linen industry of the seventeenth and early eighteenth centuries. In the Russian case, research on the textile industries (other than the palace workshop called *khamovnyi dvor*) has just begun and has not yet investigated the relations of the weavers with merchants.[6] There is, however, considerable research on the salt industry, and some archival evidence of the salt trade for Kaluga and the lower Volga (for the 1620s). This available information provides a view of salt production that is fairly complete, as well as some idea of the salt trade. In particular, it illuminates the role of the Moscow merchants, and suggests that it is the salt industry, rather than the iron industry, to which historians should turn their attention.

The earliest information about trade in salt is a list of merchants trading in salt at Kaluga in 1628, giving only names and places of origin. Table 8.1 gives no indication of the quantities of salt traded, although at least in the case of the Stroganovs they were undoubtedly large. Kaluga was one of the places where the Volga and Kama (Stroganov) salt was transferred from boats to carts to be shipped to Moscow and to the steppe region. The significance of this list lies in the hint it provides about the way merchants entered into investments in salt and the way they became *gosti*. Both of the Murom merchants, Tsvetnoi and Venevitinov later became *gosti*, and in the 1630s and 1640s invested in salt works, Tsvetnoi in Solikamsk and Venevitinov in Staraia Russa. When they made these investments, they were already Moscow *gosti*. Clearly there was a certain diversion of profits made by trading in salt to salt extraction, a process in which Moscow played a crucial role. Another provincial merchant who seems to have

Table 8.1. *Merchants trading in salt at Kaluga, 1628*

Maksim, Ivan, and Petr Stroganov
gost' Nadeia Sveteshnikov
gost' Tretiak Sudovshchikov
Nizhnii Novgorod:
    Stepan Alekseev, Dmitrii Pankrat'ev, Maksim Sherepkin
Kolomna:
    Mikhail Volkov
Murom:
    Bogdam Tsvetnoi, Fedor Venevitinov
Moscow:
    Leontii Andreev, Denis Mikulin, Iakim Patokin, Ivan Sinii, Aleksei
    Zolotov (*kadashevets*)
Kashira:
    Demid Kirillov
Soligalich:
    Stepan Grigor'ev
Kaluga:
    Zhdan Alfer'ev, Efrem Klimov, Stepan Mikhailov, Nikon Iakovlev, Sila
    Koptev, Ivan Petrov Kuchin (with Zolotov)

Source: TsGADA, fund 210, no. 37, part 1, pp. 221–2.

become a *gost'* through the salt trade is Tret'iak Sudovshchikov. His place in the list of merchants seems to imply that, although a *gost'*, he was really from Kaluga ("koluzhan . . . gostiakh Tret'iaka Sudovshchikova," whereas Sveteshnikov was listed at the beginning after the Stroganovs). In the *Utverzhennaia gramota* for the election of Mikhail Romanov as Tsar (1613) Kaluga sent a "vyboronoi chelovek Smirnoi Sudovshchikov," who turned up in Archangel in 1630 as a Muscovite.[7] Iakim Patokin invested in Solikamsk as a merchant of Nizhnii Novgorod before 1628. Thus, Moscow seems to have absorbed the most prominent traders in salt from Murom, Kolomna, and Kaluga, as well as such prominent Yaroslavl salt traders as Sveteshnikov, a fact that indicates the importance of the trade in salt before the 1630s, when the investments in salt works of these same men and other Muscovites began. It is to these investments that we must now turn.

In the Russia of the seventeenth century there were several great salt producing regions: The Perm' district centered in Solikamsk, the lower Volga, the North, the various towns of the center, such as Balakhna, and finally, Staraia Russa. Our knowledge of these districts is quite uneven, being particularly limited in the case of Balakhna. By and large it may be said that two groups dominated the salt industry: the merchants and the monasteries. The state and the boyars and gentry played a very minor role, if any at all. The role of these two groups was quite different in the various regions. Generally, the monasteries may be said to have played a minor role everywhere except in the North, where their role was undoubtedly great, although how great is very difficult to assess. The literature of Russian economic history tends to assert that virtually all salt production in the North was monastic, but because only monastic salt production has been extensively studied, the argument is circular. Savich and other writers on the sixteenth century repeatedly refer to peasant salt boiling, if only to indicate where the monasteries purchased their salt works. However, the extent of peasant salt boiling (especially for the seventeenth century) has never been examined, so that it must be said that the predominance of monastic salt boiling in the North, however likely, rests on pure assertion. Finally, the monasteries faced a serious challenge after 1650 in the salt-producing enterprises of the Pankrat'ev family.

With this limitation in mind, we shall examine the extent of the salt production and trade in the North. The most convenient index of the size of salt production is the number of salt boilers or *varnitsy* in each place where the work was done. The technology of salt boiling in the seventeenth century was generally uniform,[8] and the productivity was dependent on the strength of the *rassol*, or salt water from the ground. A pipe or a salt boiler was a considerable investment for the time, especially because it could take several years of drilling to sink a pipe to the proper level, and there was always the possibility that it could turn out to be dry.[9] This fact meant that in peasant or small merchant salt boiling, several men would own shares in one pipe or salt boiler, often with rather complicated systems of sharing and inheritance. In the North it was probably the case, as is usually asserted, that the Solovetskii monastery was the most important of the monasteries engaged in the sale and production of salt at least outside the cities. In 1590 the monastery possessed twenty-six salt pans, which means (at one pan to the boiler) twenty-six salt boilers, in various places in the North. Many of them were along the coast of the White Sea, and thus had a very high salt content to the *rassol*. In 1639 the monastery owned twenty-eight boilers, and by the end of the 1660s it had increased the number to fifty-four.[10] In contrast, the Spaso-Prilutskii monastery (near Vologda) had in 1612–13 in Tot'ma four boilers, in Una (on the White Sea) two, and in Sol' Vychegodsk one operating and two not operating, a total of seven functioning boilers. By mid-century the monastery had in Tot'ma still only four, in Una three, in Sol' Vychegodsk two, making a total of nine. By the end of the century there were in Tot'ma seven, in Una four, and in Sol' Vychegodsk still two, making in all thirteen.[11] Clearly the Spaso-Prilutskii monastery was a much smaller salt producer, and as a result put much of its capital into trading in salt produced by others, mostly at the mouth of the Northern Dvina.

The well-preserved account books of the two monasteries allow us to present in Table 8.2 exact figures for the salt sold at Vologda, the main market for northern salt. The great drop in sales in 1646–8 was the result of the tax policies of the Morozov government in the early years of the reign of Aleksei Mikhailovich in which two grivnas per ruble tax on salt was collected. After the recovery in 1649–50, sales remained at this level until 1690.

The Spaso-Prilutskii monastery's sales of salt in Vologda are shown in Table 8.3 (a large proportion of which was not produced by the monastery but rather bought in Kholmogory and shipped to Vologda). Once again, the great drop in sales in 1647 is the result of Morozov's salt tax.

These figures not only provide information on the two monasteries, but also give a standard of comparison for other producers and dealers in salt. As we shall see, whereas the Solovetskii monastery certainly sold amounts of salt that could be described as large, the Spaso-Prilutskii monastery must be described as a rather middling trader in salt; its sales in Vologda were only about a third larger than Aleksei Zolotov's sales in Kaluga in the same period (1620s), and Zolotov was certainly not an important salt merchant on the national scale.[12] We have no reason to think that the other monasteries that were involved in salt production and sales in the North (Antoniev-Siiskii, Nikola-Korel'skii, and others) were not of roughly the same importance as the Spaso-Prilutskii monastery in salt production and trade.

Some other indications of the size of the salt industry and the partici-pants in it are given by Zaozerskaia for the Nenoksa *volost'* near the mouth of the Northern Dvina, Tot'ma and Sol' Vychegodsk. Zaozerskaia is an adherent of the view that the monasteries were the only significant group in the northern salt industry, but the data she presents do not wholly back up her view. For the majority of the northern *pogosty* and *volosti* where salt was produced she merely gives an account of the development of monastic landholding in the sixteenth century, leaving the reader with the idea that

Table 8.2. *Sales of salt by Solovetskii monastery at Vologda*

Decade (averages)	Puds salt	Money received (in rubles)
1580s (five years)	62,217	5,335
1590s (three years)	91,907	5,155
1601–9 (nine years)	97,191	7,104
1617–20 (four years)	78,526	8,952
1621–30 (ten years)	92,692	8,784
1631–40 (ten years)	105,228	11,177
By years:		
1641	119,879	13,567
1642	139,959	20,457
1643	131,410	15,175
1644	125,056	14,793
1645	126,194	12,930
1646	94,437	10,005
1647	2,277	649
1648	1,909	550
1649	146,808	15,846
1650	127,917	12,700

Source: Savich, *Solovetskaia*, pp. 147–9, note 2.

by 1600 all northern salt was produced by monasteries. However, when she gives complete data, it does not support her contention. The *volost'* of Nenoksa was one of the main centers of the salt industry along the coast of the White Sea. In 1552-3 there were fifteen salt boilers. Two belonged to monasteries (Nikola-Karel'skii and Arkhangel'skii na Dvine) and the other thirteen were split up among more than forty-four owners, with shares being owned by monasteries, local townsmen, peasants (the majority), and some owners from Beloozero, Kholmogory, and Moscow.[13] This is the first case yet known of Muscovites owning shares in salt works. However, the merchants who in the seventeenth century had shares in the Nenoksa industry were all northerners: from Vologda, Ustiug Velikii (Timofei Usov, of the *gost'* hundred family, but firmly anchored in Ustiug), and the Pinega district. By 1586-7 there were only thirteen salt boilers, and in 1621-4 only twelve. Of these, four were entirely owned by four different monasteries, and the other eight were owned in shares. Of the shares, 52.4 percent were in the hands of monasteries, and 20.6 percent in the hands of merchants from outside the *volost'*. Twenty-seven percent were in the hands of local men.[14] Thus, some 70 percent of the salt works in Nenoksa were in the hands of the monasteries, which of course supports Zaozerskaia's conclusion. What is at issue, however, is not the great role of the monasteries in the North, at least in rural districts, but an accurate assessment of the extent of that role. Nenoksa was in the heart of districts

Table 8.3. *Sales of salt by the Spaso-Prilutskii monastery at Vologda*

Decade (averages)	Puds salt	Price (in rubles)
1603-9 (six years)	21,078	1,755
1624-30 (six years)	22,786	2,067
1631-40 (ten years)	25,287	2,707
By years:		
1641	24,178	2,734
1642	14,659	2,194
1643	21,654	2,739
1644	28,701	3,606
1646	22,534	2,497
1647	3,755	1,086
1650	28,494	2,812

Source: Prokof'eva, *Votchinnoe*, Table V, pp. 197-8.

of monastic landholding, near Archangel and the White Sea, and it is only to be expected that the monasteries played the major role. In this regard it is striking that in the 1640s the *gost'* hundred merchant Vasilii Usov (of Ustiug) still had substantial holdings in Nenoksa (worth 1,500 rubles), which he left to the Anton'ev–Siiskii monastery.[15] This fact suggests that merchant investment in the northern salt industry was more stable than Zaozerskaia is willing to admit, especially because she did not extend her study beyond the 1620s. The Solovetskii monastery increased its holdings in Nenoksa from shares equal to one *tsren* or salt boiling pan (equal roughly to one *varnitsa*) in the 1590s, to two in the 1620s, to two and two-thirds in the 1660s, of which, however, only one and a half still worked at the end of the century.[16] This does not appear as a massive increase, and indeed, the great period of acquisition of land and other property by the Russian monasteries was the sixteenth century; in the seventeenth century the process dropped off, and continued only for specially favored monasteries (like Troitse-Sergeev or Solovetskii). It would be surprising if the seventeenth century saw a great increase in the buying up of rural salt works in the North. We should instead conclude that the predominance of the monasteries over the merchants, which prevailed in the 1620s, lasted to about 1670. After 1670, the Pankrat'ev enterprise shifted the balance in rural areas again in favor of the merchants, as we shall see.

If we turn to the towns of the North we find a different situation from that of the rural districts like Nenoksa. None of the northern towns were as rich in salt as the country districts along the White Sea, but some of them, mainly Tot'ma and Sol' Vychegodsk were, in the sixteenth century, important centers of salt production. It is not unlikely that before about 1570, when the monasteries began to take the leading role in the northern salt industry, and the first important wells were beginning to produce in Solikamsk, that Sol' Vychegodsk and Tot'ma produced the greater proportion of the salt in the Russian North. It is surely not without significance that the Stroganov family came from Sol' Vychegodsk and built there the original family stronghold.

Tot'ma was one of the oldest centers of salt production in the North, having apparently flourished in the early sixteenth century.[17] The number of salt boilers and their owners in the first half of the seventeenth century are listed in Table 8.4. The monasteries are the Spaso-Prilutskii monastery, and also the Nikola-Ugreshskii monastery (near Moscow), which had four and two salt boilers, respectively, in 1619 and 1620. The four boilers of the Spaso-Prilutskii monastery had been its property since at least 1568 (the monastery was founded only in 1554).[18] Much more important for us is the presence of six boilers owned by merchants from outside of Tot'ma. These merchants were members of the families of the Moscow *gosti* Grudtsyn (the branch of the Ustiug Velikii Usovs that settled in Moscow), the Gusel'nikovs (or Fedotov-Gusel'nikovs, also originally from Ustiug Velikii), and the Bulgakovs, an old Moscow merchant family. By the end of the seventeenth century the Moscow merchants controlled 67 percent of the salt works in Tot'ma.[19]

The situation in Sol' Vychegodsk was completely different because it was the stronghold of the Stroganovs, descendants of Anika Fedorov Stroganov (1497–1570). The town itself was apparently founded only after about 1450, and the Stroganovs lived there, it seems, from very early in the town's history. There is some evidence that the Stroganovs came from the *dvinskie boiare*, a theory which Vvedenskii rejects, but which seems likely in view of the large number of merchants from the Dvina district who came from that class.[20] Anika started his career, as far as it can be traced, in 1526, with the purchase of two salt boilers in the town, and by his death he had accumulated ten.[21] By the end of the sixteenth century the family had accumulated fourteen. In 1625, however, the family had only six, whereas the Spaso-Prilutskii monastery had two, which it had acquired in the sixteenth century. Three salt boilers belonged to townsmen of Sol' Vychegodsk. In contrast to Tot'ma, the Sol' Vychegodsk salt industry went into a deep decline by the 1640s: In 1644–5 only two Stroganov salt boilers and the two belonging to the Spaso-Prilutskii monastery remained, of the nine that had been in operation in 1625.[22] Here, the Moscow merchants had no role.

Table 8.4. *Operating salt-boilers in Tot'ma, 1600–50*

Owners	1619–20	1623–5	1646
Townsmen of Tot'ma	5	8	11
Monasteries	7	8	10
Stroganovs	4	2	0
Townsmen of other towns	0	0	6
Total	16	18	27

Source: Zaozerskaia, *U istokov*, p. 164.

Finally there is one more important example of Muscovites playing an important role in the salt industry of the North – the Pankrat'ev enterprise in Seregova in the Iarensk district. The founder of this salt works was Grigorii Grigor'ev Pankrat'ev, originally from Soligalich, who by 1630 was trading in Archangel as a Muscovite.[23] Pankrat'ev started the works in 1637, but it took a long time to get started because there was only one salt boiler by 1646. It was not until the time of Grigorii Pankrat'ev's grandson, Ivan Danilovich, in the last quarter of the seventeenth century, that it became an important enterprise, having six salt boilers in 1678 and thirteen by the end of the century, with a yearly productivity of nearly 300,000 puds.[24] The founder of the salt works, Grigorii, was one of the small number of merchants to enter the state administration, as an official of the Treasury Office from 1648 to 1662.[25] Apparently the Pankrat'evs broke their ties with Soligalich, for in 1628 they did not appear among the owners of salt wells and boilers in that town.[26] By the end of the century the Pankrat'evs produced three times as much salt as the Solovetskii monastery, and thus ended the predominance of the monasteries in northern salt production.

During the seventeenth century, however, the North no longer was the main center of Russian salt production. The main centers were the Perm' area and Solikamsk, the lower Volga and perhaps Balakhna. Solikamsk is usually associated with the Stroganovs. Indeed they were among the first to develop the area and were by far the largest investors there, having not only wells and boilers but large tracts of land provided by the state, which supplied them with the wood for their furnaces. However, the Stroganovs did not actually invest in the town of Solikamsk, but rather concentrated their vast holdings to the south of the town along the river Chusovaia. As we shall see, however, in the period 1630–50 the Moscow merchants were almost as important as the Stroganovs. In Solikamsk the industry was derived by the census takers into five "articles," the first being the most valuable and the fifth the least valuable. The census of 1623–4 revealed the pattern of ownership in the town and district of Solikamsk, where the Stroganovs did not operate. In the Solikamsk district there were only two salt boilers, on the river Zyrianka, which both belonged to the Moscow merchant of the palace settlement, Bol'shie Luzhniki, Bogdan Ivanov Levashev.[27] In the town in the same year there were thirty-five boilers, distributed thus:

First article: nine boilers, none owned by Muscovites, one owned by Ivan Anofreev of Solikamsk, later in the *gost'* hundred.

Second article: nine boilers, two owned by the Nizhnii Novgorod merchant Iakim Sergeev Patokin (in Kaluga 1628 listed as a Muscovite, and later in the *gost'* hundred). The Muscovite Grigorii Cheboksarets had a share in one boiler with two men of Solikamsk.

Third article: six boilers, two owned jointly by the Moscow *gosti* Ivan and Vasilii Ivanov Iur'ev, one by the Muscovite (*gost'* hundred) Maksim Iakovlev Doshchanikov.

Fourth article: eight boilers, two of them jointly owned by the Muscovite Anikei Grigor'ev Tsybin (later *gost'* hundred) and Ermolai Posel'skii of Solikamsk.

Fifth article: two boilers, none owned by Muscovites. One boiler was not placed in an article, as it was too small.[28]

Although the Muscovites had no boilers of the first article, their importance is made clear by two facts. One is that only four cases existed of two boilers being in the same hands. Two of these cases were those of complete ownership by Muscovites (Levashev on the Zyrianka and the Iur'evs), one was a partnership including a Muscovite (Tsybin), and the last was Patokin's property. Thus, Muscovites were involved in all cases of larger property. Patokin paid the highest tax of all the owners (six rubles per year).[29] The second important fact is that the Muscovites formed the great majority of the merchants from outside Solikamsk; the only other non-Muscovite besides Patokin being Petr Merkur'ev of Nizhnii Novgorod, who had a share in the smallest, "nonarticled" boiler.

In the Solikamsk area Muscovite investments continued to expand. In 1632 the *gost'* Grigorii Nikitnikov bought the two boilers on the Zyrianka from Levashev, and by 1637–8 he already had thirteen boilers. In 1635, when the town burnt down, eighteen of the town boilers were destroyed and seventeen survived. Of these, four were the property of Gerasim and Ivan Cherkasov (*gost'* hundred, Moscow), one of Bogdan Tsvetnoi (*gost'* hundred, Moscow), one of the *gost'* Nadeia Sveteshnikov, one of the *gost'* Vasilii Iur'ev, and two of Izmailo Dubenskii (*gost'* hundred, Moscow). That is, eight of thirty-five boilers were now owned by Muscovites, and the only other outsider to the town was the *okol'nichii* Vasilii Ivanovich Streshnev.[30] By 1644–5, after rebuilding and more fires, twenty-seven boilers remained. Among the Muscovites, Sveteshnikov, Iur'ev, and Dubenskii had dropped out, so that the Cherkasov brothers owned five, Tsvetnoi three, and Klement Iakimov Patokin, the son of Iakim, two. Moscow thus had ten of the remaining twenty-seven boilers, the townsmen of Solikamsk had twelve, Streshnev had three, and the Voznesenskii monastery (of Solikamsk) had two. (The number of boilers owned by monasteries never exceeded two; there was only one in 1623-4 and one in 1635.)[31]

By 1649 the Muscovites were still expanding their investments, and owned a total of thirteen boilers: Tsvetnoi still had three, the Cherkasovs now had six, Sveteshnikov's son Semen had rebuilt two, and Izmailo Dubenskii had rebuilt his two. Nikitnikov still owned thirteen boilers on the Zyrianka. Hence, all of the increase in the number of boilers in the town since the fires was due to expansion by Muscovites, and the total of boilers in the town had reached thirty-two. If the possessions of Muscovites on the Zyrianka and the town are added together, the Muscovites possessed twenty-six of the fifty-three boilers in the district, about half. The Solikamsk district was thus effectively dominated by Moscow merchants by mid-century.[32]

The second half of the seventeenth century is, of course, beyond our scope, but it is not irrelevant to follow the fortunes of the area down to the Stroganov takeover of the 1690s. In the town of Solikamsk, there was a great expansion of production, and by the 1680s Muscovites owned nineteen of the fifty-eight boilers in the town. Six were owned by the Sokolov brothers of Balakhna, the Muscovites' most effective rival in the town. On the Zyrianka the situation was more complicated. In the 1640s, the Pyskorskii monastery had expanded an enterprise consisting of one boiler in 1623-4, to eight boilers. In the 1650s the treasury confiscated five of these for nonpayment of taxes, and at the same time inherited the Nikitnikov interests when the plague of 1654 left the family without heirs. The result of these events was a state salt enterprise which grew to forty boilers by the 1680s. Significantly, Moscow merchants were normally sent to administer it. On another nearby river, the Lenva, Muscovite merchants started a wholly new enterprise after the 1650s, which by the 1680s comprised twenty boilers owned by the Moscow *gost'* families Filat'ev and Shustov.[33]

During all this time the Stroganovs were active to the south of the Solikamsk district on the river Chusovaia and other areas of their vast holdings. In 1579 they had fourteen salt boilers, in the 1620s only fifteen, by 1646-7 thirty-one. That is, in the 1640s their holdings were only slightly larger than those of the Moscow merchants taken as a group. In the second half of the century they also expanded their holdings, and Grigorii Stroganov (the richest) had seventy-eight in the 1680s. The Stroganovs really became the masters of the Urals salt industry in the

1690s, when they started a suit against the Filat'evs and Shustovs claiming that the Lenva was their land. They won the suit, and by 1700 the Stroganovs had a total of 162 boilers and were the masters of the Urals. (It should be noted that the Filat'ev-Shustov group had done the same thing to the Sokolov brothers some fifteen years before.)[34] Finally, for the 1680s Ustiugov was able to make a rough estimate of the productivity of the Urals industry. He estimated the yearly production at about 7,000,000 puds, of that about 2,000,000 coming from the river Lenva.[35] These figures are surely a bit high because he estimates that the yearly production of one boiler is 18,000 to 30,000 puds, which gives a maximum of 1,300,000 puds for the Lenva. Earlier in the century (1615) the Stroganovs sold some 333,000 puds when they had fifteen boilers, which gives an average of 20,000 puds yearly per boiler.[36] If we take the lower figure for safety, then in the 1640s when there were eighty-four boilers in the Urals, the area produced about 1,680,000 puds of salt, or approximately fifteen times the yearly sales of the Solovetskii monastery in Vologda. Clearly, by this time, the monasteries were not the leading force in the Russian salt industry.

The state of the whole Urals salt industry in the 1640s and its later evolution are made clearer by Table 8.5 showing the ownership of salt boilers in the Urals, derived from Ustiugov's work. The share of the Moscow merchants fell from about 31 percent in the 1640s to about 19 percent in the 1680s, but they still were the second largest group in the Urals, after the Stroganov family. The only other merchant groups, those of Balakhna (six boilers) and of Solikamsk (at least thirteen boilers but no more than thirty-three) were considerably behind the Muscovites. Although the Stroganovs were beginning to pull ahead, they did not hold virtual monopolies until the 1690s. Only then did the Moscow merchants disappear from the Urals salt industry.

Besides the salt industry of the Urals, the other great salt industry of seventeenth-century Russia was that of the salt marshes of the lower Volga. This industry was distinct from the other salt industries of Russia in two respects, the technological and the legal. Technologically the main distinction was that the salt around Astrakhan was to be found not in underground salt water springs but in salt marshes and lakes, with a very high salt content, so that it was only necessary to let the salt water dry out in the sun to get at the salt. Obviously, this procedure was both cheaper and more certain than sinking a well. However, it then had to be transported north a very great distance over a route that was by no means safe because the boats were always open to attack from the Nogais, Tatars, or Russian cossacks. The other distinct feature (the legal) was that the Volga salt works were the property of the state, and were run as such, with *vernye tseloval'niki* from at least 1614 until the 1620s, when they were farmed out to merchants along with the fisheries. After the 1670s, some of the salt works and fisheries reverted to direct exploitation by the state. Besides the merchants and the state, a number of monasteries in Astrakhan and the Sviiazhsk Bogoroditskii monastery had the right to extract salt and trade in fish, but this monastery trade amounted to only 11 percent of the whole salt trade in 1624 and 15 percent in 1674.[37]

Table 8.5. *Ownership of salt works in the Urals, various years*

Years and owners	Number of boilers	Percentage
1644–5 and 1649		
Nikitnikov (Muscovite)	13	15.5
Moscow merchants	13	15.5
Total Moscow	26	31.0
Merchants of Solikamsk and other towns	14	16.5
Boyar Streshnev and the Voznesenskii monastery	5	6.0
Stroganovs	31	37.0
Pyskorskii monastery	8	9.5
Total	84	100
1680s		
Moscow merchants (on the Lenva River)	20	
Moscow merchants (in Solikamsk)	19	
Total Moscow	39	19.0
Other merchants	19	9.0
Unknown	20	10.0
Stroganovs	78	38.0
Treasury	34	16.0
Monasteries	17	8.0
Total	207	100

Note: Most of the owners in the "unknown" category were probably merchants of Solikamsk. The Stroganov holdings were somewhat larger, as some smaller holdings were not counted.
Source: Ustiugov, *Solevarennaia*, pp. 63–5,75–7, 138–41.

Consequently, between the 1620s and the 1670s the monasteries and merchants of various towns were the only people involved in the salt trade. The role of Moscow merchants is not absolutely clear. Stepanov maintains that they played a major role both in the fisheries and the salt industry.[38] It is true that the only two Muscovites to trade in salt in 1622–3 were *gosti*, G. Nikitnikov and N. Sveteshnikov, but it is not at all clear that they played a major role in the salt trade. In 1622–3, twenty-one merchants shipped salt north from Astrakhan and the breakdown of their share in the trade is shown in Table 8.6. Of those merchants who shipped over 10,000 puds, the specific shipments are: Timofei Stupin (Yaroslavl), 85,000; A. M. Gorokhov (Vladimir), 60,000; Bogdan Tsvetnoi (Murom) and Petr Volkov (Kolomna), 73,685; Luka Markov (Nizhnii Novgorod), 36,125; *gost'* Nadeia Sveteshnikov (Moscow), 28,500; and Gurii (the brother of Druzhina) Nazar'ev (Yaroslavl), 17,000. The *gost'* Grigorii Nikitnikov shipped only 1,000 puds of salt, so it is clear that the participation of the *gosti* in the Astrakhan salt trade was quite modest (9 percent).[39] Of the other large-scale salt traders, only Nazar'ev of Yaroslavl (Nazarii Chistoi's son?) had any possible connections with Moscow or *gosti*. Bogdan Tsevtnoi of Murom later became a member of the *gost'* hundred, and his associate Petr Volkov of Kolomna is certainly a relative (the brother?) of the Mikhail Volkov of Kolomna who traded in salt at Kaluga in 1628, and later entered the *gost'* hundred in Moscow. On the other hand, Stu-

Table 8.6. *Salt trade in Astraktan, 1622–3*

Town	Number of merchants	Puds salt	Percent
Moscow	2	29,500	9.0
Nizhnii Novgorod	7	51,245	15.3
Yaroslavl	2	102,000	30.0
Murom/Kolomna	3	78,685	23.5
Vladimir	1	60,000	18.0
Iurevets	1	3,805	1.1
Tetiushi	1	3,000	0.9
Pavlovo (peasant)	1	2,900	0.9
Kazan	2	2,200	0.7
Sviiazhsk	1	2,000	0.6
Total	21	334,835	

Source: LOII, fund 178.

pin, Gorokhov, and Markov apparently stayed in their respective towns and did not move to Moscow or become *gosti*. Thus, we must conclude that the Moscow *gosti* were involved in the salt trade of Astrakhan, but not nearly to the extent that Stepanov imagined. Even if all the merchants who farmed fisheries for the treasury were indeed important salt traders, the list of Muscovites would not expand greatly. Sveteshnikov disappeared from the fisheries some time after 1626, whereas Nikitnikov remained an important figure until at least 1649. Smirnoi Sudovshchikov (a *gost'*) held one fishery in 1626, Nazarii Chistoi (a *gost'*) held one in 1629–34, Iakim Patokin held one in 1628–9, and Vasilii Shorin had several fisheries from 1646 to the 1660s.[40] If we accept Stepanov's assertion that they were all involved in the salt trade, this does not add much because Nikitnikov already was involved in 1622–3.

The only other important salt industry in the Volga area was the *gost'* Nadeia Sveteshnikov's salt works near Samara, described by Bakhrushin. This place, the Nadeino Usol'e, was an entire settlement with a small fortress and Sveteshnikov's private army (with artillery!) to defend the settlement against the nomads. This was a salt works involving salt boilers fed by underground springs, as in the North, and had only six operating boilers in 1646.[41] It was apparently started in 1631, and lasted until Sveteshnikov's death in 1646. His son Semen inherited it then (after some troubles with the treasury over Nadeia's debts) and it stayed in the family until the plague of 1654 killed Semen and all of Nadeia's other direct descendants. In 1659–60 Semen's widowed sister, Antonida, sold it to the treasury (who gave it to the Savvo-Storozhevskii monastery). This was a typical large salt works of the period, similar to Levashev/Nikitnikov's salt works on the river Zyrianka near Solikamsk. In spite of not having (apparently) any share in the salt pans near Astrakhan, Sveteshnikov remained important in the salt trade until his death; he even shipped 50,000 puds of salt from Astrakhan in 1644.[42] Thus, it seems that the role of the Muscovites in the salt trade from Astrakhan, in spite of their importance in the fisheries, was modest. Yaroslavl, Nizhnii Novgorod, Murom, and even Vladimir were more important in the 1620s, and there is no reason to think the situation changed radically, in spite of the evident expansion of Muscovite investment in the 1630s and 1640s. Certainly they did not play the unique role that they played in Solikamsk.

One important region of salt production that stood somewhat apart from the basic Russian salt market was Staraia Russa. Staraia Russa was one of the oldest centers of salt production in Russia. It was already flourishing at the end of the fifteenth century, when the North was just beginning to produce large amounts of salt and Solikamsk was unheard of. It remained an important regional center in the seventeenth century, supplying mainly the Northwest and the Lithuanian border: Pskov, Novgorod, Toropets, and Velikie Luki. This area was the kernel of the town's salt market, and the area to which it was largely restricted in the latter part of the seventeenth century, when the competition of the Urals salt began to hurt the salt production of Staraia Russa. In the first half of the century, salt from Staraia Russa went as far afield as the upper course of the Volga (above Tver'), Mozhaisk, Viaz'ma, and even Moscow on occasion.[43] The size of the production of salt in the town is evident from the figures shown in Table 8.7 (only working salt boilers are included).

The rather violent fluctuations are the result of two different facts. The great drop in salt production in 1625 was the result of the Time of Troubles. There were in 1625 some 180 "empty" salt boilers, practically all of them belonging to townsmen as in the 1607 census.[44] These abandoned salt boilers were extremely important in starting up production again in the 1630s because they were as a rule already in the best locations near the salt pipes. (An example of this fact is the eleven boilers of the Iverskii monastery in 1662, which came from the old state boilers of 1607, granted to the monastery through Nikon's influence, and started up again.) Thus, the fact that most of the Staraia Russa townsmen had held on to the wrecked salt boilers was of considerable significance, and meant that their importance was greater than the four operating boilers owned by townsmen in 1625 would indicate. In the case of the figures of 1662, the small number by comparison with 1607 was the result of a technological

Table 8.7. *Salt boilers in Staraia Russa, various years*

	Owners				
Year	State	Monasteries	Boyars	Townsmen	Total
1607	15	9	—	150	174
1625	1	3	—	4	8
1662	2	13[a]	1[b]	36	52

[a]Of these, eleven belonged to the Iverskii monastery in the Valdai hills, favored by Patriarch Nikon.
[b]I. V. Morozov.
Source: Rabinovich, *Gorod soli*, pp. 28, 34, 67.

change. Generally speaking, most Russian salt works changed little in
their technology in the course of the century. All the changes had taken
place in Perm' and Balakhna at the end of the sixteenth century. In Staraia
Russa, where the process was more conservative, no doubt because of the
greater age of the local industry, the change did not come until the 1630s
when the industry was finally reconstructed from the devastation of the
Time of Troubles. The change involved an increase in the size of the
boiler and the subsidiary buildings and the pan. These changes, together
with the innovation of preheating the salt water, resulted in a considerable
increase in production: One boiling operation took four days (24 hours)
rather than seven to eight and produced twice as much salt in the same
period of time. Roughly speaking, the new system doubled production in
each salt boiler.[45]

The introduction of the new system came at the same time that merchants from outside the town began to invest in Staraia Russa salt production, some from Novgorod, but most from Moscow. In 1625, of the four
boilers owned by townsmen, two were owned by the Novgorod *gost'*
Andrei Kharlamov, the son of Ivan Kharlamov, a merchant of Staraia
Russa. Apparently Andrei had moved to Novgorod during the Time of
Troubles. The process of investment by outsiders in Staraia Russa was far
advanced by 1662. The Venevitinov family, the *gosti* Nikifor and Afanasii
Venevitinov and the merchant of the *gost'* hundred Vasilii Venevitinov
owned all together eleven boilers, and the *gost'* Ivan Buikov owned four.
These were the most important salt producers in the town by 1662 because only the Iverskii monastery had as many as the Venevitinovs. The
eighteen boilers of these prominent Moscow merchants made up half of
the total of thirty-six boilers owned by merchants. The Venevitinovs were
important salt producers and traders throughout Russia; they had traded
at Kaluga in 1628, and were related to the Dubenskii family of Murom
(their own place of origin) who invested in Solikamsk in the 1630s. When
the first Venevitinov (Fedor) invested in Staraia Russa in 1635, he was
working with Sava Dubenskii, his father-in-law. Fedor was the same
Venevitinov who had traded in salt at Kaluga, but by the 1630s he was a
gost' of Moscow. Judging from the case of Izmailo Dubenskii in Solikamsk,
that family had moved to Moscow from Murom along with the Venevitinovs. Ivan Buikov was a Moscow *gost'*, apparently from Vladimir
originally, whereas Smyvalov was certainly descended from an old
Moscow merchant house active in the trade with Poland before 1604, and
later in Archangel (see Chapter 1). These Moscow families remained the

richest merchant group among the salt producers until the end of the century, when the town began to experience serious economic reverses. Besides these Muscovites, there were some Novgorod *gosti* who were important, such as the *gost'* V. Stoianov, who had three salt boilers in 1655, but by 1662 no longer owned any in Staraia Russa. In the 1670s, other Novgorod *gosti*, such as Maksim Voskoboinikov and Semen Gavrilov, began to invest in Staraia Russa.[46] In the 1690s, all of these men experienced difficulties or died, leaving the field to local merchants, who did as well as they could in the declining market that had resulted from heavy competition from the cheaper salt of the lower Volga and Perm'. Rabinovich explains this fact as an example of the "instability" of seventeenth-century Russian merchant houses, but her own account of the crisis of the Staraia Russa industry in the 1690s suggests that the Moscow and Novgorod merchant families were rather cutting their losses in an investment that could no longer yield any profit.[47]

Finally, something should be said about the salt industry of Central Russia. The whole importance of the salt trade in Russia was based on the geological fact that most of the rich sources of salt were far from the centers of population, but the central regions of Russia were not wholly bereft of sources of salt. There were a number of minor sources (of one or two boilers each) in a large number of towns of Central Russia that apparently had played an important role in the fourteenth and fifteenth centuries, but later declined in importance with the appearance of the Perm salt. Some of these places were Pereiaslavl' Zalesskii, Suzdal', the lower Uvod River near Vladimir, and Galich.[48] None of these centers were very important, however, and most ceased to even exist by the seventeenth century. More important were the centers in Balakhna and the Kostroma district (Nerekhta and Soli Bol'shie), neither of which has ever been thoroughly studied. Balakhna in particular is a serious omission because in the sources of the seventeenth century there are repeated references comparing Perm and Balakhna salt in importance to the market. Furthermore, what little information there is on Balakhna points to the complete predominance of merchant investment in the salt works there. The only serious consideration of Balakhna is in a section of the article of S. Kolominskii (1912) in which, on the basis of the 1674 census, he finds the following pattern of ownership (including "empty" salt works): small producers of the Balakhna *posad*, 57 percent; *gost'* hundred, 22 percent; woolen drapers' hundred, 4 percent (total merchants: 83 percent; the state, 8 percent; and the monasteries, 9 percent.[49] Probably most of the 26 percent in the hands of members of the _gost'_ hundred and woolen drapers' hundred were in the hands of Muscovites, although nearby Nizhnii Novogorod was one of the few towns with local _gosti,_ so we cannot be sure of this.[50]

Another fairly important center of salt production in the central district was Soli Bol'shie (with Soli Malye) in tbe Kostroma district. More familiar to historians are the salt works in Nerekhta, near Soli Bol'shie, which are invariably used as examples of monastic salt enterprises (they were the property of Troitse-Sergeev monastery). However, in sixteenth-century Nerekhta there were only two operating boilers, which ceased to operate by 1609, and remained inoperative throughout the seventeenth century.[51] In Soli Bol'shie the situation was a bit different. Here there were twenty boilers in 1539: and nineteen in 1598, when the ownership was divided among some 200 townsmen of Soli Bol'shie. During the seventeenth century the number declined: There were only four in the reign of Aleksei Mikhailovich, and one in the reign of Peter (belonging to the _gost'_ Shorin).[52] We have no way of knowing the reasons for the change between 1598 and the 1650s, but it is possible that the same technological change had taken place in Soli Bol'shie as in Staraia Russa, again rather late in an isolated and backward area like the Solonitsa River. The Moscow merchants were involved in salt trade and production in Soli Bol'shie since at least the 1630s because the _gost'_ Nadeia Sveteshnikov was trading there in 1637–9. In 1646, at his death, he had five boilers, valued at 7,000 rubles, and seized by the treasury for debt.[53] His son Semen clearly recovered them; In 1648 the townsmen of Soli Bol'shie complained that they had not paid their share of taxes because they were not rich enough, as Semen Sveteshnikov owned all the salt boilers in town.[54] Thus, by 1646, a Moscow merchant had wrested control of all local salt production from the townsmen of Soli Bol'shie. Even when production declined at the end of the century, the Moscow _gost'_ Shorin had the sole remaining salt works.

Finally, the last important salt-producing area in the Russian center was Soligalich, on the northern fringe of the area that was considered part of Central Russia. According to Zaozerskaia, the ownership of salt boilers in the town developed in the manner illustrated in Table 8.8. Soligalich continued to be an important salt-producing town well into the eighteenth century, but apparently at no time did Moscow merchants invest in Soligalich. The only connection of the town with the Moscow merchant class was to provide recruits for that class: In the 1590s the salt merchants of Soligalich – Afanasii Mamychev and Tret'iak Kasatkin – moved to Moscow.

the latter entering the woolen drapers' hundred.[55] It has been noted that the Moscow merchant family of the Pankrat'evs, prominent since the 1620s (and involved in salt production), came from Soligalich. Soligalich thus provides an example to the reverse of most of the other Russian towns, for instead of Muscovite salt merchants investing in the town, the town sent out salt merchants to Moscow, who made their investments in some other salt center (e.g. Pankrat'ev).

The most basic conclusion to emerge from the history of the salt industry in early seventeenth-century Russia is the great importance of this industry to the Moscow merchant class. A large number of the most important Moscow merchants either made their fortunes in the salt trade, or were closely involved in· it when they became wealthy Moscow merchants. Only later did they begin to invest in the production of salt. The trade and production of salt was one of the important sources of wealth for the Moscow merchants.

It is more difficult to assess the importance of the Muscovites to the salt industry. Their importance varied by time and region. In the North, they were important before 1650 only in Tot'ma, and the six salt boilers owned by Muscovites in Tot'ma could hardly compete with those owned by the Solovetskii monastery or even the much smaller Spaso-Prilutskii monastery. After 1650, however, the situation changed, and the yearly production of the Pankrat'evs' salt works in the Iarensk district was about three times the yearly production of the Solovetskii monastery.

Table 8.8. *Ownership of salt boilers in Soligalich*

	1614	1628	1640
Townsmen	13	7½	9
Monasteries	6	8¼	6[b]
Michurins[a]	3	2	2
Peasants	0	1	0
Total	22	18¾	17

[a] The Michurin family was a curious (and rare) example of townsmen who became *deti boiarskie*. In 1581 they were still townsmen, but by 1611 they were *deti boiarskie*, and how they made the transition is unknown (like Kuz'ma Minin?).
[b] Simonov, 3; Troitse-Sergeev, 2; Avraam'ev in Gorodets, 1.
Source: Zaozerskaia, *U istokov*, pp. 31–2, 60.

In the Urals the Muscovites appeared on the same scene only in the 1630s, but quickly acquired possessions in the salt industry equal (taking all Muscovites together) to the possessions of the Stroganovs, and greater than the townsmen of Solikamsk, the monasteries, or (after 1650) the state. It was only in the 1690s, when the Stroganovs pushed the Filat'evs and Shustovs out of production on the Lenva River, that the Stroganovs began to approach a monopolistic position in the Urals salt industry. A similar situation existed at the other end of Russia, in Staraia Russa, where Muscovites started to invest in the 1630s, and controlled some 30 percent of the industry by mid-century, which they maintained until the 1690s.

The Muscovites were somewhat less important on the lower Volga. In the 1620s, we can estimate that they shipped only about 10 percent of the salt to Central Russia, whereas Nizhnii Novgorod merchants shipped 15 percent and Yaroslavl merchants 30 percent. The role of the Muscovites probably increased in the 1630s, because that seems to have been the time of Muscovite expansion in the salt trade. Even so, we hear later in the century of Nizhnii Novgorod merchants like Kalmykov rather than of Muscovites. In the center of Russia – in Balakhna, Nerekhta-Soli Bol'shie, and Soligalich – the role of the Muscovites was even more modest. In Soligalich they played no role at all, in Balakhna a very small one, and could only dominate tiny Soli Bol'shie with its four or five salt boilers in mid-century.

This regional pattern suggests some of the inner workings of the relation of the Moscow merchants to the salt industry. Two of the families that made the most wide-ranging investment, the Venevitinov-Dubenskii group, started as traders in salt from Murom. Their investments date only from the 1630s, when they were already in the *gost'* hundred of Moscow. Conversely, we hear of few townsmen in the salt towns moving to Moscow from owning salt wells or boilers. In Solikamsk, for example, the merchant Anofreev was taken into the *gost'* hundred, but apparently remained in Solikamsk, like the Usovs and Reviakins of Ustiug Velikii. Apparently the Moscow merchants were investing in production the profits made in trade. The regional pattern is also revealing. In the North the relative weakness of the Muscovites has an obvious cause: The monasteries got there first, in the sixteenth century, and held on to the most valuable property. Also, the merchants of the North were wealthy or entrenched enough to control the remainder of the salt production until the beginning of the seventeenth century. For Moscow, the North was closed until after 1650. In the Volga and Central Russia the Muscovites also faced stiff competition from local merchants. Their penetration of Soligalich was nonexistent, of Balakhna small. In the Urals, however, the Muscovites were the most powerful group until the 1690s, and even in the Volga they made their presence felt, in spite of the competition from Yaroslavl and the other river towns. Their investments in Staraia Russa were also successful, although they never dominated the town. In general, it seems that the farther from Moscow were the salt works, the better the Muscovites did, certainly as the result of the Muscovites' commercial power. The Moscow merchants had far more available capital than local merchants, and thus, as a rule, had more property per man in the salt towns. In the lower Volga, where the process of production was much cheaper, the Muscovites did not play an important role, evidently because the size of the investment required less and thus was within the reach of more modest fortunes. Because the salt trade was largely a matter of shipping salt from the edges of Russia to the center, the importance of the Muscovites as large-scale merchants must have played a role. They had the best contacts in the markets of Central Russia, and also already had in existence a large network of agents and traditional contacts with the boatmen and carters of the Russian rivers and roads, the size of which only a few provincial merchants could match. Finally, the Moscow merchants had better contacts with the administration in Moscow. One suspects that the Pankrat'evs would hardly have been so successful in Iarensk without relatives in the important offices in Moscow. On the other hand, in the lower Volga where the state had the final say on the distribution of the salt works, the Muscovites were not able to put themselves in a dominant position, although undoubtedly individual merchants in Moscow used their government connections. Evidently the favor or disfavor of government officials was not necessarily a decisive factor. And, as the example of Kalmykov shows, a merchant did not have to be a Muscovite to have important connections in tbe government.

The Muscovites were the only group of merchants in Russia who possessed interregional ties in the salt industry and in the salt trade. Nizhnii Novgorod merchants did not invest in Staraia Russa or Solikamsk, unless they became Muscovites, for example, Iakim Patokin. This fact suggests that the investment in the salt industry that started in the 1630s was important in the formation of the Moscow merchants' wealth and their position as the most important (if not the dominant) group in the Russian merchant class. On the basis of this fact alone, we must conclude that the Moscow merchants did play an important role in the development of

Russian industry in the seventeenth century until the decline in importance of the salt industry after the 1690s. Furthermore, because the other main groups investing in salt production were not the monasteries, the state (whose role was trivial), or even the Stroganovs, but dozens of merchants and salt producers of varying wealth and importance scattered throughout the salt towns and the provincial cities of Russia, it is clear that the merchants, Muscovites and others, played more than a secondary role in Russian industry.

9

The Moscow merchants and the state

In a centralized monarchy like seventeenth-century Russia, the state could have a great influence on trade and industry and on the formation of the merchant class. But was this influence decisive? Did it help or hinder the merchant? The older view, advanced by Kostomarov and Dovnar-Zapol'skii is that the state everywhere hindered and obstructed trade and industry through bureaucratism, oppressive monopolies, and the competition of its own trade. Recently, Samuel H. Baron has extended this analysis with reference to Weber's views of the obstacles to capitalist development. Another viewpoint cautiously advanced by the Soviet historians Bazilevich and others in the 1930s, was that during the period 1650–70 the state made a decisive move toward protectionism in its tariff policy and began to establish state industries, so that Russia could compete in the military-political struggles of the time on a more equal basis.[1] On the whole, both points of view are found in the current Soviet writing. The purpose of the present discussion is not to pronounce a definitive judgment, but rather to show that the notion that the state only hindered the merchants excludes important evidence to the contrary, and to indicate phenomena that suggest a two-sided relationship between the merchants and the state.

The state trade

All aspects of the relationship of the Russian state to the merchant class cannot be investigated here. Although numerous statements have been made on the subject, most of the central problems have never been touched. No systematic account has ever been made of the state's trade, in spite of the fact that this is probably the only aspect of seventeenth-century Russian trade for which almost complete documentation survives (from 1615). A greater difficulty is presented by the complete absence of work on the process of the collection of tolls, which provided the largest single item in the state income (combined with the income from the state taverns), and most directly affected the merchant class. Even the tariff policy has mainly been studied in relation to the decree of 1653 and the New Commercial Edict of 1667. Earlier, I indicated that already in the reign of Boris Godunov and Mikhail Romanov the government took a protectionist position by merely refusing to extend to the Dutch the privileges of the English merchants, when the Dutch had effectively captured the market from the English. In 1646, the raising of the tolls at Archangel for foreign merchants pointed in the same direction.

The trade of the state with foreign powers was one of the more important areas in which the merchants and the state were connected. The nature of the relationship is not clear. Starting at least in the middle of the sixteenth century, if not before, the state had the right to make the first choice among foreign wares offered for sale, but it is not known how often this right was exercised, with which goods, and what effect it had on trade. At Archangel the purchases and sales were usually made by the head of the toll-collecting administration (the *tamozhennyi golova*) who was invariably a *gost'* from Moscow. This form of state service is often described as an onerous burden, but it is difficult to see how the great merchants of Moscow, with their dozens of clerks and slaves scattered throughout the country carrying on their affairs, could have been so adversely affected. Because they also traded in Archangel on their own account while they were serving, the possibilities for graft must have been enormous. Indeed, the prosecution of the *kadashevets* Aleksei Zolotov was based on the fact that he was able to conduct a considerable smuggling trade with Poland by obtaining for his brother-in-law the position of tavern keeper and toll collector on the Polish border near one of the main roads.[2] It is difficult to imagine that the Moscow merchants in Archangel restrained themselves from similar activities. In the case of the state trade, where the control was tighter, there were probably fewer abuses, but the knowledge of the size of the state trade and the exact time that it would take place in the course of the Archangel fair must have been important information.

Our sources give us little direct information on these aspects of the state trade, but they do give us considerable information on its scale at Archangel, which can be compared with the estimates of the total size of the trade that have been made in Chapter 3. (For the trade to Poland and Persia, less information is available.) Before the Time of Troubles there is little information on state trade as there is little information on any trade. One of the largest amounts of furs exported by the state was sent with Vel'iaminov's embassy to Emperor Rudolf II in 1595. The embassy was assigned 1,009 forties (*soroka*) of sables worth 28,097 rubles and 337,235 squirrel skins worth 6,744 rubles, among other items, the total amounting to 44,720 rubles, an enormous sum, probably the equal of twice or three times the amount in the 1640s. But this huge sum was not only to be sold for revenue; an unspecified part was to pay the travel expenses of the large embassy and another unspecified part was for gifts to the Emperor and bribes to his courtiers.[3] Our first real data start in 1613–14, when the administration of the young Tsar Mikhail was trying to repair the damage to the court's supplies wrought by the years of turmoil. Consequently, these purchases may have been somewhat larger than usual. In the summer of 1614, the *gosti* Bakhteiar Bulgakov and Grigorii Iudin bought at Archangel for the Tsar 3,396 rubles, 18 altyny, and 3 dengi worth of cloth, gold, and jewels (*uzorochnye tovary*). Of this, 98 percent was purchased from Dutch merchants. One merchant of Hamburg sold to the treasury 64 rubles, 5 altyny, and 4 dengi worth of satin, and the Kazan merchant Vavila Konishchev sold 60 rubles and 16 altyny worth of *kamka* cloth.[4] In the period from July 13, 1613, to August 21, 1614, the treasury bought in Moscow about 10,000 rubles worth of cloth of various types including woolen cloth from the West, and some oriental cloths, such as velvet and satin (but because velvet and satin were already being produced in Venice and the Low countries, these too could have been from the West). Of this cloth, the English and Dutch merchants (mainly the latter) sold 6,020.5 rubles worth, or about 60 percent. Moscow merchants were the next largest suppliers, selling 1,890.8 rubles worth, or about 19 percent. Yaroslavl merchants accounted for 1,326.2 rubles worth, or 13 percent (a large part of which was the sales of Nadeia Sveteshnikov, who was still entitled *iaroslavskii gost'*). The other 8 percent was sold by merchants from various provincial towns, all in very small quantities. Unfortunately, there is not such extensive data as that published for later years and we have no standard of comparison.[5] However, the proportion of cloth shipped south from Archangel in 1630 by the foreign merchants was far smaller (11 percent, cf Chapter 3, Table 3.11) and it is probably fair to conclude that the high proportion of sales by foreigners was the result of the Time of Troubles: The Russian merchants had not yet recovered their resources of capital.

The next year for which there is a record of state trade at Archangel is 1620. In this year, the Moscow merchants, *gost'* Ivan Sverchkov and Bogdan Shchepotkin, in their capacity as toll collectors, bought 3,936 rubles, 20 altyny, and 3 dengi worth of cloth and valuables. In 1622, the treasury sold forty-six *soroka* of sables at Archangel for 1,004 rubles. This was evidently only the remainder of the sales for the previous year, 1621. In 1625, there were more state purchases in Archangel, of unknown size. In 1624, however, we know that the *gost'* Nadeia Sveteshnikov had traded in caviar for the state in Archangel. The wording of the document is not absolutely clear, but it seems that in 1623 and 1624 he sold about 14,000 rubles worth of caviar. He had bought the caviar in Astrakhan for 24,000 rubles (over two years) and sold it for a total of 28,000. Because the 24,000 rubles were apparently supposed to cover costs, he made the treasury a profit of almost 17 percent. He also made a contract with unnamed Western merchants to sell caviar for the next six years, until 1630, estimating at first sales of 13,000 rubles a year (he later retracted the estimate). For this service to the Tsar he received a reward of various gifts, including an inscribed silver chalice worth 16 rubles, 30 altyny, and 5 dengi. The total value of the various gifts was 126 rubles, 30 altyny, and 5 dengi.[6]

The year for which we have the fullest data until 1648 is 1626. In that year the state purchases in Archangel amounted to 200 rubles for tin, 859 rubles, 23 altyny, and 2 dengi for wine and spices (all purchased from the Dutch except for the Moscow merchant Kharlam Obrosimov and the Moscow German Baldwin Zakhar'ev who sold spices equal in value to 51 rubles and 2 altyny), and 2,084 rubles, 12 altyny, and 1 denga for cloth and jewelry; the total amounting to 3,144 rubles, 2 altyny, and 1 denga. In the same year, the treasury bought from the *gost'* Nadeia Sveteshnikov 1,516 rubles, 23 altyny, and 3 dengi worth of gold and diamonds (no doubt also imported through Archangel). The sales in Archangel that year were of wax and caviar, and 924 rubles in tolls were collected from the buyers, which means a value of 46,200 rubles. If Sveteshnikov was approximately right in his estimate that 13,000 rubles of caviar would be sold, then wax made up 72 percent of the sales and caviar 28 percent. This means that even if the purchases at Archangel and from Sveteshnikov are added together (making 4,660 rubles, 25 altyny, and 4 dengi) then the purchases by the state in Archangel for the court were only a tenth of the sales by the state. Clearly, the treasury was doing rather well. However, in a few years, the Smolensk War and the military purchases would upset this situation. In the following year, 1627, the treasury bought 3,566 rubles worth of cloth and jewelry at Archangel, and in 1628 the Commercial House (*Kupetskaia palata*) of the Siberian Office was able to present a total of 11,346 rubles and 11 altyny of jewelry, gold and silver, precious stones, and cloth to the Tsar for the court. This would include not only purchases at Archangel but also in Novgorod, along the Polish border, and in Astrakhan. Apparently, Archangel contributed about 30–40 percent of the total purchases for the court.[7]

From 1628 until 1648, when the figures provided by Kurts in his edition of de Rodes's work are available, the published information is scanty. It is in any case probable that in the years of the Smolensk War (1632–4) and its preparation, the government concentrated its financial efforts on obtaining supplies for the army. In these years the grain sales to Sweden, which were likewise ties to Russian military and diplomatic activity, also fell. A sale of silk at Archangel in 1630 may have had the function of covering some of the expenses of these years, such as the sale of silk and caviar in 1633 by the Commercial House.[8] In May of 1633, the Novgorod Quarter ordered the toll administration in Archangel to pay the English merchant Abraham Ash 1,700 rubles from their funds, as part payment on a debt of 3,200 rubles incurred by treasury purchases of cloth and precious stones in Moscow. Evidently in wartime the treasury was low on cash in Moscow. In the next year, 1634, the Ustiug Quarter was ordered to pay the English merchant John Aborn 570 more rubles of Abraham Ash's debt. Clearly, the treasury was hard pressed in those years. We hear of wine purchases in Archangel in 1636, and in 1637 the English sold the treasury 1,613 rubles worth of pearls, as well as an unspecified quantity of wine. In 1637 there was a sale of 120 puds of silk to the Dutch for 6,250 rubles.[9]

The next solid information comes in 1648, and the interval can be only partially filled in by Ogloblin's survey of the documents of the Siberian Office because the records of the Novgorod and Ustiug Quarters (fund 141) are silent on these years. The Sable Treasury (*Sobolinaia kazna*) of the Siberian Office has left records, beginning only with the year 1638, of any sales of furs (usually for cloth, gold, and precious stones) in Archangel. In view of the difficulty the government had in paying its debt to Ash, and the well-known fact that the Smolensk War was a financial as well as military disaster, it is not at all unlikely that the Sable Treasury really did only begin its operation in Archangel in 1638; especially because the records of the Siberian Office and its subordinate departments are particularly well preserved. Probably there was a decline for about eight years (1630-7), as military needs absorbed the treasury's resources, and then defeat in the war brought with it empty coffers for several years.

In any case, the size of the Sable Treasury's sales, and those of other offices, as well as the size of the purchases will remain unknown until there is further research on the question. Ogloblin records the existence of such activity only for 1638-40, and a resumption only in 1648. For these years, however, there was a great increase in activity in the trade at the Svinsk fair near Briansk, with Polish, Ukrainian, Greek, and Armenian merchants exporting furs to Constantinople, as well as an increase in state trade with Persia,[10] so that in the period 1641-7 these routes may have absorbed the treasury's resources. For the period since 1648, there is again more detailed information, thanks to the extensive extracts from the records of the Sable Office published by Kurts in his notes to de Rodes. In 1648 two merchants working for the government, Vladimir Borzov (*gost'* hundred) and Mineia Pushnikov (woolen drapers' hundred) were sent to Archangel with 10,373 rubles worth of sables and martens' tails. In 1649 three merchants of Moscow, led by Dmitrii Fedoseev (*gost'* hundred) went to Archangel with 20,000 rubles worth of furs and an escort of twenty musketeers, but were only able to sell about half of the furs. They had been ordered to get Thalers or Ducats, plus the usual cloth and precious stones, but were not able to sell any of their furs for currency and instead had to exchange the goods for imported cloth, equal in value to 9,925 rubles. In 1650 there was another expedition of the same kind, of unknown value, but in 1651 the Archangel toll collector, the Yaroslavl *gost'* Anikei Skrypkin, bought 14,077 rubles 92.5 kopecks worth of goods for the state. In 1654 the Archangel administration was ordered to buy 15,000 rubles worth of goods, but the success or failure of that year's trade remains unknown.[11]

In this context the state's trade in other towns can be quickly summarized, for so few bits of information have been published that it is difficult to draw a clear picture. Toward the west, two centers, Mozhaisk and the Svinsk fair, were the main ones. It seems that the treasury traded first in Mozhaisk with the Poles, and only began to trade heavily at the Svinsk fair later. In 1619 the treasury sold 1,009 rubles, 23 altyny, and 2 dengi worth of furs, not a very extensive operation. In 1625 two Moscow merchants were sent to Mozhaisk but were unable to sell the furs, and had to go to the Svinsk fair. From 1641 on there was extensive trade by the treasury in Viaz'ma and the Svinsk fair, and also occasionally in Toropets or Putivl'.[12] In 1648 three merchants sold 18,568 rubles worth of furs at the Svinsk fair, including 136 *soroka* of sables. It was noted in Chapter 6 that the purchases of sables in the early 1640s for the Ottoman treasury were on the order of 30–40 *soroka*. If the year 1648 was representative, the sales of the Russian government were larger in the Svinsk fair than in Archangel. This appears to be the case because most of the surviving data for the period after 1648 are on the sale of furs, which were sold more easily to the Turks than to Western merchants, because the demand for fur was declining in Western Europe. Given the problems of transportation, it is unlikely that caviar was sold to the Turks, and silk they imported directly from Persia; so in fact, it was more likely that the 18,000 rubles of furs sold to the Turks constituted practically the whole trade of the Russian treasury with the Turks, whereas the fur sales at Archangel of 10,000–15,000 rubles were only a part of the treasury's transactions, which included caviar and Persian silk.

The state's purchases of Persian goods took place in Persia, Astrakhan, and occasionally Moscow. In 1615 these purchases took place in Astrakhan under the direction of Nadeia Sveteshnikov. In 1621 they took place in Persia. In 1627 the *gost'* Bakhteiar Bulgakov received forty *soroka* of sables worth 1,673 rubles for trade with the Persians. In 1641 Grigorii Nikitnikov traded with the Persians for the treasury in Moscow, and from 1642 on there are regular records of state trade with Persia.[13]

From this description it is clear that the state did trade extensively, in the sense that the geographic scope of the trade was considerable. However, it is also fairly clear that the value of the state's trade was by no means tremendous, if the regular export of furs, caviar, and a few other goods in order to supply the Tsar's court is considered. In 1626, for example, the total of purchases at Archangel was only a little over 3,000 rubles, and the sales about 45,000 rubles. In 1626 the toll collection at Archangel was about 17,000 rubles, which at the 2 percent toll rate gives a gross value of the trade of 850,000 rubles. Thus, the state's exports at the most could have amounted to 10 percent of the exports of Russia, and the purchases at Archangel to less than 1 percent. Of course, imported goods could be and were later purchased in Moscow, but in smaller quantities, because the prices were higher in Moscow than in Archangel. This proportion of state exports to private exports is almost exactly the same as the proportion in the period 1700–10, calculated by Kozintseva,[14] 10–12 percent. It would seem that the state's trade in seventeenth-century Russia was fairly stable.

It is a figure that is only somewhat larger than the average sales of even such a great merchant as Nikitnikov (cf. Chapter 4). The treasury sold about as much as did two to four Moscow merchants of middle wealth, such as Aleksei Zolotov. Thus, it can hardly be said that the state and its trade were serious competitors to the merchants of Moscow or any other town. It should also be kept in mind that nothing is known of the internal workings of this state trade: Did the merchants who carried it out receive only the salary in the form of "gifts" or did they make some sort of profit, legal or illegal? Nor was the amount of money involved in the sale and purchase of grain for the Smolensk War tremendous, when compared with the total turnover at Archangel. The largest purchases recorded by Stashevskii are two contracts for weapons and artillery supplies let to van Ringen and de Moulijn in 1630, for a total of about 50,000 rubles.[15] The grain sales by the treasury in the 1620s and 1630s to Sweden, which were partly an attempt to support the Swedish effort in the Thirty Years' War, were also not very large by Archangel standards, although the total of all this activity in the years 1627–34 was larger than usual. In 1632 the grain sales amounted to 32,276.5 rubles, and in 1633 to 25,000 rubles, so that in addition to helping the Swedish war effort, Russia was partly covering its own military expenses.[16] In general, the trade carried on by the state, in imported luxuries, the export of caviar and (occasionally) silk, and the purchase of military supplies, all took place on the margin of Russian trade at Archangel, and does not deserve the place it has been given in the historiography.

The Moscow merchants and the collection of taxes

The most important relationship of the Moscow merchants to the Russian government was in the area of the collection of taxes.[17] The state derived its income from a Russian town in the seventeenth century from three sources: the *tiaglo* (or direct tax), the toll collection, and the revenue from the taverns (indirect taxes). As explained in Chapter 1, the collection of all three taxes was the main service obligation of the town population, an obligation that usually fell on the richest townsmen, the merchants. The system of electing a toll and tavern chief or an elder and various assistants to collect the taxes was known as collection "on faith" (*na veru*). The other possible system, that of farming the taxes (*otkup*) was also widespread, but very little is known about it. Of the three types of taxes, the two indirect taxes brought in far more money than the direct tax. It is obvious from a glance at the account books of the tax collection offices of the seventeenth century that the amount of direct taxes in proportion to the other two, indirect taxes, is best described as trivial. For example, at the ordinary taxation rates, Vladimir paid in 1614 in direct taxes (the *tiaglo*) 44 rubles, 22 altyny, and 3 dengi. In spite of the destruction of the Time of Troubles, these taxes were collected by the 1607 rates. In the same year, the farming of the tavern to a group of Vladimir townsmen brought in 548 rubles, 3 altyny, and 2 dengi. Apparently, the tolls were not collected that year.[18] In Nizhnii Novgorod, which had not been destroyed by warfare, the direct taxes for the year 7123 (1614–15) amounted to 460 rubles and 2 altyny, whereas the toll collection was 12,153 rubles and 5 altyny, and the farm for the tavern was 5,000 rubles. In other words, from the town of Nizhnii Novgorod the government collected in 1614 (and expected to collect in 1615) the sum of 17,613 rubles, 7 altyny, of which 2.6 percent came from direct taxation. In a small town like Shuia, the farm of the tavern brought in 300 rubles even in 1612, and direct taxes only about 24.5 rubles in a relatively good year like 1631.[19] Naturally, the direct taxes from the countryside raised the proportion of direct taxes for the whole district, but for the city the tolls and the tavern were what counted. The high proportion of tolls to the revenue from the tavern was characteristic of the larger towns; in smaller places the tavern brought in far more than the tolls on trade.

The only total budget that was made for the income and expenses of the state is the 1680 budget analyzed by Miliukov, which shows more than half of the revenue to come from indirect taxes (mainly the toll collection and the taverns).[20] In wartime, extraordinary taxes would increase the proportion of direct taxation, but the ordinary budget (*oklad*) that is revealed by the account books of 1614–15 (during wartime) show that the direct taxes were still a small proportion. Of course, the indirect taxes are not in these books, but for the fifth tax of 1634 Stashevskii gives the Nizhnii Novgorod contribution as 8,376 rubles, 14 altyny, and 4 dengi.[21] Certainly the Nizhnii Novgorod income from tolls and the taverns had risen since 1615, so that from the towns the direct taxes were still less than half. At the very minimum, it must be recognized that the tolls and tavern collection were the largest single item of income in the Russian budget from the 1580s to the end of the seventeenth century.

The origins of the system of tax farming combined with the collection by elected officials on faith lies in the period of the so-called reform of the land – the institution of limited forms of elective self-government on the local level in the 1550s. The government tried to combine the two systems, but the financial pressure of the Livonian War compelled extensive farming of the tolls. Starting in the 1580s, the farming of the tolls gave way to collection on faith in the majority of cases, so that the government could hope to collect a larger part of the revenue than before. However, the revenue from the tolls was not enough, and the tavern revenue appeared to supplement the tolls. Previously, the taverns had not been an important source of revenue, but from the time of Tsar Fedor onward they formed an ever-increasing part of the government's income. This income was usually farmed, even when the tolls were not, so that the merchants' interest in exploiting the state's revenue merely shifted to another sphere. From the 1550s onward, the farmers or officials collecting the tolls were usually merchants, and with the addition of the taverns, the administrative system of the seventeenth century was born.[22] One notable point, which appears also in the data for the later period, is the apparent lack of a pattern.

For the period 1614–50 there is, in contrast, a great deal of material. Unfortunately, little of it is published (especially on the taverns), and the archival material on the administration of the collecting of these taxes is immense. In particular, there are more surviving records of the tavern administrations than there are of any other part of the government's financial efforts in the towns (reflecting perhaps its priorities?). Until detailed research is done on these records, any judgments must be rather tentative, but some can be made. Generally, it is clear that the Moscow merchants played the main role in the farming of taxes, and a major role in their collection on faith. In view of the large number of examples, it will be possible to dwell only on a few.

The first important example is derived from the published account books of the Vladimir and Novgorod (or Nizhnii Novgorod) Quarters for 1614–15. These are the years immediately succeeding the election of Tsar Mikhail Romanov, and to a certain extent represent the reconstruction of the state finances after the chaos of the previous years. The method of reconstruction was to determine the traditional amount and kind of the taxes owed in each district, and use them as the basis for assessment. By fall, 1613, this task seems to have been completed. Incomplete account books only appear in districts not yet recaptured (Novgorod) or ruined in the fighting (Tver'). For other districts, the system is again in full force. In the towns of the Vladimir Quarter, which collected taxes from a patchwork of Central Russian towns, a pattern is difficult to find, but it seems that most of the larger towns collected both tolls and tavern revenue on faith; this was true of Kaluga, Tver', and Pereiaslavl' Riazanskii. In Vladimir itself, the tolls are not mentioned, and the tavern was farmed to a group of local merchants. In Torzhok (Novyi Torzhok) both were farmed in 1613, and then changed to collection on faith for 1614. However, the tolls were again farmed in the spring of 1614. In Tula, information on tolls is lacking, but the tavern was administered on faith in 1613, but farmed to Prokhor Trifonov, a Moscow *kadashevets*, in December 1613 for the coming year. Of the smaller towns and larger villages, in eleven the revenue was exclusively farmed, in four it was collected on faith, and in eight it was changed, generally toward farming all or part of the revenue. The holders of the farms were of various towns and origins, among them a number of Muscovites. The Muscovites were: Semen Denisov, *kadashevets* of Moscow, who had the beer and *braga* farm for Pereiaslavl' Riazanskii in 1614 for 100.5 rubles (whereas the main tavern revenues and the tolls were collected on faith for 809 rubles); I. Kostsov, of the *gost'* hundred of Moscow, who farmed both the tolls and the tavern in the small town of Perevitsk for 70.5 and 75 rubles in 1613 and 1614 respectively; the same *kadashevets* Prokhor Trifonov, who farmed the tavern in Dorogobuzh for 1613–14 for 42 rubles for the two years; Vas'ka Kharitonov of the Tagannaia settlement in Moscow, who farmed the tolls and tavern of the village of Struzhany (Riazan' district) in 1614 for 27 rubles and 10 altyny; and the Muscovite Isaak Iur'ev, who with a stonemason, a cossack, and an artilleryman, farmed the tavern and tolls of Sapozhsk (southeast of Riazan') in 1614 for 35 rubles, 6 altyny, and 4 dengi. These Muscovites are the only men from large towns to farm taxes in another town: The other farmers of the taxes were merchants who farmed the taxes of their own city (Vladimir) or a half-dozen peasants who farmed small taverns in nearby villages.[23]

For the Novgorod Quarter the account books have been published for 1614–15. This Quarter collected the taxes from the Novgorod area (occupied by Sweden), most of the North, and Nizhnii Novgorod. Of the towns around Nizhnii Novgorod, Gorokhovets had its tavern and tolls farmed in 1613 (for later years the information is not recorded); the village of Pavlovo's tavern was farmed in 1614 and again in 1615 for 492 rubles to a group of merchants from Gorokhovets. In Nizhnii Novgorod itself, the tolls were collected on faith and the three taverns in the town were farmed to a group of townsmen of Nizhnii Novgorod for an annual sum of 5,000 rubles. In the North there were no cases of tax farming at all, neither in the large towns, Archangel, Kholmogory, Solikamsk, and Vologda, nor in the smaller villages and country districts along the White Sea and the Northern Dvina. This pattern seems to have existed right up to 1650: The taxes of the North were never farmed, either by local men or by outsiders. For Archangel, Ustiug Velikii, and Sol' Vychegodsk there are sufficiently numerous indications to be able to say that there was no tax farming, even of the taverns, or at the very least that it was a rare occurrence. For the towns and villages of Central Russia, on the other hand, it seems that the practice of farming, especially of taverns, was fairly common.[24]

One other pattern that should be noted is the relative predominance of tax farming in the steppe frontier towns. These were administered by the *Razriad*, the Military Office in Moscow, whose accounts survive and are published for the period 1615–17. All of the taverns and all the tolls collected (some were not collected in those years) were farmed to local townsmen, soldiers, cossacks, or peasants. The only exception was Elets, where both tavern and toll revenue were collected on faith in 7125 (1616–17), under the administration of the Moscow merchant Nesmeian Gavrilov. There does not seem to be a pattern because all of the farms were for less than seventy rubles and the collections in Elets amounted to about 27.5 rubles.[25]

Among the places where the tolls were never farmed, besides the North, the most important was Moscow itself. The same was true of Archangel and Astrakhan, although our information on Astrakhan is very sparse. Novgorod's tavern, in contrast, was farmed, in the one case where there is information.[26]

The farming process will be somewhat clarified by a more detailed account of one of the important cases of farming: the tolls and taverns of Mozhaisk and Viaz'ma. These two towns were of economic importance for two reasons: They were the centers of important areas of hemp production and they were on the road to Poland. Indeed, most of Russia's trade with Poland after 1614 took place in Viaz'ma. Let us look first at Viaz'ma. In 1617, the tolls were farmed to a peasant of the boyar Ivan Nikitich Romanov. In 1624 and 1625, both sorts of revenue were collected on faith, but under the jurisdiction of Muscovites: Aleksei Levashev in 1624 and Ivan Volodimirov in 1625, who continued in office into 1626. In 1623, the Muscovite Abram Syreishchikov held the office. From 1633 through the first half of 1637, however, the tavern was farmed out to Frol Merkur'ev Rebrov, a *kadashevets*, and one of the most important tax farmers of the 1630s and 1640s. The rate was 2,000 rubles annually. Again in 1641–42,

Rebrov held the farm of the tavern, both in Mozhaisk and in Viaz'ma, but by now for only 2,100 rubles for both towns annually. According to Rebrov, the smaller sum was necessary because competition from smuggled Polish vodka had cut into the receipts of the tavern. The Ustiug Quarter agreed to the lower sum.[27]

In the case of Mozhaisk from 1617 to 1620 the tolls were collected on faith by three different men, at least two of whom, Iakov Lada, woolen drapers' hundred, and Nikita Tarutin, also woolen drapers' hundred, were Muscovites. In 1624 the chief of the collection (on faith) was Stepan Iakovlev (Iakov's son?) under whose administration a dispute arose over the farming of the *kvas* and *suslo*. Iakovlev apparently delayed solving the problem of who was to administer the *kvas* and *suslo*, and Muscovite merchants began to petition the Ustiug Quarter in Moscow asking for the farm. The office did give it to Ivashko Aksent'ev of the *Sretenskaia* hundred for six rubles, only to find that Iakovlev had already given it to a Mozhaisk townsman for five rubles. The official of the Ustiug Quarter, who was the ex-merchant Mikhailo Smyvalov, began to suspect that something was wrong, recalled Iakovlev, and sent Frol Patulkov from Moscow to replace him shortly before his term was up on August 31, 1624. Iakovlev had been caught stealing from the treasury in Mozhaisk. The Ustiug Quarter was clearly not expecting much from its merchant-administrators because when Patulkov later asked for a copy of the rules for toll collection he was told that Iakovlev had been required to hand it over, as he (Patulkov) had been told, and if Patulkov had lost it "by your own stupidity or drunkenness" he should have written for a copy much sooner.[28] In 1626 the Ustiug Quarter tried another Muscovite, Matvei Merkur'ev of the woolen drapers' hundred, as toll and tavern administrator. In 1634 Mozhaisk's tolls and tavern were farmed by Rebrov, for 1,936.5 rubles, but in 1635 the Ustiug Quarter again tried collection on faith by the Muscovite Vasilii Zheravkin.[29] For the farm on the next two years they got a number of bids. Rebrov was the first to bid, offering fifty rubles more than 1,936.5 rubles, the amount that he gave in 1634 and the amount collected by Zheravkin in 1635. The townsman of Kaluga, Iushka Martynov, offered to pay as an increase whatever the officials asked. However, Rebrov made a concrete offer of sixty rubles, and Martynov only forty-five rubles, so Rebrov got the farm for the two years. At this point boyar I. N. Romanov's peasant, Sen'ka Mikhailov, from Spasskoe, offered ten rubles more than anyone else, and the case was reconsidered. Rebrov countered with a petition signed by the official Ivan Gavrenev of the Great

Treasury praising Rebrov's past services in producing revenue for the treasury, and the final decision was to let Rebrov have it for a seventy-rubles-a-year increase over the previous income, and Rebrov ended up paying 2,006.5 rubles a year for the farm. The last we hear of the farm of the taxes in Mozhaisk is the farm of Viaz'ma and Mozhaisk's taverns in 1642, mentioned above.[30]

The history of the collection of the tolls and tavern revenues in these two towns is typical of the whole complex of problems. It is difficult to tell what the motives of the Ustiug Quarter were in the process, but the fact is that the years when the taxes were farmed fall right after the Time of Troubles and during the Smolensk War, although the practice continued in peacetime. The administration of the collection on faith was performed by Muscovites in the 1620s, and the Ustiug Quarter had difficulties with this practice. They could not easily ensure the proper control to prevent graft and general misadministration, even when the chief of the administration was not a local man.[31] The farming system produced revenue, but even less control: When the taxes were farmed, the officials had little idea how much the town could actually produce. But why the officials should switch back and forth from the one system to the other is a question that cannot be answered in the present state of research.

Finally, one more example of the process of tavern revenue collection by Moscow merchants is to be found in the case of the tavern of Bol'shie Soli, mentioned in Chapter 8 as a minor source of salt near Kostroma. In Bol'shie Soli, the toll collection was collected on faith in 1614, 1615, 1616, 1617, and 1618, the largest sum collected (in 1617) being 19 rubles and 25 altyny. In 1626–7, however, the toll collection was farmed to the local merchant Grigorii Ploshchinin for twenty-seven rubles, but in March 1627 changed to collection on faith. In 1628, the farm went, with that of Malye Soli nearby, to two more merchants, apparently also natives of the town, for a total of 28 rubles, 5 altyny, and 3 dengi. In 1629, it was collected on faith for twenty-five rubles, and in 1630, again farmed for 29 rubles, 9 altyny, and 2 dengi to a local man. In 1631 and 1632, the farm was given to different men, apparently also local, and by 1632 had reached forty-five rubles. In 1637, the collection was made on faith, but in 1641 the tavern (which we hear of for the first time) was farmed by Petrunka Semenov Panov of Iurevets Povolzhskii.[32] On August 15, 1641, a group of peasants from the district belonging to Afanasii Mikitich Cheliustkin, a minor nobleman, attacked the tavern, stole 52.5 rubles from Panov, and destroyed the tavern. A week later, they attacked Panov's servant on the road near Bol'shie Soli and stole another fifty rubles. The next record of the tavern is of the same type: In April 1645, another group of peasants attacked, wrecked, and robbed the tavern in Bol'shie Soli. This year it had been farmed to two Moscow merchants, V. Borovitinov (*gost'* hundred) and Pil'ka Savel'ev (*kadashevets*). In spite of this incident, Borovitinov persisted, and in January 1647, when he held the farm alone, another group of peasants led by one Vas'ka Fedorov-Zavorui smashed the tavern and stole 157.5 rubles. Borovitinov complained to the land elder (*zemskii starosta*) of Bol'shie Soli, but there is no record of any action.[33] In that same year, the tolls were collected on faith to the sum of 24 rubles, 29 altyny, and 5 dengi. The year 1648 brought a crisis in Bol'shie Soli, like the crises in so many Russian towns in that year, but of lesser extent. The townsmen objected to the farming of the tolls (not the tavern) to one Putilo Sorokin, a *gost'* hundred merchant from Balakhna. What they specifically objected to was his introduction of the new salt tax, at a time when the salt industry of Bol'shie Soli was in decline and run largely by the *gost'* Semen Sveteshnikov. Sveteshnikov paid his tax directly to the treasury in Moscow, causing the town even more trouble as Sorokin was determined to collect. Sorokin tried in later years to sue the townsmen for the taxes they supposedly owed, but apparently he was unsuccessful. The problem was eventually solved in 1649 by the grant of a three-year farm of the tolls to the town as a whole for a total of 100 rubles.[34] Evidently, in the atmosphere of urban unrest in 1648–50, the officials in Moscow decided to relent. Besides, by this time the new salt tax had been abolished (indeed, it was abolished in spring 1648, midway in Sorokin's tenure).

The history of Bol'shie Soli is significant because it is based on the surviving records of the *posadskaia izba*, the town administration. These records give an inside view of the whole problem of the farming of taxes that is rarely available. Evidently, the system excited conflict. In the case of the tavern, it was the peasants who rebelled, and with remarkable persistency. Whether these were simply riots, raids of bands of "social bandits" in the area, or outbursts of rage against the tavern keepers, we cannot tell. But they certainly were a focus of social conflict. In the case of the tolls, it was the townsmen who objected to the exactions of a merchant from another town that was, in fact, a rival salt-producing town, known for its wealth. The combination of this fact and the new salt tax produced a campaign of petitions and systematic nonpayment of taxes. In the tense atmosphere of 1649, the government gave in to the townsmen of Bol'shie Soli.

Fragmentary though it be, this survey of the farming of taxes and the administration of the collection of tolls and tavern revenues does allow some limited conclusions. The most obvious is that the practice of farming out the taxes, especially of the tavern monopoly, was extremely widespread, except in the Russian North. In this process of tax farming, the Moscow merchants seem to have been the most active, and perhaps held the majority of the richest sources of income. To be sure of the latter assertion, a detailed study would have to be made of the situation in the larger towns, such as Nizhnii Novgorod, Vladimir, or Yaroslavl in those years. Among the Moscow merchants, the active farmers of taverns and tolls were the *kadashevtsy* first, followed by the *gost'* hundred. It is to be noted that no *gosti* are ever found to have farmed these taxes. Another important fact is the widespread use of Moscow merchants in the provinces to head the collection of tolls on faith. This certainly provided the central government with a check on the local merchants, but the example of Mozhaisk suggests two things: that the Moscow offices were not very effective in controlling their own agents, and that it is not obvious that this "service" was as financially onerous as the traditional historiography would have it. Finally, the example of Bol'shie Soli suggests that this system led to a variety of social conflicts, and had the effect of putting the government and the merchants involved in farming the taxes in one camp. This grouping appears recurrently in the urban revolts of 1648-9, and the effects of this system of collecting what were obviously the main taxes on the urban populations must have been a major factor in the origin of these revolts. In any case, it should be clear that the collection of tolls and the administration of the state monopoly of the production and sale of vodka is more than a question of administrative history.

Finally, the whole relationship of the state to the merchant class in Russia must be reexamined. It is not possible merely to repeat the analogy of Bakhrushin that the state squeezed the merchants dry "like a lemon"; in some cases, the merchants squeezed the state dry, as well as the townsmen and peasants who paid the tolls and bought the vodka. Nor can the trade of the state be seen as a serious source of competition to the merchant class. On the whole, it amounted to a constant figure of about 5-10 percent of the trade at Archangel, and was not enough to make a serious impact on the trade, except in the period of the Smolensk War, and even then the impact was not overwhelming. In addition, none of these elements were unique to Russia. In the other Eastern European countries, merchants collected and farmed taxes, and suffered from state competition. Indeed, the Russian merchants suffered far less from state competition than did the merchants of the Habsburg lands. Caviar and vodka were virtually the only items subject to a permanent monopoly of the treasury before 1650, whereas salt, silver, mercury, and copper were all brought under state control by the Habsburgs long before Peter the Great introduced the third permanent trade monopoly (salt) in 1705.

This examination of the relationship of the merchants to the state is not sufficient to define that relationship in all its particulars. However, it does provide evidence that the most widespread traditional view – that the merchants were crushed by the state – cannot be sustained without a great deal of research that has not yet been done. As a hypothesis, I propose that this relationship was two-sided, with the merchants to some extent prospering from their relationship with the state, primarily by farming certain taxes. Furthermore, I suggest that the tax-farming system must have provided a motive for the merchants' subservience to the state as great or greater than the fear of arbitrary treatment: the dependence of part of their profits on the power of the state to enforce and defend the collecting of taxes. Naturally, a definitive account of this problem must await a detailed examination of the taxation system, something that does not now exist.

CONCLUSION

Many of the basic questions that recur in the history of the Moscow merchants – and indeed in the history of the Russian economy as a whole – can now be answered. In the first place, the structure of Russian trade, foreign and domestic, is now much clearer. The most important sectors of Russia's commerce were the Archangel and Baltic trades, whose fundamental similarity requires that they be treated together. In both cases, Russian hemp, linen, and leather were exchanged for cloth, colonial wares, silver coin, and bullion, and a variety of small manufactured goods from Western Europe. In the Baltic, merchants of Lübeck, Holland, and the Livonian towns traded with Russian merchants of Pskov and Novgorod, and only rarely dealt with Muscovites. The Baltic trade remained relatively small, however, because the merchants had to contend with both Swedish fiscal policies and the economic problems of transport and shipping, both in the Baltic and on the Russian rivers. Consequently, Archangel emerged at the end of the sixteenth century as the main port of Russia, attracting first (1553–80) mainly English ships, and later mainly Dutch ships (from 1580 to the end of the seventeenth century). Russia was part of the far-flung network of Dutch trade, a part perhaps not as significant as Danzig or the Indies, but important nevertheless, because Russia supplemented the Baltic trade and supplied some unique goods (Russian leather) and naval stores. The Archangel trade was the branch of Russia's foreign trade that attracted the Moscow merchants in the largest numbers, especially the richer merchants. Other branches of foreign trade were less important. Next in importance to Archangel was probably the trade with Persia at Astrakhan. Russia was the fourth great purchaser of Persian silk, after the Dutch and English East India Companies and the Armenians trading at Aleppo. Besides silk, the Russians also bought large quantities of cheaper textiles and *saf'ian*, the finely worked Persian leather. This branch of the Russian trade was less concentrated in Moscow because the merchants of the towns (and even villages) of the Volga purchased the great majority of Persia's wares. With other countries Russia's trade was more restricted. The trade with Poland remained set in the pattern of the early sixteenth century: Russian furs for Central and West European cloth, transported in small quantities by a few wealthy merchants. With the Ottoman Empire, although it too provided a market for Russian furs, there is no evidence that the trade was conducted on a large scale, and in any case it was not in the hands of important Russian merchants.

On the one hand, this pattern of commerce is very backward because the Moscow (and other Russian) merchants rarely traveled abroad with their goods. Trips were made to Stockholm, Reval and Dorpat, Wilno and Kiev, as well as to the Persian silk towns in Azerbaijan (Shemakha), but in no case were they frequent or important enough to establish a pattern of active and large-scale trade beyond Russian borders. Most important of all, Russia had no trading fleet at Archangel. On the other hand, the backwardness of this pattern should not be exaggerated, and most of all should be considered in the light of the commercial patterns of Eastern Europe and the Baltic as a whole. The greatest entrepôt of the Baltic was Danzig, and its fleet was relatively small, so that most of its trade was carried on in Dutch ships. The same was true of Elbing and Königsberg, Riga and Reval, and most Scandinavian ports. Although Polish and other East European merchants in this period were more active than the Russians, they too could not fight the dominance of Holland and England and remained set in the pattern of trading from native soil or making small trips across the border (e.g. Poznań to Breslau). The backwardness of Russia was part of the backwardness of the whole of Eastern Europe. But Russia and Eastern Europe were not only "backward" and stagnating. Indeed, "backward" is not a term that adequately describes the position of the region. The evolution of Russia and Eastern Europe was complicated, not to say contradictory, in the sixteenth and seventeenth centuries. Integration into the emerging commercial empires of the West brought great prosperity to the merchants and nobles of the East, who produced and exported native goods. However, this new prosperity grew against the background of servile agriculture, and even the prosperity turned to poverty in the towns after the middle of the seventeenth century. The cloth and metal industries of Poland and Hungary also lagged behind the West to an ever-increasing degree. Russia was also part of this process: Integrated into the pattern of Dutch trade after 1580, Russia saw ever-increasing prosperity for the merchant, particularly the Moscow merchant. At the same time, in the very years of the expansion of the Dutch trade at Archangel, the instruction of serfdom was changing the character of rural life more profoundly than any change since the tenth century. If a judgment is to be made on Russia's "backwardness" it must be made not against the standard of Holland, which serves only to illuminate the features of Russian society common to the region, but against the standard of Poland and Hungary, Brandenburg and the Habsburg lands. The question is, how did Russia fare in comparison with its neighbors?[1]

The history of the Moscow merchants provides some important answers to this, the second important question in the history of the Russian economy. The Moscow merchant family was no less "unstable" than the merchant family of Krakow or Buda, although farther west in towns like Hamburg the situation was beginning to change. In Russia and Eastern Europe merchant families usually did not last more than three generations, which had been the rule in the West at the end of the Middle Ages. Hamburg merchant families already lasted longer, and the same was true in Amsterdam. Moscow merchants probably had few sources of credit and more primitive bookkeeping techniques than were the rule elsewhere, but these disadvantages did not stop them from being the main force in Russian trade at Archangel and significant in virtually all branches of Russian foreign trade. If the Russian merchant did not go abroad, neither did he allow the foreign merchant to push him out of the internal markets of Russia, even in goods destined for export to the West. Neither the foreign merchants trading in Moscow nor the "Moscow Germans," the immigrants from the West, were able to control a large proportion of Russia's trade inside the border, even in goods that they themselves had imported. The importance of the foreigners in introducing certain new technical processes into the Russian armaments industry was not matched by a comparable role in Russian trade. Nor did the foreigners make any investment at all in Russia's most important industry, salt, and most of the iron industry not engaged in the production of arms was outside their sphere. The Moscow merchants responded to the new opportunities for enrichment with an activity unprecedented in Russian history. They were the leaders in the newest branches of the economy: the Archangel trade, the salt trade and industry, the purchase of furs brought from Siberia, the supplying of the steppe frontier. And the rest of Russia followed

Moscow's lead. By 1710, the provincial cities were trading at Archangel on a scale unknown in 1630, and a multitude of village traders were drawn in, coming thousands of miles away by cart and boat to trade with the Dutch and the English.

The history of the Moscow merchants and their trade stands in distinct contrast to the history of Poland's merchants, as well as that of a number of other territories of Eastern Europe. The high point of the merchant classes' influence and prosperity in Eastern Europe as a whole was the beginning of the sixteenth century. This was the great time of the Krakow financiers such as Jan Boner, of the Fugger (and other) mining operations in Upper Hungary (Slovakia), of the burghers of Prague and Breslau, and of the Italian and German merchants of Buda and Pressburg. The last third of the century was a period of stagnation, in spite of the growing export of agricultural commodities, such as Danzig's export of grain. The mines of Hungary and the Habsburg lands began to stagnate and close down, and Polish iron production fell off and came into the hands of Italians producing for the needs of the King's army. But the real crisis came after the middle of the seventeenth century, when the grain exports of Danzig began first to stagnate and then to decline, pulling the whole structure of Polish urban life into ruin. The disastrous wars of the mid-century aided this process, but fundamentally it was an economic decline. Russia, in contrast, did not decline or stagnate after 1650. Coming from a much more "backward" level in 1500, when the Moscow merchant and his exchange of luxury goods with Poland and Turkey was still reminiscent of the Krakow or Prague merchant of 1250, the Moscow merchant moved into a qualitatively different stage of development, one that put him on a footing of rough equality with his immediate neighbors. After 1650, there was no catastrophic decline. The trade at Archangel remained about the same, but by the end of the century the English at Narva were increasing the level of the Baltic trade and the trade with Persia may have increased as well. Russia began to trade (on a small scale) with China after the 1680s. There is no discernable sign of decline in the Russian towns: Indeed, the increase in number of trading villages suggests the very opposite. If the period 1650–1710 was not as expansive as that of 1580–1650, it was still a period of general prosperity. Even the decline of the salt industry in the 1690s was more than compensated for by the rise of the iron industry in Tula and the Urals. Backward by Western European standards, Russia was relatively successful in the context of the more similar societies of Eastern Europe.

The older view of the "backwardness" of the Russian economy, although true in the broadest sense, does not adequately grasp the complexities of life in Russia and Eastern Europe in the early modern era. But what factors account for the relatively strong position of Russia? Certainly Russia did not have any technological advantage over its neighbors; rather, the reverse is likely. Russia lacked any system of education adequate to the demands of the time in any field, which was not generally the case in Eastern Europe, even if Krakow and Prague could not boast a university equal to Leiden. Indeed, the Moscow merchants made their achievement in spite of their apparent ignorance of the bookkeeping techniques that were used in the West. A complete answer to the question must await further research, but some suggestions can be made. The more favorable consequences of Russian exports noted in Chapter 4 certainly had something to do with Russia's advantageous position: Russian exports pumped more money into the towns than the export of Polish grain or Livonian timber. Another reason for the persistence of Russian commerce after 1650 may be the importance in Russia of the peasant-trader, who widened the base of commerce. The peasant-trader was in turn a result of the feature of Russian serfdom that distinguished it from the agrarian systems of Poland or Prussia: Many, if not most, serfs in seventeenth-century Russia did not have to perform labor services (universal farther west) and merely paid a money rent called *obrok*. This gave them the freedom to engage in small-scale trade and handicrafts, and prevented Russian trade and crafts from being locked up in closed urban guilds, jealous of their monopolistic privileges. The very "backwardness" of the Russian town may have been an advantage for Russian trade and craft industries.

One of the most striking signs of the "backwardness" of the Russian merchants, especially the wealthiest merchants in Moscow, was their supposed political weakness. It has been claimed that two factors were behind this weakness – the economic insignificance of the merchants and the supposedly all-powerful Russian state. However, "backwardness" is inadequate not only in describing the economic situation of the merchant, but also in describing the relation of the merchants, especially those of the capital, to the state. The history of the toll and tavern administration has been dismissed as a mere record of how the state exploited the merchant, but there is no proof that this was so. The merchant may have exploited the state as much as the state exploited the merchant. Certainly the status of the Russian merchant in the seventeenth century was an improvement over his earlier position. The medieval Russian merchant was merely a merchant, and if he served the Prince, that was the choice of a personal career: Taxes were collected by the Prince's servitors. In the seventeenth century, merchants continued to enter the ranks of the officials as individuals, but the existence of the tax-farming system meant that much actual control of the state's finances was being lost to the merchants. The intertwining of the practice of tax farming with the "service" of the merchant in the elective offices of the toll and tavern administration meant that the service character of the office remained a legal theory, adhered to in some years and in some towns, but bypassed in others. The Russian state was continually short of money to maintain its military ventures, and not until Peter the Great introduced the head tax did the treasury break free of partial dependence on the merchants to collect the main part of the state's income.

From one point of view, the absence of a legally enshrined system of political rights and privileges did not prevent the merchant from exercising such power as his wealth gave him. The result was that the wealthiest merchants, the Moscow merchants, had the best chance at the most lucrative investments in the taverns. Seen from another point of view, this exercise of power weakened the merchant class because it made them dependent on the power of the state for a portion of their profit. Without the authority and even the military power of the Tsar behind them, they could not collect and safeguard the taxes farmed to them. The result was a split in the towns, and a drawing of the merchant tax farmers, mostly men of middle wealth, into the camp of the government, as in the revolts of 1648–50. The Russian merchant was able to exploit the weakness of the state, but he nevertheless grew up under its shadow. This particular configuration of forces in the first century of great prosperity for the Russian merchants may go far in explaining their political passivity in the ensuing centuries.

Appendix 1

Moscow *gosti*, 1566–1650

The gosti *of 1566:*

Iurii Borisov Glazeev

Ivan Ivanov Afanasev

Aleksei Khoznikov

Vasilii Petrov Nikitin

Vasilii Suzin

Afanasii Ivashev

Dmitrii Ivashev

Mikhailo Petrov Podushkin

Grigorii Fedorov Tarakanov

Ivan Kotkov

Prokofii Tsvilenev

Bulgak Savanin

Source: SGGD 1 (192): 553.

The gosti *of 1598:*

Ivan Mikhailov Chiurkin

Petr Vasil'ev Miakotin

Grigorii Ivanov Tverdikov

Afanasii Ivanov Iudin

Ivan Iur'ev (Bulgakov)

Men'shoi Semenov Bulgakov

Bogdan Semenov Bulgakov

Stepan Ivanov Kotov

Aleksei Konstantinov Patrushin

Bazhen Ivanov

Ivan Faleleev

Bogdan Trofimov Poryvkin

Ivan Semenov Koshurin

Vasilii Dmitreev Chiulkov

Fedor Sozonov Skrobnitskii

Kirilo Sozonov Skrobnitskii

Sotnik Ignat'ev

Vasilli Koptev

Iurii Bolotnikov

Timofei Vykhodets

Tret'iak Favorov

Source: AAE 2 (7): 45.

The gosti of the 1620s:

Iurii Bolotnikov
Bakhteiar Bulgakov
Kirilo Bulgakov
Nazarii Chistoi
Smironoi Eroksalimov
Andrei Kotov
Fedot Kotov
Rodion Kotov
Vasilii Lytkin
Fedor Maksimov
Grigorii Myl'nikov
Grigorii Nikitnikov
Gavrilo Oblezov
Vtoroi Ozerov
Grigorii Shorin
Smirnoi Sudovshchikov

Ivan Sverchkov
Nadeia Sveteshnikov
Naum Sveteshnikov
Tomilo Tarakanov
Grigorii Tverdikov
Maksim Tverdikov
Andrei Vasil'ev
Andrei Iudin
Ivan Iudin
Vasilii Iudin
Vasilii Ivanov Iur'ev
Vasilii Vasil'ev Iur'ev
Ivan Vasil'ev Iur'ev
Il'ia Vasil'ev Iur'ev
(Mikhailo Smyvalov)

Source: Baron, *"Gosti,"* p. 25; see also Chapter 1.

The gosti of the 1630s:

Bakhteiar Bulgakov
Anikei Ivanov Chistoi
Vasilii Lytkin
Tret'iak Lytkin
Grigorii Nikitnikov
Ivan Vtorov Ozerov
Dem'ian Smirnov Sudovshchikov
Matvei Ivanov Sverchkov
Nadeia Sveteshnikov
Semen Nadein Sveteshnikov

Tomilo Tarakanov
Maksim Tverdikov
Anufrii Vasil'ev
Andrei Iudin
Vasilii Iudin
Il'ia Iur'ev
Vasilii (?) Il'in Iur'ev
Vasilii Iur'ev
Bogdan Tsvetnoi
(Smirnoi Sudovshchikov)

Source: Baron, *"Gosti,"* p. 25; see also Chapter 1.

The gosti of the 1640s:

Kiril Bosoi
Semen Cherkasov

Vasilii Fedotov-Gusiatnikov
("Skoraia Zapis'")

Ivan Kolomiatin
Grigorii Nikitnikov
Ivan Vtorov Ozerov
Daniil Pankrat'ev
Bogdan Shchepotkin
Vasilii Grigor'ev Shorin
Andrei Sprirdonov
Smirnoi Sudovshchikov
Matvei Sverchkov

Nadeia Sveteshnikov
Semen Sveteshnikov
Tomilo Tarakanov
Matvei Vasil'ev
Afanasii Venevitinov
Petr Volkov
Fedor Vasil'ev Iur'ev
Ivan Iur'ev
Vasilii Iur'ev

Source: Baron, *"Gosti,"* p. 26; see also Chapter 1.

Appendix 2

Manuscript sources

The great majority of the relevant unpublished sources are to be found in several funds of the Central State Archive of Ancient Acts, Moscow, (TsGADA). The most important of these is fund 141 (*Prikaznye dela starykh let*). This fund was put together in the nineteenth century from the various fragmentary archives of the Russian offices of the seventeenth century, and does not reflect the archive of any one office. The main components of fund 141 for the period before 1650 are the Ustiug and Novgorod Quarters, which collected taxes and administered the taverns and toll collections in the areas under their jurisdiction. The holdings consist of correspondence of the central offices in Moscow with their local representatives. The records of these offices are also to be found in fund 137 (*Gorodovye knigi*), which includes not only the books of the censuses of the towns but also those records of the taverns and toll collection that were collected into books, usually to provide a precedent for later officials. Some information is to be found in funds 210 (*Razriad; prikaznoi stol*) and 396 (*Oruzhennaia palata*). The suit against the Zolotovs is in fund 210, presumably because taverns in the steppe were under the jurisdiction of the *Razriad*, and the case involved such a tavern.

The Leningrad Section of the Institute of the History (LOII) of the USSR has among its collection fund 178 (*Astrakhanskaia prikaznaia izba*), the records of the local administration of Astrakhan and thus one of the few surviving local archives of the period. It records the affairs of the Astrakhan fisheries and salt marshes as well as trade. Finally, the Reval City Archive in the Staatliche Archivlager Göttingen (West Germany) contains a contemporary German translation of the Pskov toll book of 1624, or rather of the part of the toll book that concerned trade with the Germans of Reval.

The majority of the sources from these various archival funds that can be used to reconstruct the history of the Russian merchant class are from the records of the toll collections, the *tamozhennyi sbor*. These tolls were collected by the system described in Chapter 2, and the records of the collection were supposed to include the name of the person who paid the toll, his place of residence, whether or not he was the agent of another man, the quantity or weight of the goods, and their price. These records were kept in the town's *prikaznaia izba* (official house), and at the end of the year (August–September), these records were made up into a toll book called a *tamozhennaia kniga*, a copy of which was sent to the appropriate financial office in Moscow.

In general, the records kept at the local level have not survived. In the important case of Archangel, they perished in a fire in the 1770s. Most local archives have remained uncatalogued until the last five to ten years, and thus have been rarely used by scholars, including Soviet scholars. The majority of holdings in local archives are in fact unknown and are just beginning to be exploited. One important exception is the archive of the Astrakhan *prikaznaia izba*, which found its way to the archive of the Leningrad Division of the Institute of the History of the USSR.

With this important exception, only those records of the toll collections that were kept in Moscow offices have been preserved and rendered usable to historians. The survival of such records has therefore been dependent on the vagaries of the fires of the seventeenth and eighteenth centuries, as well as the fire of 1812. Because most of the offices were wooden until well into the eighteenth century, the fires took a heavy toll. In this process, the Siberian Office's records survived most fully, whereas the records of the Kazan Palace, which administered the whole Volga region from Kazan south, were irreparably lost in the seventeenth century. For the rest of Russia, losses are more irregular. For the period 1613–50, the records of the Ustiug Quarter have survived very well, whereas the Novgorod Quarter (responsible for Novgorod, the North including Archangel, and the Nizhnii Novgorod district) are more irregular. Central Russia is most poorly represented. For the important commercial town of Yaroslavl there is little for the whole of the seventeenth century. For the historian of Moscow, however, the situation is especially bad because the loss of records of the Great Toll Office (*Bol'shaia Tamozhnia*), which collected tolls in Moscow, is virtually complete. Few records of the Land Office (*Zemskii prikaz*), the administration of the city of Moscow, have survived. The loss is to some extent repaired by the survival of the records of the palace settlements (*dvortsovye slobody*), the Great Treasury (*Bol'shaia kazna*), which judged *gosti*, and the Foreign Office (*Posol'skii prikaz*), which judged cases involving foreign merchants. These last three groups, however, provide only occasional items for the historian of the Moscow merchants.

The basic archival materials remain the correspondence of the Novgorod and Ustiug Quarters with provincial towns, and the Astrakhan records. Published materials include the partial censuses of Moscow made by the Land Office and published in the nineteenth century and especially the toll collection books of Ustiug Velikii and other northern towns published by Iakovlev. In general, it may be said that virtually all information on Russian trade from Russian sources comes from the records of the toll collection, whether directly or from the work of other scholars.

NOTES

Preface

1 N. Kostomarov, *Ocherk torgovli Moskovskogo gosudarstva v XVI i XVII stoletiiakh* (St. Petersburg, 1862), especially Chapter 4.

2 M. V. Dovnar-Zapol'skii, "Torgovlia i promyshlennost' Moskvy," *Moskva v ee proshlom i nastoiashchem* 3(2) (Moscow, circa 1912): 5-67.

3 A. D. Gradovskii, "Obshchestvennye klassy v Rossii do Petra I," *Zhurnal ministerstva narodnogo prosveshcheniia* 138-9 (April-September 1868): 1-91, 405-56, 631-98 in vol. 138; 72-241 in vol. 139; V. O. Kliuchevskii, "Istoriia soslovii v Rossii" *Sochineniia 6* (Moscow, 1959): 414-17. This latter work is a course of lectures given in 1886.

4 K. V. Bazilevich, "Krupnoe torgovoe predipriiatie v moskovskom gosudarstve v pervoi poloviny XVII v.," *Izvestiia Akademii Nauk SSSR* VII series, no. 9 (1932): 783-812; id., "Kollektivnye chelobit'ia torgovykh liudei i bor'ba za russkii rynok v pervoi polovine XVII veka," Ibid., VII series, no. 2 (1932): 91-123; id., "Novotorgovyi ustav 1667 g. (K voprosu o ego istochnikakh), Ibid. VII series, no. 7 (1932): 589-622; S. V. Bakhrushin, *Nauchnye trudy*, 3 vols. ed. A. A. Zimin et al, (Moscow, 1952-5):

5 *Perekhod ot feodalizma k kapitalizmu v Rossii* (Moscow, 1969), pp. 29-30. Pavlenko was the editor of the main report delivered at the 1965 conference whose proceedings appear in this volume.

6 N. V. Ustiugov, *Solevarennaia promyshlennost' Soli Kamskoi v XVII veke: K voprosu o genezise kapitalisticheskikh otnoshenii v russkoi promyshlennosti* (Moscow, 1957); K. N. Serbina, *Ocherki iz sotsial'no-ekonomicheskoi istorii russkogo goroda: Tikhvinskii posad v XVI-XVII vv.* (Moscow-Leningrad, 1951); id., *Krest'ianskaia zhelezodelatel'naia promyshlennost' severo-zapadnoi Rossii XVI-pervoi poloviny XIX v.* (Leningrad, 1971); E. I. Zaozerskaia, *U istokov krupnogo proizvodstva v russkoi promyshlennosti XVI-XVII vekov: K voprosu o genezise kapitalizma v Rossii* (Moscow, 1970); A. Ts. Merzon and Iu. A. Tikhonov, *Rynok Ustiuga Velikogo v period skladyvaniia vserossiiskogo rynka (XVII vek)* (Moscow, 1960); R. I. Kozintseva, "Uchastie kazny vo vneshnei torgovle Rossii v pervoi chetverti XVIII v.," *Istoricheskie zapiski* 91 (Moscow, 1973): 267-337; N. N. Repin, "K voprosu o sviazi vneshnego i vnutrennogo rynka Rossii vo vtoroi polovine XVII-pervoi chetverti XVIII v. (Po materialam Arkhangel'ska)," *Vestnik MGU: seriia istorii* 6 (1970): 56-72; id., "Vneshnaia torgovlia cherez Arkhangel'sk i vnutrennii rynok Rossii vo vtoroi polovine XVII-pervoi chetverti XVIII v." (*Kandidatskaia* dissertation, Moscow University, 1970).

7 Erik Amburger, *Die Familie Marselis: Studien zur russischen Wirtschaftsgeschicte*, Osteuropastudien der Hochschulen des Landes Hessen: Reihe 1: Giessener Abhandlungen zur Agrar-und Wirtschaftsforschung des europäischen Ostens 4 (Giessen, 1957); Samuel H. Baron, "Who Were the *Gosti?*," *California Slavic Studies* 7 (1973): 1–40.

8 Wolfgang Knackstedt, *Moskau: Studien zur Geschichte einer mittelalterlichen Stadt*, Quellen und Studien zur Geschichte des östlichen Europa 8 (Wiesbaden, 1975); id. "Moskauer Kaufleute im späten Mittelalter: Organisationsformen und soziale Stellung," *Zeitschrift für Historische Forschung* 3, Heft 1 (1976): 1–19.

Chapter 1. Moscow and its merchant, 1580–1650

1 B. Chicherin, *Oblastnye uchrezhdeniia Rossii v XVII veke* (Moscow, 1856); A. D. Gradovskii, "Obshchestvennye klassy v Rossii do Petra I," *Zhurnal ministerstva narodnogo prosveshcheniia* 138 (April–September 1868): 631–98; P. P. Smirnov, *Posadskie liudi i ikh klassovaia bor'ba do serediny XVII veka*, 2 vols. (Moscow-Leningrad, 1947–1948); M. D'iakonov, *Ocherki obshchestvennogo i gosudarstvennogo stroia drevnei Rusi (do kontsa XVII veka)* 1 (Iur'ev, 1907); P. P. Smirnov, *Goroda Moskovskogo gosudarstva v pervoi polovine XVII veka. Kievskie universitetski izvestiia* 58, (Kiev, 1918).

2 M. N. Tikhomirov, *Srednevekovaia Moskva v XIV–XV vekakh* (Moscow, 1957); Knackstedt, *Moskau*, pp. 12–65; S. V. Bakhrushin et al., eds., *Istoria Moskvy* 1 (Moscow, 1952) pp. 446–91.

3 On merchants' houses and related problems see A. A. Tits, *Russkoe kammennoe zhiloe zodchestvo XVII veka* (Moscow, 1966).

4 Bogoiavlenskii is the author of the relevant section in *Istoriia Moskvy* 1, p. 456.

5 S. K. Bogoiavlenskii, "Moskovskie slobody i sotni v XVII veke," *Moskovskii krai v ego proshlom* 2, Trudy Obshchestva Izucheniia Moskovskoi Oblasti 6 (Moscow, 1930): 119–26.

6 L. V. Cherepnin, ed., "Ukaznaia kniga zemskogo prikaza," *Pamiatniki russkogo prava* 5 (Moscow, 1959): 376–82.

7 P. P. Smirnov, "Okladnoi spisok gostei gostinnoi i sukonnoi sotni 1632 g.," *Chteniia v Istoricheskom obshchestve Nestora-letopistsa* 23 (1) (Kiev, 1912): 12–15. Most of the foreigners in Moscow were clerks or agents for greater men than themselves and were not an important group among the merchants of Moscow. A few settled permanently in Russia and became russified, entering the Moscow merchant class. In spite of remarks in the literature to the contrary, they were not especially wealthy or powerful, as shown in Chapter 3. Most of these foreigners who rose to great wealth did so through influence at court, even if that influence was the result of commercial and industrial services to the Tsar. Such was the case of the Vinius family at the end of the century. In contrast, the Vestov/Westhoff family was more purely merchants. On the foreigners see Erik Amburger, *Die Familie Marselis: Studien zur russischen Wirtschaftsgeschicte*, Osteuropastudien der Hochschulen des Landes Hessen: Reihe 1; Giessener Abhandlunger zur Agrar- und Wirtschaftsforschumg des europäischen Ostens, 4 (Giessen, 1957).

8 *Dopolneniia k aktam istoricheskim* 10 vols. (St. Petersburg, 1846–75) 3 (44): 150–1 (hereafter DAI).

9 Paul Bushkovitch, "Taxation, Tax Farming, and Merchants in Sixteenth-Century Russia," *Slavic Review* 37, (3) (Sept. 1978): 381–98.

10 E. D. Stashevskii, "Piatina 142-go goda i torgovo-promyshlennye tsentry Moskovskogo gosudarstva," *Zhurnal ministerstva narodnogo prosveshcheniia* n.s. 38 (April 1912): 283–5.

11 Samuel H. Baron, "Who were the *Gosti?*," *California Slavic Studies* 7 (1973): 1–40.

12 Richard Ehrenberg, *Das Zeitalter der Fugger: Geldkapital und Creditverkehr im 16. Jahrhundert*, 2 vols. (Jena, 1896), 1, p. 384; W. G. Hoskins, "English Provincial Towns in the Early Sixteenth Century," *Transactions of the Royal Historical Society*, Fifth Series 6 (1956): 8.

13 András Kubinyi, "Die Städte Ofen und Pest und der Fernhandel am Ende des 15. und am Anfang des 16. Jahrhunderts," in *Der Aussenhandel Ostmitteleuropas 1450–1650: Die ostmitteleuropäischen Volkswirtschaften in ihren Beziehungen zu Mitteleuropa*, ed. Ingomar Bog (Köln, 1971): 386; Janina Bieniarzówna, *Mieszczaństwo krakowskie XVII w.: z badań nad strukturą społeczną miasta* (Krakow, 1969): 155–72; Hermann Kellenbenz, *Unternehmerkräfte im Hamburger Portugal und Spanienhandel 1590–1625* Veröffentlichungen der Wirtschaftsgeschichtlichen Forschungsstelle Hamburg, vol. 10 (Hamburg, 1954); Martin Reissmann, *Die hamburgische Kaufmannschaft des 17. Jahrhunderts in sozialgeschichtlicher Sicht*, Beiträge zur Geschichte Hamburgs, vol. 4 (Hamburg, 1975): 267–68.

14 *Sobranie gosudarstvennykh gramot i dogovorov*, 5 vols. (Moscow, 1813–94): 1 (192): 553 (hereafter SGGD); *Akty arkheograficheskoi ekspeditsii*, 5 vols. (Saint Petersburg, 1836) 2 (7): 45 (hereafter AAE); Bushkovitch, "Merchants." See Appendix 1.

15 S. G. Tomsinskii ed., *Materialy po istorii Tatarskoi ASSR: Pistsovye knigi goroda Kazani 1565–8 gg. i 1646 g.* Trudy istoriko-arkheograficheskogo instituta akademii Nauk SSSR: Materialy po istorii narodov SSSR, no. 2, p. 34.

16 M. N. Tikhomirov, "Pskovskoe vosstanie 1650 g.," *Klassovaia bor'ba v Rossii XVII v.* (Moscow, 1969): 38–40; id., "Novgorodskoe vosstanie 1650 g" Ibid., pp. 142–4. These articles first appeared in 1935 and 1940 respectively. K. V. Bazilevich, "Krupnoe torgovoe predpriiatie v moskovskom gosudarstve v pervoi polovine XVII v.," *Izvestiia Akademii Nauk SSSR*, VII series, no. 9 (1932): 3–4.

17 The Yaroslavl *gost'* Mikhail Gur'ev (the founder of Gur'evsk on the Caspian Sea) was the son of Gurii Nazar'ev, and was probably the nephew of the Yaroslavl *gost'* Druzhina Nazar'ev active on the lower Volga in the 1630s. Gurii Nazar'ev was apparently related to the merchant and later government official Nazarii Ivanov Chistoi (perhaps his nephew or even son). Nazarii Chistoi was killed in the Moscow revolt of 1648, and was closely related to Anikei (Almaz) Ivanov Chistoi, another important official. An Ivan Chistoi was still a Yaroslavl merchant in 1638. See *Sovietskaia istoricheskaia entsiklopediia* 4, s.v. "Gur'evy" by S. K. Bazhanova; I. V. Stepanov. "Khoziaistvennaia deiatel'nost' Moskovskogo pravitel'stva v Nizhnem Povolzh'e v XVII veke," *Uchenye Zapiski LGU: seriia istoricheskikh nauk* 48 (5) (1939): 96; *Russkii biograficheskii slovar'* s.vv. Chistogo, Almaz (Anikii) Ivanovich, and Chistogo Nazar Ivanovich, by E. Likhachev (St. Petersburg, 1905); P. P. Smirnov, *Posadskie liudi* I. p. 454.

18 Besides the signatures of the *gosti*, this document was also signed by *smol'niane* (cf. Chapter 1) and ordinary merchants.

19 A. A. Zimin, *Oprichnina Ivana Groznogo* (Moscow, 1964), pp. 181–3.

20 Ivan Iur'ev signed the document "Ivan Iur'ev Men'shogo Semenov Bulgakov," and indicated that he signed for his cousin. *AAE* 2 (7): 53. Churkin's son, Al. Ivanov Churkin sold an estate in the Moscow district sometime before the 1620s. Cf. Iu. Got'e, *Zamoskovnyi krai v XVII veke: Opyt issledovaniia po istorii ekonomicheskogo byta Moskovskoi Rusi* (Moscow, 1906): 423.

21 Zimin, *Oprichnina*, pp. 183–6; *AAE* 1 (223): 213.

22 Tsentral'nyi gosudarstvennyi arkhiv drevnikh aktov (hereafter TsGADA), f. 141 (Prikaznye dela starykh let), no. 2, 1613; Baron, "*Gosti*," p. 25; A. Orlov, *Domostroi po konshinskomu spisku* (Moscow, 1908): 37.

23 TsGADA, f. 141, 1611, no. 1; p. 10 ff.; *Perepisnye knigi goroda Moskvy, sostavlennye v 1738–1742 (s prilozheniem Perepisnoi knigi 1626 g.)* 1 (Moscow, 1881): 12. Ivan Kashurin was prominent in the Time of Troubles and was Moscow Toll Chief in 1615, but had no known descendants. Cf. *Akty zapadnoi Rossii* 4 (182) (St. Petersburg, 1846–53): 319; S. B. Veselovskii and S. F. Platonov, eds., "Prikhodo-raskhodnye knigi moskovskikh prikazov," I, *Russkaia istoricheskaia biblioteka* (RIB) 28 (Moscow, 1912): 265.

24 Vtoroe otdelemie sobstuennoi E. I. V. kantselianii, ed. *Pamiatniki diplomaticheskikh snoshenii drevnei Rossii s derzhavami inostrannymi* 1 (St. Petersburg, 1851), pp. 1076–7, 1109, 114, 1219.

25 Got'e, *Zamoskovnyi*, p. 423; *Perepisnye Knigi goroda Moskvy, sostavlennye v 1738–1742 (s prilozheniem Perepisnoi Knigi 1626 g.)*. (Moscow, 1881): 12; Baron, "*Gosti*," pp. 25–31.

26 Andrei, Rodion, and Fedot Kotov were the *gosti*. Fedot went on a famous mission to Persia in 1628. Cf. N. A. Kuznetsova ed., *Khozhdenie kuptsa Fedota Kotova v Persiiu*, (Moscow, 1958).

27 S. V. Rozhdestvenskii, ed. *Pamiatniki istorii nizhegorodskogo dvizheniia v epokhu smuty i zemskogo opolcheniia 1611–1612 gg.* Deistviia Nizhegorodskoi Gubernskoi uchenoi arkhiv-noi kommissii 11 (1912): 104, 167–8, 172–3.

28 A. I. Timofeev, ed., "Prikhodo-raskhodnye knigi kazennogo prikaza," *Russkaia istoricheskaia biblioteka* 9 (St. Petersburg, 1884): 2; E. S. Ovchinnikova, *Tserkov' Troitsy v Nikitnikakh: Pamiatnik zhivopisi i zodchestva XVII veka* (Moscow, 1970), pp. 5–12 (an art historian's description of the church built in the Kitaigorod by the Nikitnikovs, with a sketch of the family); S. V. Bakhrushin, "Promyshlennye predpriiatiia russkikh tor-govykh liudei v XVII veke," *Istoricheskie zapiski* 8 (Moscow, 1940): 98–128.

29 "Pamiatniki diplomaticheskikh snoshenii drevnei Rossii s derzhavami inostrannymi," K. N. Bestuzhev-Riumin, ed., Pamiatniki diplomaticheskikh snoshenii moskovskogo gosudarstva s Anglieiu, vol. 2, *Sbornik russkogo istoricheskogo obshchesvta* 38 (St. Petersburg, 1883): 209. In 1583 the English merchant Anthony Marsh had contracted a debt of 525 rubles to Semen Shorin; Samuel H. Baron, "Vasilii Shorin: Seventeenth Century Russian Merchant-Extraordinary," *Canadian-American Slavic Studies* 6: 4 (1972): 506; L. S. Abetsedarskii and M. Ia. Volkov eds., *Russko-belorusskie sviazi: Sbornik dokumentov (1570–1667)* (Minsk, 1963), pp. 42, 45–6.

30 *RIB* 28: 8, 333; S. A. Belokurov ed., "Utverzhdennaia gramota ob izbranii na Moskovskoe gosudarstvo Mikhaila Fedorovicha Romanova," *Chteniia v obshchestve istorii i drevnostei pri Moskovskom universitete* (hereafter *ChOIDR*), 218 (3) (Moscow, 1906): 83.

31 Leningradskii otdel Instituta Istorii (hereafter LOII), f. 178, 1622–3, nos. 679, 722. On the Oblezovs see *Perepisnye kniga goroda Moskvy 1638 goda* (Moscow, 1881): 63.

32 *Perepisnye... 1626:* 12; *Perepisnaia 1638 goda* (Moscow, 1881): 14.

33 Bazilevich, "Krupnoe," pp. 3–4.

34 LOII, f. 178, 1622–3, no. 722.

35 LOII, f. 178, 1622–3, no. 651; TsGADA, f. 210 (Razriad: Prikaznoi stol), 1631, no. 37, part 1, p. 222; N. V. Ustiugov, *Solevarennaia promyshlennost' Soli Kamskoi v XVII veke: K voprosu o genezise kapitalisticheskikh otnoshenii v russkoi promyshlennosti* (Moscow, 1957): 7.

36 On the Moscow revolt of 1648 see S. V. Bakhrushin, "Moskovskoe vosstanie 1648 g." *Nauchnye trudy* 2 (Moscow, 1954).

37 The text of this order is in M. Bogoslovskii, *Zemskoe samoupravlenie na Russkom Severe v XVII v.* 1 (Moscow, 1909), p. 104, note 2. See also Bazilevich, "Krupnoe," passim; A. Ts. Merzon and Iu. A. Tikhonov, *Rynok Ustiuga Velikogo v period skladyvaniia vserossiis-kogo rynka (XVII vek)* (Moscow, 1960): 372. Kirill and Vasilii Bosoi claimed to be Muskovites only when it suited them. See Chapter 3, note 22.

Chapter 2. The conditions of trade in seventeenth-century Russia

1 Philippe Dollinger, *La Hanse (XIIe-XVIIe siecles) (Paris, 1964):* 177-8; A. L. Khoroshkevich, *Torgovlia Velikogo Novgoroda s Pribaltikoi i Zapadnoi evropoi v XIV-XV vv* (Moscow, 1963); I. E. Kleinenberg, "Serebro vmesto soli: Elementy rannego merkantilizma vo vneshnetorgovoi politike Russkogo gosudarstva kontsa XV-nachala XVI veka," *Istoriia SSSR* 2 (1977): 115-24; N. A. Kazakova, *Russko-livonskie i russko-ganzeiskie otnosheniia: Konets XIV nachalo XVI v.* (Leningrad, 1975); Walter Kirchner, *Commercial Relations between Russia and Europe, 1400 to 1800: Collected Essays,* (Bloomington: Indiana University Publications, Russian and East European Series, vol. 33, 1966): 26-42, 59-77.

2 V. A. Kordt, "Ocherk snoshenii Moskovskogo gosudarstva s Respublikoi Soedinennykh Niderlandov po 1631 g.," *Sbornik Imperatorskogo Rossiiskogo Istoricheskogo Obshchestva* 116 (St. Petersburg, 1902): lvi-lvii. See also Jorma Ahvenainen, "Some Contributions to the Question of Dutch Traders in Lapland and Russia at the End of the Sixteenth Century," *Studia historica Jyväskyläensia* 5 (Jyväskylä, Finland, 1967): 5-53.

3 Simon Hart, "Amsterdam Shipping and Trade to Northern Russia in the Seventeenth Century," *Mededelingen van de Nederlandse Vereniging voor Zeegeschiedenis* 26 (1973): 8.

4 Ibid., pp. 17-19; see also Chapter 3.

5 N. A. Baklanova, "Privoznye tovary v Moskovskom gosudarstve vo vtoroi polovine XVII veka," *Ocherki po istorii torgovli i promyshlennosti v Rossii v 17 i v nachale 18 stoletiia,* Trudy gosudarstvennogo istoricheskogo muzeia 4, Otdel istoricheskii obshchii (Moscow, 1928): 12.

6 The stone Merchants' House built after 1667 was much more elaborate. It contained 116 storage rooms in the "German" (i.e. foreign) section and 102 in the Russian section. It had two towers at each end and a fortified gate tower, the whole forming an irregular quadrilateral of 177 by 73 by 90 sazhens (about 378 by 155 by 192 meters). Each of the storage rooms was about 17.1 square meters in area. The building was about 11 meters high. Baklanova, "Privoznye," p. 8.

7 TsGADA, f. 141, 1614, no. 8, pp. 13-14, 42-45.

8 Baklanova, "Privoznye," p. 10.

9 A. A. Vvedenskii, *Dom Stroganovykh v XVI-XVII vekakh* (Moscow, 1962): 251-5. The Hunters' Settlement in Moscow was one of the palace settlements, which at this time contained merchants rather than the servants of the Tsar's hunt.

10 The earliest evidence of Indian merchants trading in Russia seems to be from 1638: *Russko-indiiskie otnosheniia v XVII veke* (Moscow, 1958): 38-9. It is not known when they first began to settle in Astrakhan.

11 LOII, f. 178, 1622-3, no. 654; N. A. Baklanova *Torgovo-promyshlennaia deiatel'nost Kalmykovykh vo vtoroi polovine XVII v.: K istorii formirovaniia russkoi burzhuazii* (Moscow, 1959): 131-5; A. A. Zimin ed., "Russkie geograficheskie spravochniki XVII veka," *Zapiski otdela rukopisei Gosudarstvennoi biblioteki SSSR im. V.I. Lenina* 21 (Moscow, 1959): 229-31.

12 For the minor role of the Tatar merchants in the seventeenth century see G. Gubaidullin, "Iz istorii torgovogo klassa Privolzhskikh tatar," *Izvestiia vostochnogo fakul'teta Azerbaidzhanskogo gosudarstvennogo universiteta im. V.I. Lenina: Vostokovedeniia* 1 (Baku, 1926): 51-4.

13 Alina Wawrzyńczyk, *Studia z dziejów handlu Polski z Wielkim Księstwem Litewskim i Rosją w XVI wieku* (Warsaw, 1956): 26-40.

14 Michał Baliński, *Historya Miasta Wilna,* 2 vols. (Wilno, 1836-7), vol. 1, p. 36; Piotr Dubiński, *Zbiór praw i przywilejów miastu stołecznemu S.X.L. Wilnowi nadanych* (Wilno, 1788): 18.

15 See Chapter 5. The trade between the Don Cossacks and the Crimean Tatars was very limited at that. A. A. Novosel'skii, "Iz istorii donskoi torgovli v XVII veke," *Istoricheskie zapiski* 26 (Moscow, 1948): 198-216.

16 I. P. Shaskol'skii, *Stolbovskii mir 1617 g. i torgovye otnosheniia Rossii so shvedskim gosudarstvom* (Moscow-Leningrad, 1967): 16-23; Sven-Erik Åström, *From Stockholm to St. Petersburg: Commercial Factors in the Political Relations between England and Sweden 1675-1700*, Studia Historica 2 (Helsinki, 1962): 76.

17 I. P. Shaskol'skii, "Ob osnovnykh osobennostiiakh russko-shvedskoi torgovli XVII v.," *Mezhdunarodnye sviazi Rossii v XVII-XVIII vv. (Ekonomika, politika i kul'tura)* (Moscow, 1966): 15-18.

18 Kordt, "Ocherk"; Iu. V. Tolstoi, *Pervye sorok let snoshenii mezhdu Rossiiu i Angliiu* 1553 - 1593 (St. Petersburg, 1875).

19 T. S. Willan, *The Early History of the Russia Company 1553-1603* (Manchester, 1956); I. I. Liubimenko, *Istoriia torgovykh snoshenii Rossii s Angliiu*, part 1, *XVI-i vek* (Iur'ev, 1912); id., *Les rélations commerciales et politiques de l'Angleterre avec la Russie avant Pierre le Grand*, (Paris: Bibliothèque de L'école des hautes études, Sciences historiques et philologiques 261, 1933).

20 Shaskol'skii, *Stolbovskii mir*, especially pp. 153-200. See also Marc Szeftel, "The Legal Condition of the Foreign Merchants in Muscovy," *Recueils de la Société Jean Bodin* 33 (Brussels, 1972): 335-58.

21 Kostomarov, *Ocherk torgovli*, pp. 29-30; P. P. Smirnov, "Novoe chelobit'e Moskovskikh torgovykh liudei o vysylke inozemtsev 1627 goda," *Chteniia v Istoricheskom obshchestve Nestora-letopistsa* 23 (1) (Kiev, 1912): 7; I. I. Liubimenko, "The Struggle of the Dutch with the English for the Russian Market in the Seventeenth Century," *Transactions of the Royal Historical Society* Fourth Series 7 (1924): 27-51.

22 Shaskol'skii, *Stolbovskii mir*, pp. 214-16.

23 Ibid., p. 158, note 36.

24 J. Scheltema, *Rusland en de Nederlanden beschouwd in derzelver wederkeerige betrekkingen* 4 vols. (Amsterdam, 1819), vol. 4, p. 330.

25 Kordt, *Ocherk*, pp. cxxviii, cliii. Such a refusal of privileges took place in 1614 and 1617.

26 Iu. A. Tikhonov, "Tamoznennaia politika Russkogo gosudarstva s serediny XVI do 60-kh godov XVII v.," *Istoricheski zapiski* 53 (Moscow, 1955): Table 1, p. 264.

27 Ibid., p. 273.

28 According to a document of November 1629, foreign merchants normally paid in Moscow a separate, higher toll of 4 percent for ordinary goods, and 5 percent for goods that had to be weighed. This rate was said to exist in the time of the Tsars Ivan IV, Fedor, and Boris Godunov. *SGGD* 3 no. 80, p. 306.

29 N. S. Chaev, ed., "Dvinskaia ustavnaia tamozhennaia otkupnaia gramota 1560 g.," *Letopis' zaniatii postoiannoi istoriko-arkheograficheskoi komissii* 1 (34) (1926) (Moscow, 1927): 199-203; *AAE* 1 no. 338, pp. 408-11.

30 "From Korela (i.e. the later Kexholm), from Novgorod, and from beyond the sea"; N. S. Chaev, ed., "Dvinskaia," p. 201.

31 Th. J. G. Locher and P. de Buck eds., Introduction to *Moscovische Reyse 1664-1665, Journaal en Aentekeningen*, by Nicolaas Witsen, Werken uitgegeven door de Linschoten-Vereniging, vols. 66-8 (The Hague, 1966-7), vol. 66, p. xxxii, note 6.

32 There is one difficulty in all this. The toll rates of 1588 refer to the payment by the foreign merchants in Archangel of an unspecified "great toll" *(bol'shaia poshlina)*. What was this? The pre-1646 toll of a maximum of 2 percent is hard to describe as a "great toll," especially in view of the higher toll paid by foreign merchants in the city of Moscow. The most likely hypothesis is that the foreigners were released from the

payment of all the smaller toll charges (for storage, for writing documents, the few kopecks paid per head or *gostinoe*, etc.), and paid a lump sum instead of these smaller charges. It is unlikely that there was a temporary raising of the tolls at Archangel in the 1580s, which later fell to the post-1613 rate.

Chapter 3. The Archangel trade

1 On the Archangel trade see: V. V. Krestinin, *Kratkaia istoriia o gorode Arkhangel'skom, sochinena Arkhangelogorodskim grazhdaninon Vasil'em Krestininom* (St. Petersburg, 1792); S. F. Ogorodnikov, *Ocherk istorii goroda Arkhangel'ska v torgovo-promyshlennon otnoshenii* (St. Petersburg, 1890); B. N. Floria, "Torgovlia Rossii so stranami Zapadnoi Evropy v Arkhangel'ske (konets XVI–nachalo XVII v.)," *Srednie veka* 36 (Moscow, 1973): 129–51; R. I. Kozintseva, "Vneshnetorgovyi oborot Arkhangelogorodskoi iarmarki i ee rol' v razvitii vserossiiskogo rynka," *Issledovaniia po istorii feodal'no-krepostnicheskoi Rossii* (Moscow-Leningrad, 1964): 116–63; N. N. Repin, "Vneshnaia torgovlia cherez Arkhangel'sk i vnutrennii rynok Rossii vo vtoroi polovine XVII–pervoi chetverti XVIII v." *Kandidatskaia* dissertation, Moscow University, 1970: Liubimenko, "Struggle," pp. 27–51.

2 Hart, "Amsterdam," p. 5.

3 A. Iziumov, "Razmery russkoi torgovli XVII veka cherez Arkhangel'sk v sviazi s neobsledovannymi arkhivnymi istochnikami," *Izvestiia Arkhangel'skogo obshchestva izucheniia Russkogo severa* 6 (1912): 250–8.

4 V. O. Kliuchevskii, "Russkaia rubl' XVI-XVIII vv. v ego otnoshenii k nyneshnemu," *Sochineniia* 7 (Moscow, 1959): 170–236; B. N. Mironov, "Revoliutsiia tsen' v Rossii v XVIII v.," *Voprosy istorii* 11 (1971): 49–61; Iu. A. Tikhonov, *Pomeshchich'i krest'iane v Rossii: Feodal'naia renta v XVII–nachale XVIII v.* (Moscow, 1974). See also: A. G. Man'kov, *Tseny i ikh dvizhenie v russkom gosudarstve XVI veka* (Moscow-Leningrad, 1951); I. G. Spasskii, "Denezhnoe khoziaistvo russkogo gosudarstva y seredine XVII v. i reformy 1654-1663," *Arkheograficheskii ezhegodnik za 1959 god* (Moscow, 1960).

5 Floria, "Torgovlia," p. 144.

6 Artur Attman, *Den ryska marknaden i 1500-talets baltiska politik* (Lund, 1944): 60.

7 B. G. Kurts, "Sostoianie Rossii v 1650-1655 gg. po doneseniiam Rodesa," *ChOIDR*, bk. 2, 253, 1915 (Moscow, 1914): 166.

8 Ibid., pp. 210–11.

9 TsGADA, f. 141, *opis'* 1, part 1, Reestr Prikaznym delam starykh let. This is a register of the mid-eighteenth century that describes numerous documents later lost.

10 Amburger, *Marselis*, p. 95.

11 Kozintseva, "Oborot," p. 131. In the percentage of merchants in 1710 Moscow and Yaroslavl were equal at 11.5 percent, and Vologda third with 7.5 percent. Ibid., table 3, pp. 128–30.

12 This title when granted to foreign merchants gave them certain privileges in return for the duty (and privilege) of supplying the court and acting as the Tsar's agent.

13 Floria, "Torgovlia," p. 146; Kozintseva, "Oborot," p. 121.

14 Floria, "Torgovlia," p. 146; Kozintseva, "Oborot," p. 121.

15 Floria, "Torgovlia," p. 150.

16 Kozintseva, "Oborot," p. 121; Floria, "Torgovlia," p. 146.

17 Floria, "Torgovlia," pp. 146–7.

18 Kozintseva, "Oborot," p. 121; Floria, "Torgovlia," pp. 146–7.

19 Before the Time of Troubles the official rate was three *efimki* to one ruble. Floria, "Torgovlia," p. 145.

20 After 1613 one ruble was officially equal to two *efimki*. Spasskii, "Denezhnoe," p. 108. If there was also an unofficial exchange rate of the ruble to the *efimka*, it is not recorded.
21 Kozintseva, "Oborot," p. 137.
22 In view of the ambiguous status of the Moscow merchants whose roots were in the town of Ustiug Velikii (see the Index), we should note that in Chapter 3 they have been included among the Muscovites, following the designation found in the documents of Archangel. In the cases of Isaak Reviakin and Ivan Iakimov Usov (Grudtsyn) this makes little difference as their trade at Archangel was small and in no case did their purchases make more than 1–2 percent of the total for Moscow merchants in Tables 3.10–3.15. Vasilii Semenov Bosov (Bosoi) was more important, as he contributed 377½ *postavs* of cloth in the total purchased by Moscow merchants of 900 (Table 3.10). I have included him as a Muscovite because (1) he is so designated in the documents and (2) he seems to have acted frequently as an agent or partner of his brother Aleksei Semenov Bosoi, who was definitely in the *gost'* hundred of Moscow rather than Ustiug. See TsGADA f. 141, 1630, no. 68, 11. 27, 36–7, 39–40. Surely the fact that Vasilii Bosoi was either himself a Muscovite or working for his brother Aleksei accounts for his greater purchases, as compared to Reviakin or Usov. The Reviakins and Usovs were evidently tied more closely to Ustiug than the Bosois, and prepared to exploit this tie when the occasion arose as in Sol' Vychegodsk or Ustiug itself. On the Bosois see Bazilevich, "Krupnoe," passim.
23 It should be noted here that the English ships were much smaller than the Dutch. In 1587 and 1588 the average tonnage works out to 115.1 and 101.8 tons respectively. Because one last was equal to two tons, the averages in lasts of the cargo was 57.5 lasts and 50.9 lasts respectively. No doubt the greater capacity of the Dutch ships was one of the secrets of their success.
24 Ahvenainen, "Contributions," pp. 17, 37.
25 Willan gives the exchange rate of the ruble to the pound in this period as 13s. 4d. to the ruble. Willan, *Russia*, p. 250. At this rate, the ruble value of the Russian exports at the official valuation in London would be:

1587	18,000 rubles
1588	8,300 rubles
1589	5,000 rubles

26 TsGADA, f. 210, no. 37, part 1, pp. 195–6; f. 141, 1633, no. 41, pp. 134–5.

Chapter 4. Russia and the Baltic trade

1 Shaskol'skii, *Stolbovskii mir*, pp. 14–29.
2 Arnold Soom, "Die merkantilistische Wirtschaftspolitik Schwedens und die baltische Städte im 17. Jahrhundert," *Jahrbücher für Geschichte Osteuropas* 2 (1963): 182–222. The right of direct trade with the Russians acquired by the English in 1665 was to change this situation to some extent,
3 Attman, *Ryska*; Elisabeth Harder, "Seehandel zwischen Lübeck und Russland in 17/18 Jahrhundert nach den Zollbüchern der Novgorodfahrer," *Zeitschrift des Vereins für Lübeckische Geschichte und Altertumskunde* 41 and 42 (1961–1962): 43–114, 5–54.
4 Nina Bang, ed., *Tabeller over skibsfart og varetransport gennem Ø resund 1497 – 1660*, parts 1 and 2 (Copenhagen, 1906–22).
5 Sven A. Nilsson, "Den ryska marknaden i 1500-talets baltiska politik," *Scandia* 16 (2) årgång 1944 (1945); 175–90; Eli F. Heckscher, "Multilateralism, Baltic Trade and the Mercantilists," *Economic History Review*, Second Series 3(2) (1950): 219–28.
6 Charles Wilson, "Treasure and Trade Balances: the Mercantilist Problem," *Economic

History Review, Second Series 2(2) (1949): 152–61; id., "Treasure and Trade Balances: Further Evidence," *Economic History Review*, Second Series 4(2) (1951) 231–42.

7 Maria Bogucka, *Handel zagraniczny Gdańska w pierwszej połowie XVII wieku* (Wrocław-Warsaw-Krakow, 1970); Antoni Mączak, *Między Gdańskiem a Sundem: Studia nad handlem bałtyckim od połowy XVI do połowy XVII w* (Warsaw, 1972); Georg Jensch, "Der Handel Rigas im 17. Jahrhundert: Ein Beitrag zur livländischen Wirtschaftsgeschichte in Schwedischer Zeit," *Mitteilungen aus der livländischen Geschichte* 24 (2) (Gessellschaft für Geschichte und Altertumskunde zu Riga, 1930); Arnold Soom, *Der Handel Revals im siebzehnten Jahrhundert*, Marburger Ostforschungen 29 (Wiesbaden, 1969); Wasilij W. Doroszenko, "Eksport Rygi na zachód w okresie przynależnosci do Rzeczypospolitej (1562–1620)," *Zapiski historyczne* 31 (1) (1966): 7–41; H. Piirimäe, "O sostoianii narvskoi torgovli v nachale XVII veka," *Skandinavskii sbornik* 11 (Tallin, 1966): 82–108; Miroslav Hroch, "Die Rolle des zentraleuropäischen Handels im Ausgleich der Handelsbilanz zwischen Ost- und Westeuropa," *Aussenhandel Ostmitteleuropas* (Köln, 1971): 1–27.

8 R. W. K. Hinton, *The Eastland Trade and the Common Weal in the Seventeenth Century* (Cambridge, 1959): 22–3.

9 Shaskol'skii, *Stolbovskii mir*, p. 20.

10 J. Denucé, *Die Hanse und die Antwerpener Handelskompanien in den Ostseeländern*, Dokumente zur Handelsgeschichte 3 (Antwerp, 1938), pp. xxiii–xxiv.

11 Ibid., pp. 13–14, 24–33.

12 Whether merchants from the city of Moscow were already trading on the shores of the Baltic is unknown. Dalz records the purchase of 746 Reichsthalers worth of elk hides from "een Moscovyt" in Pskov. Generally, German and Dutch merchants called the Russians "Russen" or "Reussen" at that time, so Dalz may have meant a man from Moscow. Denucé, *Hanse*, p. 28.

13 Per Nyström, "Mercatura Ruthenica," *Scandia* 10:2 (December 1937): 263.

14 Soom, "Wirtschaftspolitik," pp. 193–4.

15 Harder, "Seehandel," 41, p. 57.

16 Harder. "Seehandel." 41, p. 100.

17 Shaskol'skii, "Ob osobennostiakh," pp. 18–20.

18 Shaskol'skii, "Ob osobennostiakh," pp. 13–14.

19 Staatliches Archivlager Göttingen, Stadtarchiv Reval, BH 12, "Verdolmetschung aus den russischen Zollbüchern in Pleskau." See also Norbert Angermann, "Zum Handel der deutschen Kaufleute in Pleskau," *Russland und Deutschland*, Georg von Rauch Festschrift, Kieler historische Studien vol. 22 (Stuttgart, 1974): 73–82.

20 TsGADA, f. 141, 1627, no. 13.

21 Carl von Bonsdorff, "Nyen och Nyenskans: Historisk skildring," *Acta Societatis scientiarum Fennicae* (Finska vetenskapsocieteten) 18 (1891): 496–7; E. V. Chistiakova, "Pskovskii torg," p. 216.

22 *Russko-shvedski ekonomicheskie otnosheniia v XVII veke*; *Sbornik dokumentov* (Moscow-Leningrad, 1960), nos. 11, 28, 30, 76, 110, 121, 50.

23 See Zsigmond Pach, *The Role of East-Central Europe in International Trade, 16th and 17th Centuries*, Studia historica Academiae Scientarium Hungaricae 70 (Budapest, 1970).

24 Sven-Erik Åström, *From Cloth to Iron: The Anglo-Baltic Trade in the Later Seventeenth polovine XVI–pervoi polovine XVII v." Istoricheski zapiski* 92 (Moscow, 1973): 223–4; N. W. Posthumus, *Inquiry into the History of Prices in Holland*, 2 vols. (Leiden, 1946–64), vol. 1, p. 360; Kozintseva, "Oborot," p. 121.

25 Sven-Erik Åström, *From Cloth to Iron: The Anglo-Baltic Trade in the Later Seventeenth Century*, Societas Scientiarum Fennica, Commentationes Humanarum Litterarum, 33, part 1, and 37, part 3 (Helsinki, 1963 and 1965).

26 The export of wine from Hungary was of course the export of a manufactured product. But the wine was produced in seigneurial wine presses.

Chapter 5. The trade with Poland

1 Alina Wawrzyńczyk, *Handlu Polski;* Roman Rybarski, *Handel i polityka handlowa Polski w XVI stuleciu,* 2 vols., 2nd ed. (Warsaw, 1958). The lack of any research on trade at Wilno greatly complicates the historian's task in analyzing Russo-Polish trade. Some insight into the economy of Wilno may be gained from Jerzy Morzy, "Geneza i rozwój cechów wileńskich do końca XVII w.," *Zeszyty naukowe uniwersytetu im. A. Mickiewicza: Historia* (z. 4, 1959): 3–93. Morzy gives no suggestion of a general decline of the town until 1648, implying that the prosperity of the sixteenth century continued until that date. But was Russian trade a factor in the continuation of that prosperity? No clue is given by J. Jurginis, V. Merkys, and A. Tautavicius, *Vilniaus Miesto Istorija* (Vilnius, 1968) where the account of economic history breaks off about 1600 and does not resume until 1760.
2 Z. Iu. Kopysskii, "Iz istorii torgovykh sviazei gorodov Belorusii s gorodami Pol'shi (konets XVI–pervaia polovina XVII v.)," *Istoricheski zapiski* 72 (Moscow, 1962): 140–83 id., *Ekonomicheskoe razvitie gorodov Belorussii v XVL–pervoi polovine XVII v.* (Minsk, 1966); L. S. Abetsedarskii, "Torgovye sviazi Belorussii s russkim gosudarstvom (vtoraia polovina XVI – pervaia polovina XVII v.)," *Belorusskii gosudarstvennyi universitet, uchenye zapiski* 36 (Minsk, 1957): 3–42; Henryk Łowmiański, "Handel Mohylewa w wieku XVI," *Studia historyczne ku czci Stanisława Kutrzeby* 2 (Krakow, 1938): 517–47.
3 Wawrzyńczyk, *Handel Polski,* pp. 10–25.
4 Łowmiański, "Handel Mohylewa," pp. 524, 538–40.
5 "Mytnaia kniga (Brest, 1582)," *Arkheograficheskii sbornik dokumentov, otnosiashchikhsia k istorii Severozapadnoi Rusi* 3 and 4 (Wilno, 1867): 289–322, 252–88 vol. 3, entry for February 27, 1583; Kopysskii, "Iz istorii," pp. 167–8; Abetsedarskii, "Torgovye sviazi," p. 37.
6 L. S. Abetsedarskii and M. Ia. Volkov, eds., *Russko-belorusskie sviazi,* pp. 20–6, 56–62.
7 Rybarski, *Handel* 1, p. 99; Kopysskii, "Iz istorii," pp. 162, 172; Abetsedarskii and Volkov, eds., *Russko-belorusskie sviazi,* pp. 56–62.
8 Rybarski, *Handel* 1, p. 98; Abetsedarskii and Volkov, eds., *Russko-belorusskie sviazi,* pp. 56–62; Kopysskii, "Iz istorii," pp. 162, 172.
9 Abetsedarskii and Volkov, eds., *Russko-belorusskie sviazi,* pp. 56, 58–9, 59–60.
10 K. G. Mitiaev, "Oboroty i torgovye sviazi smolenskogo rynka v 70-kh godakh XVII v.," *Istoricheskie zapiski* 13 (Moscow, 1941): 54–83.
11 Doroszenko, "Eksport Rygi," pp. 24–5.

Chapter 6. The trade with the South: The Ottoman Empire and Persia

1 M. V. Fekhner, *Torgovlia russkogo gosudarstva so stranami Vostoka v XVI veke,* 2nd ed., Trudy gosudarstvennogo istoricheskogo Muzeia 31 (Moscow, 1956): 98–112; Syroechkovskii, *Gosti-surozhane,* pp. 50–1.
2 Mihnea Berindei, "Contributions a l'étude du commerce ottoman des fourrures moscovites: La route moldavo-polonaise 1453–1700," *Cahiers du monde russe et soviétique* 12 (4) (1971): 399.
3 Alexandre Bennigsen and Chantal Lemercier-Quelquejay, "Les marchands de la cour ottomane et le commerce des fourrures moscovites dans la seconde moitié du XVI siecle," *Cahiers du monde russe et soviétique* 11 (3) (1970): 369.

4 Ibid., p. 370; Fekhner, *Torgovlia*, p. 85.

5 A. N. Kopylov, *Russkie na Enisee v XVII v.: Zemledelie, promyshlennost', i torgovye sviazi eniseiskogo uezda* (Novosibirsk, 1965): 233.

6 Kurts, *de Rodesa*, pp. 162, 214, 216. The figures for the treasury's fur trade come from Kurts's extracts from the archives of the Siberian Office, not from de Rodes. Furthermore, a large proportion of the furs sold at the Svinsk fair certainly went to merchants from the Ukrainian towns within the Polish Commonwealth. Fragmentary data suggest that furs were one of the main exports of the Russian state to the Ukraine. In return, the Ukrainian merchants mainly supplied the Russian steppe frontier with grain, cattle, and (illegally) liquor. Ukrainian merchants did bring Near Eastern products such as silk, pearls, and other goods, as far north as Moscow but they had to compete with the importation of the same goods coming in at Archangel and Astrakhan. The total number of furs leaving Russia for the southwest may have been larger than the Ottoman figures suggest, but many of these furs were not destined for Ottoman markets and remained in the Ukraine or Poland. All trade at Svinsk or Kiev was not Russo-Ottoman trade; much was Russo-Ukrainian or Russo-Polish, but the exact proportions cannot be determined. See: *Vossoedinenie Ukrainy s Rossiei* 1 (1620–47), (Moscow, 1654), docs. no. 244, 260.

7 Maurycy Horn, *Walka klasowa i konflikty spoleczyne w miastach Rusi czerwonej w latach 1600–1647 na tle stosunków gospodarczych*, Prace opolskiego towarzystwa przyjaciól nauk, Wydzial nauk historyczno-spoleczynch (Wroclaw-Warsaw-Krakow-Gdańsk, 1972): 43. See also Władysław Loziński, *Lwów starozytny*, 2 vols. (Lwow, 1889–90), especially vol. 2.

8 E. N. Kusheva, *Narody severnogo Kavkaza i ikh sviazi s Rossiei* (Moscow, 1963): 250–1.

9 Fekhner, *Torgovlia*, pp. 52, 60–1.

10 On these documents see: E. N. Kusheva, "Materialy astrakhanskoi tamozhni kak istochnik po sotsial'no-ekonomicheskoi istorii Rossii XVII–XVIII vv," *Iz istorii ekonomicheskoi i obshchestvennoi zhizni Rossii* (Festschrift for N. M. Druzhinin), (Moscow, 1976): 261–72.

11 LOII, fund 178, 1622–3, no. 738.

12 LOII, fund 178, 1622–3, nos. 635, 689, 726, 732.

13 LOII, fund 178, 1622–3, nos. 726, 648, 693. Some conception of Russia's role in the silk trade of Persia can be derived from the reports of the agents of the Dutch East India Company in Persia for the 1630s. The company's agent Nicholaes Jacobsz Overschie traveled back and forth from Ormuz to Isfahan and even ventured into Gilan and other northern districts where the silk was manufactured. One of his duties was to spy on the English and other nations who traded in silk. His summary of the number of bales of silk exported from Persia was the following (one bale was 200 Dutch pounds):

1635:		1636:	
Dutch	743	Dutch	1,000
English	100	English	373
Djulfa Armenians	150	Djulfa Armenians	100
Russians	80		—
Total	1,073	Total	1,473

Source: H. Dunlop ed., *Bronnen tot de Geschiedenis der Oostindische Compagnie in Perzie 1611–1638*, Rijksgeschiedkundige Publicatien 72 (The Hague, 1930): 547–612.

The Djulfa Armenians shipped silk to Aleppo in Syria. The year 1622–3 was already a good year for the Persian silk trade through the Persian Gulf, but the real boom came only in the 1630s, followed by a decline in the 1640s. The caravan trade to Aleppo may have been more viable than supposed. See Nils Steensgaard, *Carracks, Caravans, and*

Companies: The Asian Trade in the Early Seventeenth Century, Scandinavian Institute of Asian Studies, Monograph Series, no. 17 (1973): 395–6.

14 LOII, fund 178, 1622–3, no. 690.

15 LOII, fund 178, 1622–3, nos. 648, 709, 702, 661.

16 LOII, fund 178, 1622–3, nos. 703, 751, 667, 733, 648. Ivan Aksenov of Kostroma shipped 265 pairs and Matvei Lopatin of Murom shipped 230 pairs of *saf'ian*.

Chapter 7. Moscow and the internal market

1 Serbina, *Krest'ianskaia*, pp. 226–8.

2 A. I. Iakovlev, ed., *Tamozhennye knigi* 1, pp. 232, 234, 386.

3 S. I. Kotov et al., eds., *Moskovskaia delovaia i bytovaia pis'mennost' XVII veka* (Moscow, 1968), p. 63.

4 TsGADA, fund 210, no. 37, part 1, pp. 224–8.

5 Ibid., p. 221.

6 TsGADA, fund 210, no. 37, part 1, p. 188.

7 TsGADA, fund 210, no. 37, part 1, pp. 445–7.

8 The trade with the Livonian Germans at Pskov in 1623–4 was wholly conducted by Pskov merchants (cf. Chapter 4).

9 Serbina, *Krest'ianskaia*, pp. 37–51.

10 A. A. Novosel'skii, "Iz istorii donskoi torgovli v XVII veke," *Istoricheskie zapiski* 26 (Moscow, 1948): 207, 209, 210, 212–13.

11 N. N. Miklashevskii, *K istorii khoziaistvennogo byta moskovskogo gosudarstva* 1: *Zaselenie i sel'skoe khoziaistvo iuzhnoi okrainy XVII veka* (Moscow, 1894): 76, 109.

12 N. I. Privalova, "Torgi goroda Kasimova v seredine XVII veka," *Istoricheskie zapiski* 21 (Moscow, 1947): 113, 122.

13 Ustiugov, *Solevarennaia*, p. 65.

14 V. S. Bakulin, "Torgovye oboroty i sotsial'nyi sostav torgovtsev na Belevskom rynke v 60-70-kh godakh XVII veka," *Trudy moskovskogo gosudarstvennogo istoriko-arkhivnogo instituta* 21 (Moscow, 1965): 297–9.

15 Kozintseva, "Oborot," pp. 124–5.

16 I. S. Makarov, "Pushnoi rynok Soli Vychegodskoi v XVII," *Istoricheskie zapiski* 14 (Moscow, 1945): 163.

17 Nadeia Sveteshnikov was a well-known *gost'* (see Chapter 1). For I. Pankrat'ev's membership in the *gost'* hundred, see TsGADA, fund 141, 1633, no. 42, pp. 69–72. For B. Filat'ev, see Merzon and Tikhonov, *Rynok*, p. 323.

18 A. I. Iakovlev, ed., *Tamozhennye knigi* 1, p. 384.

19 On the *gost'* hundred families of Ustiug see Chapter 1. The ambiguous status of the Bosois was very unusual among Russian merchants, who can usually be clearly fixed in one town or another in the records, whatever commercial ties may have existed. The merchants who came to Moscow from Yaroslavl seem to have broken the formal ties and were always listed as Muscovites after a certain year, although of course family ties still existed.

20 For Siberia's administration see George V. Lantzeff, *Siberia in the Seventeenth Century: A Study of the Colonial Administration* (University of California Publications in History 30, Berkeley and Los Angeles, 1943); *Istoriia Sibiri* 2 (Leningrad, 1968): 124–37, 300–11. On the fur trade see Raymond H. Fisher, *The Russian Fur Trade 1550–1700* (University of California Publications in History 31, Berkeley and Los Angeles, 1943). Fisher's work has been in large part superseded by Soviet work of the last twenty years that has relied on the unusually rich Siberian archives.

21 Lantzeff, *Siberia*, pp. 1–18.

22 Lantzeff, *Siberia*, pp. 47–61, 171–3.
23 See A. N. Kopylov, "Tamozhennaia politika v Sibiri v XVII v.," *Russkoe gosudarstvo v XVII v.: Novye iavleniia v sotsial'no-ekonomicheskoi, politicheskoi i kul'turnoi zhizni* (Moscow, 1961).
24 Kopylov, *Russkie na Enisee*, pp. 232–3.
25 Aleksandrov, "Rol' krupnogo kupechestva," p. 195.
26 O. N. Vilkov, *Remeslo i torgovlia zapadnoi Sibiri v XVII veke* (Moscow, 1967): 322–3.
27 Aleksandrov, "Rol' krupnogo kupechestva," p. 191.
28 S. V. Bakhrushin, "Pokruta na sobolinykh promyslakh XVII v.," *Nauchnye trudy* 3 (1) (Moscow, 1952–5): 203–204.
29 Kopylov, *Russkie na Enisee*, p. 232.
30 Kopylov, *Russkie na Enisee*, p. 233.
31 P. N. Pavlov, "Ob uchastie i roli razlichnykh kategorii naseleniia v sibirskom pushnom promysle v 40–70-e gody XVII v.," *Ekonomika, upravlenie i kul'tura Sibiri XVI–XIX vv.*, Sibir' perioda feodalizma 2 (Novosibirsk, 1965): 26.
32 Aleksandrov, "Rol' krupnogo kupechestva," p. 191; Pavlov, "Uchastie," p. 35.
33 Pavlov, "Uchastie," p. 27.
34 Kopylov, *Russkie na Enisee*, p. 244.
35 Vilkov, *Remeslo*, pp. 122–4.
36 Ibid., pp. 296–8.

Chapter 8. Salt production and the internal market

1 P. G. Liubomirov, *Ocherki po istorii russkoi promyshlennosti* (Moscow, 1947): 209–255, especially p. 520.
2 Zaozerskaia, *U istokov*, p. 198; cf. Amburger, *Marselis;* Joseph T. Fuhrmann, *The Origins of Capitalism in Russia: Industry and Progress in the Sixteenth and Seventeenth Centuries* (Chicago, 1972).
3 Benedykt Zientara, *Dzieje małopolskiego hutnictwa żelaznego XVI-XVII wiek*, Badania z dziejów rzemiosła i handlu w epoce feudalzmu, 1 (Warsaw, 1954).
4 Ferdinand Tremel, *Wirtschafts- und Sozialgeschichte Osterreichs* (Vienna, 1969): 255–6. See also Tremel, *Der Frühkapitalismus in Innerösterreich* (Graz, Austria, 1954).
5 Heinrich Ritter von Srbik, *Der staatliche Exporthandel Osterreichs von Leopold I. bis Maria Theresia: Untersuchungen zur Wirtschaftsgeschichte Osterreichs im Zeitalter des Merkantilismus* (Vienna, 1907).
6 L. L. Murav'eva, *Derevenskaia promyshlennost' tsentral'noi Rossii vtoroi poloviny XVII v.* (Moscow, 1971).
7 S. A. Belokurov, ed., "Utverzhdennaia gramota," p. 83; TsGADA, fund 141, 1630, no. 68.
8 Ustiugov, *Solevarennaia*, pp. 34–40; Vvedenskii, *Dom Stroganovykh*, pp. 156–214.
9 Vvedenskii, *Dom Stroganovykh*, p. 165.
10 A. A. Savich, *Solovetskaia votchina XV-XVII vv.: opyt izucheniia khoziaistva i sotsial'nykh otnoshenii na krainem russkom severe v drevnei Rusi* (Perm, 1927): 115–16.
11 L. S. Prokof'eva, *Votchinnoe khoziaistvo v XVII veke: Po materialam Spaso-Prilutskogo monastyria* (Moscow, 1959): 41, 52, 55.
12 Zolotov sold 14,000 puds of salt in Kaluga in 1628. TsGADA, fund 210, no. 37, part 1, p. 221.
13 Zaozerskaia, *U istokov*, pp. 115–66.
14 Ibid., pp. 125, 132, 133.
15 Ibid., p. 134.
16 Savich, *Solovetskaia*, p. 117.
17 Zaozerskaia, *U istokov*, p. 162.
18 Ibid., p. 163.

19 Ibid., p. 168.
20 Vvedenskii, *Dom Stroganovykh*, pp. 16-17; N. E. Nosov, *Stanovlenie soslovno-predstavitel'nykh uchrezhdenii v Rossii: Izyskaniia o zemskoi reforme Ivana Groznogo* (Leningrad, 1969): 240-84. The Dvina boyars (*dvinskie boiare*) were the local landholding aristocracy of the Northern Dvina valley in the fourteenth and fifteenth centuries. Their wealth was little greater than that of a prosperous peasant, and in the sixteenth century the group disappeared. Some became simply prosperous peasants, some moved south and joined the gentry, and some became merchants in the North.
21 Vvedenskii, *Dom Stroganovykh*, pp. 20, 24.
22 Zaozerskaia, *U istokov*, pp. 155, 156-7, 158, 160.
23 TsGADA, fund 141, 1630, no. 68.
24 V. G. Geiman, "Solianoi promysel gostia I. D. Pankrat'eva v Iarenskom uiezde v XVII veke (Materialy po istorii russkoi promyshlennosti)," *Letopis' zaniatii postoiannoi istoriko-arkheograficheskoi kommissii* 35 (Leningrad, 1929): 11, 16-17; Zaozerskaia, *U istokov*, p. 172.
25 Ibid., p. 172.
26 Ibid., p. 45.
27 Ustiugov, *Solevarennaia*, p. 45; Stashevskii, "Piatina," p. 283.
28 Ustiugov, *Solevarennaia*, pp. 45-55.
29 Ibid., p. 45.
30 Ibid., pp. 63-4.
31 Ibid., pp. 64-5.
32 Ibid., p. 65.
33 Ibid., pp. 71-82, 97-102, 107-9, 111-21.
34 Ibid., pp. 110-23.
35 Ibid., p. 292.
36 *AAE*, vol. 3, no. 68.
37 I. V. Stepanov, "Organizatisiia solianykh promyslov v nizov'iakh reki Volgi v XVII v.," *Uchenye zapiski LGU: seriia istoricheskikh nauk* 8 (1941): 152.
38 I. V. Stepanov, "Khoziaistvennaia deiatel'nost'," p. 97; id., "Organizatsiia," p. 153.
39 LOII, fund 178, 1622-3, nos. 737, 630, 722, 701, 688, 697, 749, 654.
40 Stepanov, "Khoziaistvennaia deiatel'nost'," p. 97.
41 S. V. Bakhrushin, "Promyshlennye predpriiatiia russkikh torgovykh liudei v XVII veke," *Istoricheskie zapiski* 8 (Moscow, 1940): 107.
42 Ibid., p. 103.
43 G. S. Rabinovich, *Gorod soli: Staraia Russa v kontse XVI-seredine XVII vv. (K voprosu o genezise kapitalizma v russkoi promyshlennosti)* (Leningrad, 1973), map, pp. 204-5.
44 Ibid., p. 28.
45 Ibid., pp. 34-61.
46 Ibid., pp. 67-8.
47 Ibid., pp. 72, 208-20.
48 A. M. Sakharov, *Goroda severo-vostochnoi Rusi XIV-XV vekov* (Moscow, 1959): 34, 41, 44, 74.
49 S. Kolominskii, "Torgovlia sol'iu na Rusi v 16-17 v. i obshchee sostoianie solianykh promyslov v ukazannyi period vremeni," *Kievskie universitetskie izvestiia* 12 (December, 1912): 45.
50 Of the eighty-six salt boilers in Balakhna in 1674 only nineteen were operating, yet Balakhna was repeatedly pointed to as an important center. Had the Volga salt already started to cut into the sales of Balakhna salt? Without a thorough study of Balakhna this problem cannot be solved. Rabinovich, *Gorod soli*, p. 38.
51 Zaozerskaia, *U istokov*, pp. 19-20.
52 N. N. Selifonov, ed., *Opisi dokumentov arkhiva byvshikh Bol'shesol'skikh posadskoi izby i*

ratushi, naidennogo v posade Bol'shie Soli, Kostromskogo uezda XVI-XVIII stoletii, published by the Kostromskaia gubernskaia uchenaia arkhivnaia kommissiia (Saint Petersburg, 1902): i–iii; Zaozerskaia, *U istokov*, pp. 19–24.
53 Bakhrushin, "Promyshlennye," p. 104.
54 *Opisi*, p. 118, no. 94.
55 Zaozerskaia, *U istokov*, pp. 31, 36–7.

Chapter 9. The Moscow merchants and the state

1 See Bazilevich, "Novotorgovyi ustav"; Samuel H. Baron, "The Weber Thesis and the Failure of Capitalist Development in 'Early Modern' Russia," *Jahrbücher für Geschichte Osteuropas* 18(3) (September 1970): 321–36.
2 TsGADA, fund 210, no. 37, part 1, p. 177.
3 N. I. Novikov ed., *Drevnaia Rossiisskaia Vivliofika*, 20 vols. (Moscow, 1788–91), vol. 15, pp. 127–8.
4 A. I. Uspenskii, *Stolbtsy byvshego arkhiva Oruzhennoi palaty*, 3 vols. (Moscow, 1912–14), vol. 1, no. 49, pp. 15–16.
5 A. I. Timofeev, ed., "Knigi Kazennogo prikaza," *RIB* 9. Author's calculations.
6 Uspenskii, *Stolbtsy*, vol. 1, nos. 513, 684, pp. 157–62; vol. 2, no. 1195, pp. 467–9.
7 Ibid., vol. 3, nos. 1391, 1406, 1410, 1263, 1467, 1490, pp. 515, 623, 645–50, 653–6, 729–32.
8 TsGADA, fund 141, 1633, no. 42; Reestr, p. 158.
9 TsGADA, fund 141, 1634, no. 82; Reestr, pp. 37 and 43 verso; 1637, no. 56.
10 Ogloblin, *Obozrenie*, *ChOIDR* 194, p. 343.
11 Kurts, *De Rodesa*, pp. 214–21.
12 Uspenskii, *Stolbtsy*, vol. 2, nos. 1192–8, pp. 467–72; Ogloblin, *Obozrenie*, *ChOIDR* 194, p. 343.
13 Uspenskii, *Stolbtsy* 1 (90) pp. 40–1; Ogloblin, *Obozrenie*, *ChOIDR* 200, p. 165; *ChOIDR* 194, pp. 199, 343.
14 Kozintseva, "Uchastie," p. 328.
15 E. D. Stashevskii, *Ocherki po istorii tsarstvovovaniia Mikhaila Fedorovicha* (Kiev, 1913): 385; B. F. Porshnev, "Russkie subsidii Shvetsii vo vremia Tridtsatiletnei voiny," *Izvestiia Akademii Nauk SSSR, Seriia istorii i filosofii* 6 (5) (1945): 319–40; id., "Bor'ba vokrug shvedsko-russkogo soiuza v 1631–1633 gg.," *Skandinavskii sbornik* 1 (Tallinn, 1956): 11–71; Lars Ekholm, "Rysk spannmål och svenska krigsfinanser 1629–1633," *Scandia* 40 (1) (1974): 57–103.
16 M. B. Davydova et al., eds., *Russko-shvedskie*, p. 89.
17 The clearest account of the system of tax collection in the towns is to be found in Chicherin, *Oblastnye*, pp. 403–49.
18 S. B. Veselovskii and S. F. Platonov, eds., "Prikhodo-raskhodnye knigi," *RIB* 28, pp. 1–4.
19 Ibid., pp. 117–118. P. G. Liubomirov, *Ocherki istorii nizhegorodskogo opolcheniia* (Moscow, 1939): 239–40; N. V. Kalachov, ed., *Akty otnosiashchiesia do iuridicheskogo byta Drevnei Rossii* 2 (St. Petersburg, 1857): no. 246, IV.
20 P. N. Miliukov, *Gosudarstvennoe khoziaistvo Rossii v pervoi chetverti XVII stoletiia i reformy Petra Velikogo*, 2nd ed. (Saint Petersburg, 1905): 74.
21 Stashevskii, "Piatina," p. 91.
22 Paul Bushkovitch, "Taxation, Tax Farming, and Merchants in Sixteenth-Century Russia," *Slavic Review* 37 (3) (Sept. 1978): 381–98.
23 "Prikhodo-raskhodnye knigi," *RIB* 28, pp. 1–116, especially pp. 1–4, 7–13, 35–46, 53–56, 46–49, 28–34, 57, 62, 64, 65.

24 S. B. Veselovskii and S. F. Platonov, eds., "Prikhodo-raskhodnye knigi," *RIB*, 28, pp. 234, 116–25, 128–30, 194, 231–232, 190–2; A. I. Iakowev, ed., *Tamozhennye knigi*, 1, pp. 11, 157, 299, 373.

25 S. B. Veselovskii and S. F. Platonov, eds., "Prikhodo-raskhodnye knigi," *RIB* 28, pp. 290–2, 515.

26 The *gost'* Grigorii Nikitnikov was the head of the tolls in Moscow in 1620 and 1631, the *gost'* Bakhteiar Bulgakov in 1622, the *gost'* Ivan Kashurin in 1615, and the *kadashevets* Frol Merkur'ev Rebrov in 1632–4. See TsGADA, fund 396, opis' 1, no. 599 and 824; fund 141, 1642, no. 92, p. 2; Veselovskii and Pletonov, eds., "Prikhodo-raskhodnye knigi," *RIB* 28, p. 265. It is well known that Archangel and Astrakhan were always under a *gost'* for the collection of tolls. For Novgorod see TsGADA, fund 141; Reestr, p. 135.

27 TsGADA, fund 141; Reestr, pp. 36, 108; TsGADA, fund 137, Ustiug no. 1, pp. 60–8, 254; fund 141, 1642, no. 92.

28 TsGADA, fund 137, Ustiug no. 1, pp. 197–202.

29 TsGADA, fund 137, Ustiug no. 1, pp. 222–3 verso; Uspenskii, *Stolbtsy* 1 (607) p. 194; TsGADA, fund 141, 1634, no. 54; Stashevskii, "Piatina," p. 271.

30 TsGADA, fund 141, 1634, no. 54, pp. 147–50.

31 The chief of the local administration, the *voevoda*, also seems to have been unable to control the toll and tavern chiefs in the town under his jurisdiction. In this uncontrolled situation graft evidently flourished. Some insight into the actual process is afforded by the report made by the merchant Nikifor Bogdanov Poryvkin, the son of the *gost'* of 1598 Bogdan Poryvkin. This report was a denunciation submitted in 1622 to the boyar Fyodor Ivanovich Sheremetev and the *d'iak* Ivan Gramotin. Evidently Poryvkin had personal grudges against prominent merchants but that does not necessarily mean that he was lying. According to him, the *gost'* Andrei Kotov "got 20,000" (rubles) by serving in the mint, and Dmitrii Oblezov "had 10,000" after his service. The *gost'* Tomilo Tarakanov had only 100 rubles left after the Time of Troubles, but after he went to Kazan where he "poprazdnoval v tamozhennykh golovakh" (was idle as a toll chief), he "had 20,000" and showed off twenty golden ducats. Smirnoi and Tret'iak Sudovshchikov were also impoverished by the Time of Troubles, but acquired 40,000 rubles in trade and had diamonds, gold, and precious stones (the implication being of illegal trade in precious stones). Ivan Fyodorov Maksimov (clearly the son of the *gost'* Fyodor Maksimov) was an assistant to the Archangel toll chief, and secretly bought a large amount of salt from Nenoksa, shipping it south without paying duties. He was found out and arrested by his colleagues in the toll administration, whom he gave huge bribes. They accepted the bribes but arrested him anyway, even taking 100 rubles "out of his pants" and sent him to Moscow under arrest. There Maksimov gave out 300 rubles in bribes so that his case was never tried. The *gost'* Kirilo Bulgakov and Elisei Rodionov of the *gost'* hundred also made illegal profits from the Nizhnii Novgorod tavern. Poryvkin gave other minor examples, but these are enough to justify the suspicions of the Moscow officials and suggest that the state administration was an important source of merchant fortunes. Cf. TsGADA, fund 141, 1611, no. 1.

32 N. N. Selifonov, ed., *Opisi*, pp. 40–1, 102–3, 111.

33 Ibid., pp. 7, 47.

34 Ibid., pp. 7, 9, 118, 121–2.

Notes to conclusion

1 Paul Bushkovitch, "Towns, Trade, and Artisans in Seventeenth-Century Russia: The View from Eastern Europe," *Forschungen zur osteuropäischen Geschichte* 27 (forthcoming).

BIBLIOGRAPHY

Abetsedarskii, L. S. "Torgovye sviazi Belorussii s russkim gosudarstvom (vtoraia polovina XVI - pervaia polovina XVII v." *Belorusskii gosudarstvennyi Universitet, uchenye zapiski* 36 (Minsk, 1957): 3-42.

Abetsedarskii, L. S. and Volkoy, M. Ia., eds. *Russko-belorusskie sviazi: Sbornik dokumentov (1570-1667 gg.)*. Minsk, 1963.

Ahvenainen, Jorma. "Some Contributions to the Question of Dutch Traders in Lapland and Russia at the End of the Sixteenth Century." *Studia historica Jyväskyläensia* 5 (Jyväskylä, Finland, 1967): 5-53.

Akty arkeograficheskoi ekspeditsii. 4 vols. St. Petersburg, 1836.

Akty zapadnoi Rossii. 5 vols. St. Petersburg, 1846-53.

Aleksandrov, V. A. "Rol' krupnogo kupechestva v organizatsii pushnykh promyslov na Enisee v XVII v." *Istoricheskie zapiski* 71 (Moscow, 1962): 158-95.

Amburger, Erik. *Die Familie Marselis: Studien zur russischen Wirtschaftsgeschichte.* Osteuropastudien der Hochschulen des Landes Hessen: Reihe 1: Giessener Abhandlungen zur Agrar- und Wirtschaftsforschung des europäischen Ostens. vol. 4. Giessen, 1957.

Angermann, Norbert, "Zum Handel der deutschen Kaufleute in Pleskau." *Russland und Deutschland* (Georg von Rauch Festschrift). Kieler historische Studien, vol. 22. Stuttgart, 1974: 73-82.

Arne, T. J. *Det stora Svitjod: Essayer om gånga tiders svensk-ryska kulturförbindelser.* Stockholm, 1917.

Åström, Sven-Erik. *From Cloth to Iron: The Anglo-Baltic Trade in the Later Seventeenth Century*. Societas Scientiarum Fennica, Commentationes Humanarum Litterarum 33, I and 37, III. Helsinki, 1963 and 1965.

From Stockholm to St. Petersburg: Commercial Factors in the Political Relations between England and Sweden 1675-1700. Studia Historica 2. Helsinki, 1962.

Attman, Artur. *Den ryska marknaden i 1500-talets baltiska politik*. Lund, 1944.

Bakhrushin, S. V. *Nauchnye trudy*. ed. by A. A. Zimin et al. 3 vols. Moscow, 1952-5.

"Promyshlennye predpriiatiia russkikh torgovykh liudei v XVII veke." *Istoricheskie zapiski* 8 (Moscow, 1940): 98-128.

Bakhrushin, S. V., Novosel'skii, A. A., Ustiugov, N. V., and Zimin, A. A., eds. *Istoriia Moskvy* 1. Moscow, 1952.

Baklanova, N. A. "Privoznye tovary v Moskovskom gosudarstve vo vtoroi polovine XVII veka." *Ocherki po istorii torgovli i promyshlennosti v Rossii v XVII i v nachale XVIII stoletiia.* Trudy gosudarstvennogo istoricheskogo muzeia 4: Otdel istoricheskii obshchii (Moscow, 1928): 5–118.

Torgovo-promyshlennaia deiatel'nost' Kalmykovykh vo vtoroi polovine XVII v.: K istorii formirovaniia russkoi burzhuazii. Moscow, 1959.

Bakulin, V. S. "Torgovye oboroty i sotsial'nyi sostav torgovtsev na Belevskom rynke v 60–70-kh godakh XVII veka." *Trudy moskovskogo gosudarstvennogo istoriko-arkhivnogo instituta* 21 (Moscow, 1965): 289–312.

Baliński, Michał. *Historya Miasta Wilna.* 2 vols. Wilno, 1836–7.

Bang, Nina. *Tabeller over skibsfart og varetransport gennem Øresund 1497–1660.* Parts 1 and 2. Copenhagen, 1906–20.

Baron, Samuel H. "Vasilii Shorin: Seventeenth Century Russian Merchant Extraordinary." *Canadian-American Slavic Studies* 6 (4) (1972): 503–48.

"The Weber Thesis and the Failure of Capitalist Development in 'Early Modern' Russia." *Jahrbücher für Geschichte Osteuropas* XVIII, 3 (September 1970): 321–36.

"Who Were the *Gosti?*" *California Slavic Studies* 7 (1973): 1–40.

Bazhanova, S. K. "Gur'evy." *Sovetskaia istoricheskaia entsiklopediia.* 16 vols., Moscow, 1961–76.

Bazilevich, K. V. "Kollektivnye chelobit'ia torgovykh liudei i bor'ba za russkii rynok v pervoi polovine XVII veka." *Izvestiia Akademii Nauk SSSR:* Seventh series 9 (1932): 91–123.

"Krupnoe torgovoe predpriiatie v moskovskom gosudarstve v pervoi polovine XVII v." *Izvestiia Akademii Nauk SSSR:* Seventh series 9 (1932): 783–812.

"Novotorgovyi ustav 1667 g. (K voprosu o ego istochnikakh)" *Izvestiia Akademii Nauk SSSR:* Seventh series 7 (1932): 589–622.

"Tamozhennye knigi kak istochnik ekonomicheskoi istorii Rossii." *Problemy istochnikovedeniia* 1. Trudy istoriko-arkheograficheskogo instituta Akademii Nauk SSSR, vol. 9. (Moscow-Leningrad, 1933): 110–29.

"K voprosu ob izuchenii tamozhennykh knig XVII v." *Problemy istochnikovedeniia* 2. Trudy istoriko-arkheograficheskogo instituta Akademii Nauk SSSR, vol. 17. (Moscow-Leningrad, 1936): 71–90.

Belokurov, S. A., ed. "Utverzhdennaia gramota ob izbranii na Moskovskoe gosudarstvo Mikhaila Fedorovicha Romanova." *Chteniia v obshchestve istorii i drevnostei rossiiskikh* 218 (3) (Moscow, 1906): 1–110.

Bennigsen, Alexandre, and Lemercier-Quelquejay, Chantal. "Les marchands de la cour ottomane et le commerce des fourrures moscovites dans la seconde moitié du XVI siecle." *Cahiers du monde russe et soviétique* 11 (No. 3, 1970): 363–91.

Berindei, Mihnea. "Contributions a l'étude du commerce ottoman des fourrures moscovites: La route moldavo-polonaise 1453–1700." *Cahiers du monde russe et soviétique* 12 (1971): 393–409.

Bieniarzówna, Janina. *Mieszczaństwo krakowskie XVII w.: z badań nad strukturą społeczną miasta.* Krakow, 1969.

Bogoiavlenskii, S. K. "Moskovskie slobody i sotni v XVII veke." *Moskovskii krai v ego proshlom* 2. Trudy Obshchestva Izucheniia Moskovskoi Oblasti 6 (Moscow, 1930): 117–31.

"Upravlenie Moskvoi v XVI–XVII vv." *Moskva v ee proshlom i nastoiashchem* 2 (1) (Moscow, no date, but c. 1910): 81–96.

Bogoslovskii, M. M. *Zemskoe samoupravlenie na russkom severe v XVII v.* 2 vols. Moscow, 1909–12.

Bogucka, Maria. *Handel zagraniczny Gdańska w pierwszej połowie XVII wieku.* Wrocław-Warsaw-Krakow, 1970.
Bonsdorff, Carl von. "Nyen och Nyenskans: Historisk skildring." *Acta Societatis scientiarum Fennicae* (Finska vetenskapsocieteten) 18 (1891): 349–505.
Bushkovitch, Paul. "Taxation, Tax Farming, and Merchants in Sixteenth-Century Russia." *Slavic Review* 37 (3) (Sept. 1978): 381–98.
"Towns, Trade, and Artisans in Seventeenth Century Russia: the View from Eastern Europe." *Forschungen zur osteuropäischen Geschichte* 27 (forthcoming).
Chaev, N. S., ed. "Dvinskaia ustavnaia tamozhennaia otkupnaia gramota 1560 g." *Letopis' zaniatii postoiannoi istoriko-arkheograficheskoi kommissii* 1 (34) 1926. (Moscow, 1927): 199–203.
Chicherin, B. *Oblastnye uchrezhdeniia Rossii v XVII veke.* Moscow, 1856.
Chistiakova, E. V. "Pskovskii torg v seredine XVII v." *Istoricheskie zapiski* 34 (Moscow, 1950).
"Remeslo i torgovlia na Voronezhskom posade v seredine XVII v." *Trudy Voronezhskogo gosudarstvennogo universiteta* 25 (Leningrad, 1954): 46–62.
Christensen, A. E. *Dutch Trade to the Baltic about 1600.* Copenhagen, 1941.
Chulkov, M. D. *Istoricheskoie opisanie rossiiskoi kommertsii.* 7 vols. St. Petersberg, 1781–8.
Davydova, M. B., Iukht, A. I., and Shaskol'skii, I. P., eds. *Russko-shvedskie ekonomicheskie otnosheniia v XVII veke: Sbornik dokumentov.* Moscow-Leningrad, 1960.
Denucé, J. *Die Hanse und die Antwerpener Handelskompanien in den Ostseeländern.* Dokumente zur Handelsgeschichte 3. Antwerp, 1938.
D'iakonov, M. *Ocherki obshchestvennogo i gosudarstvennogo stroia drevnei Rusi (do kontsa XVII veka).* Vol. 1. Iur'ev (Tartu), 1907.
Dillen, J. G. van. *Van rijkdom en regenten: Handboek tot de economische en sociale geschiedenis van Nederland tijdens de Republiek.* The Hague, 1970.
Dollinger, Philippe. *La Hanse (XIIe–XVIIe siecles).* Paris, 1964.
Dopolneniia k aktam istoricheskim. 12 vols. St. Petersburg, 1846–1872.
Doroszenko, Wasilij W. "Eksport Rygi na zachód w okresie przynależności de Rzeczypospolitej (1562–1620)" *Zapiski Historyczne* 31 (1) (1966): 7–41.
Dovnar-Zapol'skii, M. V. "Torgovlia i promyshlennost' Moskvy." *Moskva v ee proshlom i nastoiashchem* 3 (2) (Moscow, no date, but c. 1912): 5–67.
Dubiński, Piotr. *Zbiór praw i przywilejów miastu stołecznemu W. X. L. Wilnowi nadanych.* Wilno, 1788.
Dunlop, H., ed. *Bronnen tot de Geschiedenis der Oostindische Compagnie in Perzie* Part 1 (1611–38). Rijks-Geschiedkundige Publicatien 72, The Hague, 1930.
Ehrenberg, Richard. *Das Zeitalter der Fugger: Geldkapital und Creditverkehr im 16. Jahrhundert.* 2 vols. Jena, 1896.
Ekholm, Lars. "Rysk spannmål och svenska krigsfinanser 1629–1633." *Scandia* 40: (1974): 57–103.
Fekhner, M. V. *Torgovlia russkogo gosudarstva so stranami Vostoka v XVI veke,* 2nd. ed. Trudy gosudarstvennogo istoricheskogo muzeia 31. Moscow, 1956.
Fisher, Raymond H. *The Russian Fur Trade 1550–1700.* University of California Publications in History 31. Berkeley and Los Angeles, 1943.
Floria, B. N. "Torgovlia Rossii so stranami Zapadnoi Evropy v Arkhangel'ske (konets XVI–nachalo XVII v.)" *Srednie veka* 36 (Moscow, 1973): 129–51.
Fuhrmann, Joseph T. *The Origins of Capitalism in Russia: Industry and Progress in the Sixteenth and Seventeenth Centuries.* Chicago, 1972.

Geiman, V. G. "Solianoi promysel gostia I. D. Pankrat'eva v Iarenskom uiezde v XVII veke (Materialy po istorii russkoi promyshlennosti)" *Letopis' zaniatii postoiannoi istoriko- arkheograficheskoi kommissii* 35 (Leningrad, 1929): 11–38.

Got'e, Iu. *Zamoskovnyi krai v XVII veke: Opyt issledovaniia po istorii eknomicheskogo byta Moskovskoi Rusi.* Moscow, 1906.

Gradovskii, A. D. "Obshchestvennye klassy v Rossii do Petra I." *Zhurnal ministerstva narodnogo prosveshcheniia* 9 (April-September, 1868). Vol. 138, 1–91, 405–456, 631–698; Vol. 139, 72–241.

Gubaidullin, G. "Iz istorii torgovogo klassa Privolzhskikh tatar." *Izvestiia vostochnogo fakul'teta Azerbaidzhanskogo gosudarstvennogo universiteta: Vostokovedenie* 1 (Baku, 1926): 49–74.

Harder, Elisabeth. "Seehandel zwischen Lübeck and Russland in 17/18 Jahrhundert nach den Zollbüchern der Novgorodfahrer." *Zeitschrift des Vereins für Lübeckische- und Altertumskunde* 41 and 42 (1961–2): 43–114, 5–54.

Hart, Simon. "Amsterdam Shipping and Trade to Northern Russia in the Seventeenth Century." *Mededelinger van de Nederlands Vereniging voor Zeegeschiedenis* 26 (March 1973): 5–78.

"De handelsbetrekkingen van Amsterdam met Archangel en Lapland (Kola) in de 17e eeuw." *Nederlands Archievenblad* 73 (2) (1969): 66–80.

Heckscher, Eli F. "Multilateralism, Baltic Trade and the Mercantilists." *Economic History Review*, Second series 3 (2) (1950): 219–42.

Hinton, R. W. K. *The Eastland Trade and the Common Weal in the Seventeenth Century* (Cambridge, 1959).

Horn, Maurycy. *Walka klasowa i konflikty społeczne w miastach Rusi czerwonej w latach 1600–1647 na tle stosunków gospodarczych.* Prace opolskiego towarzystwa przyjaciół nauk: wydział nauk historyczno-społecznych. Wrocław-Warsaw-Krakow-Gdańsk, 1972.

Hoskins, W. G. "English Provincial Towns in the Early Sixteenth Century." *Transactions of the Royal Historical Society*, Fifth Series, vol. 6 (1956): 1–21.

Hroch, Miroslav. "Die Rolle des zentraleuropäischen Handels im Ausgleich der Handelsbilanz zwischen Ost- und Westeuropa 1550-1650." *Der Aussenhandel Ostmitteleuropas 1450-1650: Die ostmitteleuropäischen Volkswirtschaften in ihren Beziehungen zu Mitteleuropa*, ed. by Ingomar Bog (Köln, 1971): 1–27.

Iakovlev, A. I., ed. *Tamozhennye knigi moskovskogo gosudarstva XVII veka.* 3 vols. Moscow-Leningrad, 1950-1.

Istoriia Sibiri, 5 vols. Leningrad, 1968.

Iziumov, A. "Razmery russkoi torgovli XVII veka cherez Arkhangel'sk v sviazi s neobsledovannymi arkhivnymi istochnikami." *Izvestiia Arkhangel'skogo obshchestva izucheniia Russkogo severa* 6 (1912): 250–8.

Jensch, Georg. "Der Handel Rigas im 17. Jahrhundert: Ein Beitrag zur livländischen Wirtschaftsgeschichte in Schwedischer Zeit." *Mitteilungen aus der livländschen Geschichte* 24 (Gesellschatt für Geschichte und Altertumskunde zu Riga, 1930).

Jurginis, J., Merkys, V., and Tautavicius, A. *Vilniaus Miesto Istorija.* Vilnius, 1968.

Kalachov, N. V., ed. *Akty otnosiashchiesia do iuridicheskogo byta Drevnei Rossii.* 3 vols. St. Petersburg, 1857-84.

Kazakova, N. A. *Russko-livonskie i russko-ganzeiskie otnosheniia: Konets XIV-nachalo XVI v.* Leningrad, 1975.

Kellenbenz, Hermann. *Unternehmerkräfte im Hamburger Portugal und Spanienhandel*

1590–1625. Veröffentlichungen der Wirtschaftsgeschichtlichen Forschungsstelle Hamburg, vol. 10. Hamburg, 1954.

Khoroshkevich, A. L. *Torgovlia Velikogo Novgoroda s Pribaltikoi i Zapadnoi evropoi v XIV-XV vv.* Moscow, 1963.

Kirchner, Walter. *Commercial Relations between Russia and Europe, 1400 to 1800: Collected Essays.* Indiana University Publications, Russian and East European Series, vol. 33. Bloomington, Indiana, 1966.

Kleinenberg, I. E. "Serebro vmesto soli: Elementy rannego merkantilizma vo vneshnetorgovoi politike Russkogo gosudarstva kontsa XV–nachala XVI veka," *Istoriia SSSR* 2 (1977): 115–124.

Kliuchevskii, V. O. *Istoriia soslovii v Rossii. Sochineniia* 6. Moscow, 1959.

"Russkaia rubl' XVI-XVIII vv. v ego otnoshenii k nyneshnemu." *Sochineniia* 7. Moscow, 1959: 170–236.

Knackstedt, Wolfgang. *Moskau: Studien zur Geschichte einer mittelalterlichen Stadt.* Quellen und Studien zur Geschichte des östlichen Europa. vol. 8. Wiesbaden, 1975.

"Moskauer Kaufleute im späten Mittelalter: Organisationsformen und soziale Stellung." *Zeitschrift für Historische Forschung* (Bd. 3, 1976, Heft 1): 1–19.

Kolominskii, S. "Torgovlia sol'iu na Rusi v 16–17 v. i obshchee sostoianie solianykh promyslov v ukazannyi period vremeni." *Kievskie universitetskie izvestiia* 12 (December 1912): 2–51.

Kopanev, A. I. "Novgorodskie tamozhennye tseloval'niki 70–80–kh godov XVI v." *Issledovaniia po sotsial'no-politicheskoi istorii Rossii: Sbornik statei pamiati Borisa Aleksandrovicha Romanova.* Trudy LOII 12 (Leningrad, 1971): 142–51.

Kopylov, A. N. *Russkie na Enisee v XVII v.: Zemledelie, promyshlennost' i torgovye sviazi eniseiskogo uiezda.* Novosibirsk, 1965.

"Tamozhennaia politika v Sibiri v XVII v." *Russkoe gosudarstvo v XVII v.: Novye iavleniia v sotsial'no-ekonomicheskoi, politicheskoi i kul'turnoi zhizni* (Moscow, 1961): 330–70.

Kopysskii, Z. Iu. *Ekonomicheskoi razvitie gorodov Belorussii v XVI–pervoi polovine XVII v.* Minsk, 1966.

"Iz istorii torgovykh sviazei gorodov Belorussii s gorodami Pol'shi (konets XVI–pervaia polovina XVII v.)" *Istoricheskie zapiski* 72 (Moscow, 1962): 140–83.

Kordt, V. A. "Ocherk snoshenii Moskovskogo gosudarstva s Respublikoi Soiedinennykh Niderlandov po 1631 g." *Sbornik Russkogo Istoricheskogo Obshchestva* 116 (St. Petersburg, 1902): III-CLXXVII.

Kostomarov, N. *Ocherk torgovli Moskovskogo gosudarstva v XVI i XVII stoletiiakh.* St. Petersburg, 1862.

Kotkov, S. I., Oreshnikov, A. S., and Filippova, I. S., eds. *Moskovskaia delovaia i bytovaia pis'mennost' XVII veka.* Moscow, 1968.

Kotoshikhin, G. *O Rossii v tsarstvovanie Alekseia Mikhailovicha.* 2nd ed. St. Petersburg, 1859.

Kozintseva, R. I. "Uchastie kazny vo vneshnei torgovle Rossii v pervoi chetverti XVIII v." *Istoricheskie zapiski* 91 (Moscow, 1973): 267–337.

"Vneshnetorgovyi oborot Arkhangelogorodskoi iarmarki i ee rol' v razvitii vserossiiskogo rynka." *Issledovaniia po istorii feodal'no-krepostnicheskoi Rossi* (Moscow-Leningrad, 1964): 116–63.

Krestinin, V. V. "Istoricheskii opyt o vneshnei torgovle gosudaria Imperatora Petra Velikogo ot 1693 po 1719 g." *Mesiatseslov istoricheskii i geograficheskii na 1795 g.* (St. Petersburg, 1794).

Kratkaia istoriia o gorode Arkhangel'skom, sochinena Arkhangelogorodskim grazhdaninom Vasil'em Krestininom. St. Petersburg, 1792.

Kubinyi, András. "Die Städte Ofen und Pest und der Fernhandel an Ende des 15. und am Anfang des 16. Jahrhunderts." *Der Aussenhandel Ostmitteleuropas 1450–1650: Die ostmitteleuropäischen Volkswirtschaften in ihren Beziehungen zu Mitteleuropa,* ed. by Ingomar Bog (Köln, 1971): 342–433.

Kurts, B. G. *Sochineniia Kil'burgera o russkoi torgovle v tsarstovanie Alekseia Mikhailovicha.* Kiev, 1915.

"Sostoianie Rossii v 1650–1655 gg. po doneseniiam Rodesa." *Chteniia Obshchestva Istorii i Drevnostei Rossiiskikh.* Book 2, 253, 1915 (Moscow, 1914): I–VII, 1–268.

Kusheva, E. N. "Materialy astrakhanskoi tamozhni kak istochnik po sotsial'no-ekonomicheskoi istorii Rossii XVII-XVIII vv." *Iz istorii ekonomicheskoi i obshchestvennoi zhizni Rossii* (N. M. Druzhinin Festschrift), (Moscow, 1976): 261–72.

Narody severnogo Kavkaza i ikh sviazi s Rossiei. Moscow, 1963.

Kuznetsova, N. A., ed. *Khozhdenie kuptsa Fedota Kotova v Persiuu.* Moscow, 1958.

Lantzeff, George V. *Siberia in the Seventeenth Century: A Study of the Colonial Administration.* University of California Publications in History 30. Berkeley and Los Angeles, 1943.

Likhachev, E. s. v. Chistogo, Almaz (Anikei) Ivanovich and Chistogo, Nazar Ivanovich. *Russkii biograficheskii slovar'.* St. Petersburg, 1896-1918.

Liubimenko, I. I. *Istoriia torgovykh snoshenii Rossii s Angliei,* part 1: *XVI-i vek.* Iur'ev (Tartu), 1912.

Les relations commerciales et politiques de l'Angelterre avec la Russie avant Pierre le Grand. Bibliotheque de l'ecole des hautes etudes: Sciences historiques et philologiques 261. Paris, 1933.

"The Struggle of the Dutch with the English for the Russian Market in the Seventeenth Century." *Transactions of the Royal Historical Society* 7 (1924): 27–51.

Liubomirov, P. G. *Ocherki istorii nizhegorodskogo opolcheniia.* Moscow, 1939.

Ocherki po istorii russkoi promyshlennosti. Moscow, 1947.

Łowmiański, Henryk. "Handel Mohylewa w wieku XVI." *Studia historyczne ku czci Stanisława Kutrzeby* 2 (Krakow, 1938): 517–47.

Łoziński, Władysław. *Lwów starożytny.* 2 vols. Lwow, 1889–90.

Mączak, Antoni. *Między Gdańskiem a Sundem: Studia nad handlem bałtyckim od połowy XVI do połowy XVII w.* Warsaw, 1972.

Makarov, I. S. "Pushnoi rynok v Sol'vychegodske XVII" *Istoricheskie zapiski* 14 (Moscow, 1945): 148–69.

Man'kov, A. G. *Tseny ikh dvizhenie v russkom gosudarstve XVI veka.* Moscow-Leningrad, 1951.

Merzon, A. Ts. and Tikhonov, Iu. A. *Rynok Ustiuga Velikogo v period skladyvaniia vserossiiskogo rynka (XVII vek).* Moscow, 1960.

Miklashevskii, N. N. *K istorii khoziaistvennogo byta moskovskogo gosudarstva* 1: *Zaselenie i sel'skoe khoziaistvo iuzhnoi okrainy XVII veka.* Moscow, 1894.

Miliukov, P. N. *Gosudarstvennoie khoziaistvo Rossii v pervoi chetverti XVIII stoletiia i reformy Petra Velikogo,* 2nd. ed. St. Petersburg, 1905.

Mironov, B. N. "'Revoliutsiia tsen' v Rossii v XVIII v." *Voprosy istorii* 11 (1971): 49–61.

Mitiaev, K. G. "Oboroty i torgovye sviazi smolenskogo rynka v 70-kh godakh XVII v." *Istoricheskie zapiski* 13 (Moscow, 1941): 54–83.

Morzy, Jerzy. "Geneza i rozwój cechów wileńskich do końca XVII w." *Zeszyty naukowe uniwersytetu im. A. Mickiewicza: Historia* (z. 4, 1959): 3–93.

Murav'eva, L. L. *Derevenskaia promyshlennost' tsentral'noi Rossii vtoroi poloviny XVII v.* Moscow, 1971.

"Mytnaia kniga (Brest, 1583)" *Arkheograficheskii sbornik dokumentov otnosiashchikhsia k istorii Severozapadnoi Rusi* 3 and 4 (Wilno, 1867): 252–89, 289–322.

Nilsson, Sven A. "Den ryska marknaden i 1500-talets baltiska politik." *Scandia* 16 (2) årgång 1944 (1945): 175–90.

Nosov, N. E. "Russkii gorod i russkoie kupechestvo v XVI stoletii (K postanovke voprosa)" *Issledovaniia po sotsial'no-politicheskoi istorii Rossii: Sbornik statei k pamiati Borisa Aleksandrovicha Romanova.* Trudy LOII 12 (Leningrad, 1971): 152–77.

Stanovlenie soslovno-predstavitel'nykh uchrezhdenii v Rossii: Izyskaniia o zemskoi reforme Ivana Groznogo. Leningrad, 1969.

Novikov, N. I., ed. *Drevniaia Rossiiskaia Vifliofika.* 2nd ed. 20 vols. Moscow, 1788–91.

Novosel'skii, A. A. "Iz istorii donskoi torgovli v XVII veke." *Istoricheskie zapiski* 26 (Moscow, 1948): 198–216.

Nyström, Per. "Mercatura Ruthenica." *Scandia* 10 (2) (December 1937): 239–96.

Ogloblin, N. N. *Obozrenie stolbtsov i knig sibirskogo prikaza (1592–1768 gg.) Chteniia Obshchestva Istorii i Drevnostei Rossiiskikh* 173, 184, 194, 200. Moscow, 1895–1902.

Ogorodnikov, S. F. *Ocherk istorii goroda Arkhangel'ska v torgovo-promyshlennom otnoshenii.* St. Petersburg, 1890.

Orlov, A. *Domostroi po konshinskomu spisku.* Moscow, 1908.

Pach, Zsigmond. *The Role of East-Central Europe in International Trade, 16th and 17th Centuries.* Studia Historica Academiae Scientiarum Hungaricae 70. Budapest, 1970.

Pavlov, P. N. "Ob uchastie i roli razlichnykh kategorii naseleniia v sibirskom pushnom promysle v 40–70-e gody XVII v." *Eknomika, upravlenie i kul'tura Sibiri XVI–XIX vv.* Sibir' perioda feodalizma 2 (Novosibirsk, 1965): 17–39. "Vyvoz pushniny iz Sibiri v XVII v." *Sibir' XVII–XVIII vv.* Sibir' perioda feodalizma 1 (Novosibirsk, 1962): 121–38.

Perekhod ot feodalizma k kapitalizmu v. Rossii. Moscow, 1969.

Perepisnye knigi goroda Moskvy, sostavlennye v 1738–1742 (s prilozheniem Perepisnoi knigi 1626 g.). Moscow, 1881.

Perepisnaia kniga 1638 goda. Moscow, 1881.

Piirimäe, H. "O sostoianii narvskoi torgovli v nachale XVII veka." *Skandinavskii sbornik* 11 (Tallin, 1966): 82–108.

Polnoe sobranie zakonov Rossiiskoi Imperii. 45 vols. St. Petersburg, 1830.

Porshnev, B. F. "Bor'ba vokrug shvedsko-russkogo soiuza v 1631–1633 gg." *Skandinavskii sbornik* 1 (Tallinn, 1956): 11–71.

"Russkie subsidii Shvetsii vo vremia Tridtstaletnei voiny." *Izvestiia Akademii Nauk SSSR, Seriia istorii i filosofii* 6 (1945).

Posthumus, N. W. *Inquiry into the History of Prices in Holland.* 2 vols. Leiden, 1946–64.

Privalova, N. I. "Torgi goroda Kasimova v seredine XVII veka." *Istoricheskie zapiski* 21 (Moscow, 1947): 105–33.

Prokof'eva, L. S. *Votchinnoe khoziaistvo v XVII veke: Po materialam Spaso-Prilutskogo monastyria.* Moscow-Leningrad, 1959.

Rabinovich, G. S. *Gorod soli: Staraia Russa v kontse XVI–seredine XVIII vekov (K voprosu o genezise kapitalizma v russkoi promyshlennosti)*. Leningrad, 1973.

Reissmann, Martin. *Die hamburgische Kaufmannschaft des 17. Jahrhunderts in sozialgeschichtlicher Sicht*. Beiträge zur Geschichte Hamburgs, vol. 4. Hamburg, 1975.

Repin, N. N. "K voprosu o sviazi vneshnego i vnutrennogo rynka Rossii vo vtoroi polovine XVII–pervoi chetverti XVIII v. (Po materialam Arkhangel'ska)" *Vestnik MGU: seriia istoria* 6 (1970): 56–72.

"Vneshnaia torgovlia cherez Arkhangel'sk i vnutrennii rynok Rossii vo vtoroi polovine XVII–pervoi chetverti XVIII v." *Kandidatskaia* dissertation, Moscow University, 1970.

Rozhdestvenskii, S. V., ed. *Pamiatniki istorii nizhegorodskogo dvizheniia v epokhu smuty i zemskogo opolcheniia 1611–1612 gg*. Deistviia Nizhegorodskoi gubernskoi uchenoi arkhivnoi kommissii 11. Nizhnii Novgorod, 1912.

Russko-indiiskie otnosheniia v XVII v.: Sbornik dokumentov. Moscow, 1959.

Rybarski, Roman. *Handel i polityka handlowa Polski w XVI stuleciu*, 2nd. ed. 2 vols. Warsaw, 1958.

Sakharov, A. M. *Goroda sever-vostochnoi Rusi XIV-XV vekov*. Moscow, 1959.

Savich, A. A. *Solovetskaia votchina XV–XVII vv.: opyt izucheniia khoziaistva i sotsial'nykh otnoshenii na krainem russkom severe v drevnei Rusi*. Perm', 1927.

Scheltema, J. *Rusland en de Nederlanden beschouwd in derzelver wederkeerige betrekkingen*. 4 vols. Amsterdam, 1819.

Selifonov, N. N. ed. *Opisi dokumentam arkhiva byvshikh Bol'shesol'skikh posadskoi izby i ratushi, naidennogo v posade Bol'shie Soli, Kostromskogo uezda*. Published by Kostromskaia gubernskaia uchenaia arkhivnaia kommissiia. St. Petersburg, 1902.

Serbina, K. N. *Ocherki iz sotsial'no-ekonomicheskoi istorii russkogo goroda: Tikhvinskii posad v XVI–XVII vv*. Moscow-Leningrad, 1951.

Krest'ianskaia zhelezodelatel'naia promyshlennost' severo-zapadnoi Rossii XVI–pervoi poloviny XIX v. Leningrad, 1971.

Shaskol'skii, I. P. "Ob osnovnykh osobennostiakh russko-shvedskoi torgovli XVII v." *Mezhdunarodnye sviazi Rossii v XVII–XVIII vv. (Ekonomika, politika i kul'tura)* (Moscow, 1966): 7–34.

Stolbovskii mir 1617 g. i torgovye otnosheniia Rossii so shvedskim gosudarstvom. Moscow-Leningrad, 1964.

Smirnov, P. P. *Goroda Moskovskogo gosudarstva v pervoi polovine XVII veka. Kievskie universiteskie izvestiia* 58 (1 and 2) (January–February, 1918).

"Novoe chelobit'e Moskovskikh torgovykh liudei o vysylke inozemtsev 1627 goda." *Chteniia v istoricheskom obshchestve Nestora–letopistsa*, book 23, no. 1, section 2 (Kiev, 1912): 3–32.

"Okladnoi spisok gostei gostinnoi i sukonnoi sotni 1632 g." *Chteniia v istoricheskom obshchestve Nestora-letopistsa*, book 23, part 1, section 1 (Kiev, 1912): 12–15.

Posadskie liudi i ikh klassovaia bor'ba do serediny XVII veka. 2 vols. Moscow-Leningrad, 1947–8.

Sobranie gosudarstvennykh gramot i dogovorov. 5 vols. Moscow, 1813–94.

Soom, Arnold. *Der Handel Revals im siebzehnten Jahrhundert*. Marburger Ostforschungen 29. Wiesbaden, 1969.

"Die merkantilistische Wirtschaftspolitik Schwedens und die baltische Städte im 17. Jahrhundert." *Jahrbücher für die Geschichte Osteuropas* 2 (1963): 183–222.

Spasskii, I. G. "Denezhnoie khoziaistvo russkogo gosudarstva v seredine XVII v. i reformy 1654–1663 gg." *Arkheograficheskii ezhegodnik za 1959 god* (Moscow, 1960): 103–56.

Srbik, Heinrich Ritter von. *Der Staatliche Exporthandel Osterreichs von Leopold I. bis Maria Theresia: Untersuchungen zur Wirtschafsgeschichte Osterreichs im Zeitalter des Merkantilismus.* Vienna, 1907.

Stashevsii, E. D. *Ocherki po istorii tsarstvovaniia Mikhaila Fedorovicha 1.* Kiev, 1913.

"Piatina 142-go goda i torgovo-promyshlennye tsentry Moskovskogo gosudarstva." *Zhurnal ministerstva narodnogo prosveshcheniia*, n. s. 38 (April-May 1912): 83-112. 250-319.

Steensgaard, Nils. *Carracks, Caravans, and Companies: The Asian Trade in the Early Seventeenth Century.* Scandinavian Institute of Asian Studies, Monograph Series No. 17. Copenhagen, 1973.

Stepanov, I. V. "Khoziaistvennaia deiatel'nost' Moskovskogo pravitel'stva v Nizhnem Povolzh'e XVII veke." *Uchenye zapiski LGU: seriia istoricheskikh nauk* 48 (5) (1939): 80-142.

"Organizatsiia solianykh promyslov v nizov'iakh reki Volgi v XVII v." *Uchenye zapiski LGU: seriia istoricheskikh nauk* 8 (1941): 147-61.

Syroechkovskii, V. E. *Gosti-surozhane.* Izvestiia gosudarstvennoi Akademii istorii material'noi kul'tury 127. Moscow-Leningrad, 1935.

Szeftel, Marc. "The Legal Condition of the Foreign Merchants in Muscovy." *Recueils de la Société Jean Bodin* 33 (Brussels, 1972): 335-58.

Tikhomirov, M. N. "Novgorodskoe vosstanie 1650 g." *Klassovaia bor'ba v Rossii XVII v.* (Moscow, 1969): 139-169. Originally: *Istoricheskie zapiski* 7 (Moscow, 1940): 91-114.

"Pskovskoie vosstanie 1650 g." *Klassovaia bor'ba v Rossii XVIII v.* (Moscow, 1969): 23-138. Originally published: Moscow-Leningrad, 1935.

Srednevekovaia Moskva v XIV-XV vekakh. Moscow, 1957.

Tikhonov, Iu. A. *Pomeshchich'i krest'iane v Rossii: Feodal'naia renta v XVII-nachale XVIII v.* Moscow, 1974.

"Tamozhennaia politika Russkogo gosudarstva s serediny XVI do 60-kh godov XVII v." *Istoricheskie zapiski* 53 (Moscow, 1955): 258-90.

Timofeev, A. I., ed. "Prikhodo-raskhodnye knigi kazennogo prikaza." *Russkaia istoricheskaia biblioteka* 9. St. Petersburg, 1884.

Tolstoi, Iu. V. *Pervye sorok let snoshenii mezhdu Rossieiu i Anglieiu 1553-1593.* St. Petersburg, 1875.

Tomsinskii, S. G. ed. *Materialy po istorii Tatarskoi ASSR: Pistsovye knigi goroda Kazani 1565-1568 gg. i 1646 g.* Trudy istoriko-arkheograficheskogo instituta Akademii nauk SSSR: Materialy po istorii narodov SSSR 2. Leningrad, 1932.

Tremel, Ferdinand. *Der Frühkapitalismus in Innerösterreich.* Graz, Austria, 1954. *Wirtschafts- und Sozialgeschichte Osterreichs.* Vienna, 1969.

Tverskaia, D. I. *Moskva vtoroi poloviny XVII veka - Tsentr skladyvaiushchegosia vserossiiskogo rynka.* Trudy gosudarstvennogo istoricheskogo muzeia 34. Moscow, 1959.

Uspenskii, A. I. *Stolbtsy byvshego arkhiva Oruzheinoi palaty.* 3 vols. Moscow, 1912-14.

Ustiugov, N. V. *Solevarennaia promyshlennost' Soli Kamskoi v XVII veke: K voprosu o genezise kapitalisticheskikh otnoshenii v russkoi promyshlennosti.* Moscow, 1957.

Veselovskii, S. B. and Platonov, S. F., eds. "Prikhodo-raskhodnye knigi moskovskikh prikazov." *Russkaia istoricheskaia biblioteka* 28. St. Petersburg, 1912.

Vilkov, O. N. *Remeslo i torgovlia zapadnoi Sibiri v XVII veke.* Moscow, 1967.

Volkov, M. Ia. "Remeslennoie i melkotovarnoie proizvodstvo iufti v Rossii vo vtoroi polovine XVI–pervoi polovine XVII v." *Istoricheskie zapiski* 92 (Moscow, 1973): 215–52.

Vossoedinenie Ukrainy s Rossiei, 3 vols. Moscow, 1954.

Vvedenskii, A. A. *Dom Stroganovykh v XVI–XVII vekakh.* Moscow, 1962.

Wawrzyńczyk, Alina. *Studia z dziejów handlu Polski z Wielkim Księstwom Litewskim i Rosją w XVI wieku.* Warsaw, 1956.

Willan, T. S. *The Early History of the Russia Company 1553–1603.* Manchester, 1956.

Wilson, Charles. "Treasure and Trade Balances: the Mercantilist Problem." *Economic History Review*, Second Series 2, no. 2 (1949): 152–61.

"Treasure and Trade Balances: Further Evidence." *Economic History Review*, Second Series 4, no. 2 (1951): 231–42.

Witsen, Nicolaas. *Moscovische Reyse 1664–1665: Journaal en Aentekeningen*, ed. by Th. J. G. Locher and P. de Buck. Werken uitgegeven door de Linschoten-Vereniging. vols. 66–68. The Hague, 1966–7.

Zaozerskaia, E. I. *U istokov krupnogo proizvodstva v russkoi promyshlennosti XVI–XVII vekov: K voprosu o genezise kapitalizma v Rossii.* Moscow, 1970.

Zientara, Benedykt. *Dzieje małopolskiego hutnictwa żelaznego XIV–XVII wiek.* Badania z dziejów rzemiosła i handlu w epoce feudalizmu 1. Warsaw, 1954.

Zimin, A. A. *Oprichnina Ivana Groznogo.* Moscow, 1964.

Reformy Ivana Groznogo: Ocherki Sotsial'no-ekonomicheskoi i politicheskoi istorii Rossii serediny XVI v., Moscow, 1960.

"Russkie geograficheskie spravochniki XVII veka." *Zapiski otdela rukopisei Gosudarstvennoi biblioteki SSSR im. V. I. Lenina* 21 (Moscow, 1959): 229–31.

Zimin, A. A., ed. "Ukaznaia kniga zemskogo prikaza," in *Pamiantniki russkogo prava* vol. 5 ed. by L. V. Cherepnin.

INDEX